Strong Hearts, Native Lands

Tribal Worlds: Critical Studies in
American Indian Nation Building

Brian Hosmer and Larry Nesper, editors

Strong Hearts, Native Lands

The Cultural and Political Landscape of
Anishinaabe Anti-Clearcutting Activism

Anna J. Willow

SUNY
PRESS

Published by State University of New York Press, Albany

For information, contact State University of New York Press, Albany, NY
www.sunypress.edu

Production by Ryan Morris
Marketing by Anne M. Valentine

Library of Congress Cataloging-in-Publication Data

Willow, Anna J.
   Strong hearts, Native lands : the cultural and political landscape of Anishinaabe
anti-clearcutting activism / Anna J. Willow.
      p. cm.— (Tribal worlds : critical studies in American Indian nation building)
   Includes bibliographical references and index.
   ISBN 978-1-4384-4202-0 (paperback : alk. paper)
   ISBN 978-1-4384-4203-7 (hardcover : alk. paper)
   1. Ojibwa Indians—Ontario—Kenora Region—Politics and government 2. Ojibwa
Indians—Ontario—Kenora Region—Social conditions. 3. Ojibwa Indians—
Ontario—Kenora Region—Ethnic identity. 4. Clearcutting—Ontario—Kenora
Region. 5. Forest protection—Ontario—Kenora Region. 6. Indian activists—
Ontario—Kenora Region. 7. Environmentalists—Ontario—Kenora Region.
8. Protest movements—Ontario—Kenora Region. 9. English River Indian Reserve
No. 21 (Ont.)—Environmental conditions. 10. Kenora Region (Ont.)—Environ-
mental conditions. I. Title.
   E99.C6W56 2012
   977.004'97333—dc23
                                          2011023185

10   9   8   7   6   5   4   3   2   1

Contents

Illustrations

Preface

Social science is a form of storytelling, and the way we tell stories largely determines who will hear them.

—Julie Cruikshank, *Life Lived Like a Story:*
Life Stories of Three Yukon Native Elders

Many stories could be told about the Grassy Narrows First Nation blockade. Some stories have made their way into the media record. Perhaps the most important blockade stories are those that continue to be retold and reimagined by the blockade's participants. This book presents my own account of the Grassy Narrows blockade and what made it possible. The events of the blockade, like the lives and motivations of the Anishinaabe activists who instigated it, are complex. The story of the Grassy Narrows blockade is a story of convergences. It takes place where cultural, political, and environmental dimensions of Anishinaabe anti-clearcutting activism intersect; where history and contemporary challenges combine with future aspirations to inspire action. I recount this multifaceted tale to the best of my ability; without question, others' interpretations—like the stories they tell—will differ from my own.

In the mid-1980s, sociologist Anastasia Shkilnyk (1985: 4) wrote the following of her time in Grassy Narrows over the previous decade:

I could never escape the feeling that I had been parachuted into a void—a drab and lifeless place in which the vital spark

ix

of life had gone out. It wasn't just the poverty of the place, the isolation, or even the lack of a decent bed that depressed me. I had seen worse material deprivation when I was working in squatter settlements around Santiago, Chile. And I had been in worse physical surroundings while working in war-devastated Ismailia on the project for the reconstruction of the Suez Canal. What struck me about Grassy Narrows was the numbness in the human spirit. There was an indifference, a listlessness, a total passivity that I could neither understand nor seem to do anything about. I had never seen such hopelessness anywhere in the Third World.

Eager to draw public attention to Grassy Narrows First Nation's plight, Shkilnyk may have been moved to hyperbole. And, to be sure, Grassy Narrows today is not without its share of problems. But the hopelessness Shkilnyk described is no longer so pervasive. Hope, determination, and perseverance now stand strong within the First Nation community. The contrast between Shkilnyk's gloomy outlook and my own reflects, first and foremost, the many positive changes that have taken place at Grassy Narrows in the twenty-five years separating our time there. But it was also catalyzed by First Nation members' resentment—made pointedly clear to me—at seeing their community portrayed in such a pessimistic light.

When any story is told, many choices must be made. Certainly, it would have been possible to craft an account of Grassy Narrows life that highlighted the harsh social realities so many Native Canadians experience firsthand. Colin Samson, for example, respectfully describes the culturally catastrophic results of Canada's "extinguishment" policy in order to advocate for Innu rights, arguing that "sustained efforts to transform and to impose external authority upon Native peoples . . . carry with them consequences that demand to be accounted for" (2003: 11). My decision to downplay the internal disagreements and social problems that exist at Grassy Narrows today should by no means be taken to excuse the generations of injustice that underlie them. But this is not how activists at Grassy Narrows choose to think about their past, present, and future. By thriving, they make a powerful statement about the inability of colonialism to complete its intended task.

Ultimately, the way I wrote about the blockade was guided by a conversation that took place during my first month of full-time fieldwork. Feeling homesick and anxious, I asked respected Grassy Narrows blockade spokesperson, trapper, and business owner J. B. Fobister if he had any suggestions for how I could "give back" to the First Nation community. J. B. did not offer an immediate answer. Gradually, though, over the course of an hour-long conversation, he returned to my question. He described the lack of self-respect and community pride he saw in many of Grassy's young people and, without missing a beat, asked me about the writing I planned to do. Giving has to come from within, J. B. said, when you do it and feel good about it you will know that you have given back in the right way. Finally, it seemed, J. B. had answered my question. The message I took from this conversation—the idea that I might be able to "give back" by writing in a way that inspires and honors the youth of Grassy Narrows—stayed with me through every page.

Acknowledgments

Without assistance from many people, this book could not have been written. I am eternally grateful for the time, patience, and friendship of activists and community leaders at Grassy Narrows First Nation (especially Judy DaSilva, Barbara Fobister, J. B. Fobister, Steve Fobister, Roberta Keesick, Andy Keewatin, and Chrissy Swain). Many thanks are also due to Bobbie Harrington, members of Christian Peacemaker Teams, and Friends of Grassy Narrows for assistance and friendship during my time in northwestern Ontario. The direction and encouragement offered by Paul Nadasdy, Larry Nesper, and Marilyn Runge (both my mother and my most devoted editor) have been extremely valuable throughout the long process of writing and revising this work. Finally, I offer my love and appreciation to Ryan, Evan, Aaron, and Autumn for their patience and understanding.

Portions of this book have appeared previously in different versions in journals: "Conceiving Kakipitatapitmok: The Political Landscape of Anishinaabe Anticlearcutting Activism," *American Anthropologist* 113(2) (2011): 262–76; "Cultivating Common Ground: Cultural Revitalization in Anishinaabe and Anthropological Discourse," *American Indian Quarterly* 34(1) (2010): 33–60; and "Clear-Cutting and Colonialism: The Ethnopolitical Dynamics of Indigenous

Environmental Activism in Northwestern Ontario," *Ethnohistory* 56(1) (2009): 35–67. This book is based on fieldwork supported by a J. William Fulbright Foreign Scholarship Award, a Canadian Embassy Graduate Research Fellowship, and a University of Wisconsin Vilas Travel Grant.

Introduction

On December 3rd of 2002, three young members of Grassy Narrows First Nation positioned a fallen tree across a snow-covered logging road just north of Ontario Provincial Highway 671 in order to impede the movement of logging trucks and equipment within Grassy Narrows' Traditional Land Use Area.[1] Their act marked the beginning of the Grassy Narrows blockade. The commencement of the blockade was supported by around sixty First Nation residents who had gathered at the Slant Lake site earlier in the day, including a busload of students and teachers from the community's Sakatcheway Anishinabe School and members of the Grassy Narrows Environmental Group. With excitement in the air, the blockaders quickly lit a fire and erected a tipi on site.

People present that cold December day told me the blockade began spontaneously. Yet the impetus for direct anti-clearcutting action had been building at Grassy Narrows for a long time. Tensions over large-scale industrial logging in the vicinity had been escalating since the late 1990s. By 2002, many people at Grassy Narrows felt their concerns—previously expressed through letter-writing campaigns and peaceful demonstrations in the small timber- and recreation-dependent city of Kenora—were being ignored by the government and the forest industry alike. When a logging truck headed north to collect a load of freshly cut trees was turned back by the protestors (Godin 2002a), the blockade at Grassy Narrows quickly

1

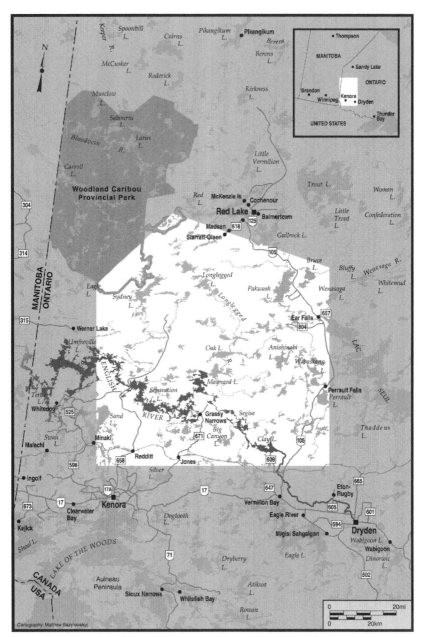

Figure I.1. Map of the Grassy Narrows Traditional Land Use Area and surrounding area (Land Use Area Boundaries from Vecsey 1987: 312).

became big news not only for those within the First Nation, but throughout the region. The blockade went on to become the longest-standing indigenous direct action protest in Canadian history.

Grassy Narrows First Nation is known to the Anishinaabe people who live there as Asubpeeschoseewagong Netum Anishinabek. The community is located in northwestern Ontario, fifty miles north of Kenora, Ontario, and approximately 170 miles northeast of Winnipeg, Manitoba. Although the First Nation's reserve is only fourteen square miles, the area Grassy Narrows residents consider their traditional territory covers 2,500. Just over 1,300 members belong to Grassy Narrows First Nation, with approximately 850 living on the reserve.

The Theoretical Landscape:
Context and Significance

The story of the Grassy Narrows blockade is interesting for several reasons. As an important episode in Canadian and Native North American history, the blockade is worthy of documentation. The blockade is also of considerable interest for area scholarship in Subarctic, First Nations, and Anishinaabe studies. And, as a case study in grassroots activism, it offers an outstanding example of a local indigenous response—and resistance—to externally imposed change.

The Grassy Narrows blockade is also theoretically significant for the field of cultural anthropology. What motivated people in this small Anishinaabe community to initiate a blockade? And what does it all mean? To most outside observers, the blockade appeared to be primarily an "environmental" movement, but answering these questions requires acknowledging that the real world is rarely so simple. "Instead of allegories about environmental activism," Stuart Kirsch recently observed, "anthropologists need ethnographic accounts that better represent the complex and potentially contradictory ambitions of indigenous movements" (Kirsch 2007: 314). This study presents a holistically contextualized account of Anishinaabe people's changing ways of comprehending and interacting with their boreal forest homeland. In doing so, it enriches anthropological knowledge about indigenous environmental movements and encourages a more complex—and more constructive—understanding of human-environment relationships.

How best to understand and represent relationships between people and the environments they live in is a question of long-standing anthropological interest. The centrality of culture in shaping human relationships to the natural world has been broadly addressed by environmental anthropology and, since the mid-1990s, numerous volumes on landscape (e.g., Tilley 1994; Hirsh and O'Hanlon 1995) and the closely related theme of space and place (e.g., Feld and Basso 1996; Gupta and Ferguson 1997; Low and Lawrence-Zúñiga 2003; MacDonald 2003) have explored relationships between peoples and places as well as the culturally specific ways of perceiving the natural world that infuse these relationships. Three main factors have guided much of this recent attention.

First and foremost, the landscape concept has the capacity to unify material and ideological ways of thinking about the world that have been separated in Western ontology since the time of Descartes. Landscape demands human perception and interpretation of a physical world. In landscape anthropology, the natural world becomes cultural through human action; nature is inseparable from culturally or mentally "socialized" landscapes (Descola 1986). In contrast to conceptions of the environment as separate and separable from human views and visions, landscape offers an integrative—and more cross-culturally valid—perspective that has proven attractive to humanistically inclined anthropologists seeking to describe a unified natural/cultural world in a nonreductionistic manner.

Second, landscape is capable of embracing the complexities of anthropological positionality (see Rosaldo 1989). In his introduction to *The Anthropology of Landscape*, Eric Hirsh (1995) traces the term's etymology to its fine art origins. In the landscape genre of painting, he explains, an artist portrays the environment from a specific and removed point of view; what a painter depicts on the canvas is a symbiosis of what is really there and what the artist believes he or she sees. Cultural and literary critic Raymond Williams (1973) offers a related observation: It is never those who are actually *in* the landscape who do the painting. This analogy contains important implications for the anthropological enterprise. Just as the reflexive trend urged those of us who "write culture" to step into our ethnographies (Clifford and Marcus 1986; see also Rosaldo 1989), locating ourselves within the landscapes we describe can shed light on how our positionality shapes our views of people, places, and their distinctive patterns of interaction. Whether a painted pastoral scene or an ethnographic portrait, landscape is about how we see the world and why we see it as we do.

Third, countering charges of earlier anthropology's lack of attention to history and individual agency, landscape is inherently processual and perspectival. Rather than a static and stationary environment, landscape is actively sensed; perceived appearances and meanings shift according to vantage point, moment in time, and observer. As Hirsh (1995) points out, landscape is best understood as a continuously unfolding cultural *process*. And, as philosopher Edward Casey (1996: 27) tells us, "landscapes not only *are*—they *happen*." Thanks to this dynamic outlook, landscape is ripe for fusing with projects in oral history and historical anthropology; several scholars have combined these trends in innovative ways (e.g., Morphey 1995; Basso 1996; Abercrombie 1998; Santos-Granero 1998).

Despite its potential, however, landscape is not a panacea. Too often, work in landscape anthropology has depended upon romantic naturalizations of indigenous peoples' connections to the places they live, thus obscuring serious historical and contemporary political inequities. Especially in the New World context, the range of relationships between indigenous peoples and the environment—like the diversity of American Indian people themselves—has not always been recognized. Since the early days of contact, Europeans and their New World descendants have imagined—and, as time passed and circumstances changed, reimagined—American Indians. Many of these portraits have been extremely unflattering. Others have depicted Natives in a romantically positive light; at times people of European ancestry have reveled in their own imitations of Indians' "primitive" glory (Deloria 1998). However opposite these images may appear, they all represent diverse peoples in simplistic and stereotypical manners.

In both popular and academic discourse, images of "Ecological Indians" have been held up for several decades as figurative—and at times literal—poster children for the mainstream environmental movement (Krech 1999; Nadasdy 2005; Willow 2009).[2] Over and above its stereotypical generalizations, the Ecological Indian image is deeply problematic. Not only does it invoke visions of a "pristine" or "virgin" precontact environment, thereby denying aboriginal peoples' historical presence and thousands of years of active modifications to the land (Wolf 1982; Cronon 1983), but romantic notions of ecological nobility also deny a sense of dynamism and "coevalness" (Fabian 1983) to indigenous people living today and invite troubling charges of inauthenticity when they do not act in accordance with unrealistic, imaginary expectations (Conklin and Graham 1995; Buege 1996; Nadasdy 2005; Lewis 2007: 328).

Even as landscape anthropology celebrates the ubiquitous role of human actors in physically and culturally shaping the landscape, its implicit binding of peoples to places had produced spatially fixed and culturally bounded portraits that are increasingly inconsistent with current anthropological understandings of human life and that disregard the political complexities of human-environment relationships. Appadurai (1988) points out that the application of the indigenous label leads dynamic cultural groups to become tied to—even "incarcerated" in—specific locales; indigenous peoples become conflated with the places they sometimes struggle to protect (see also Malkki 1997: 58–61). To assume a one-to-one correlation between disappearing cultures and endangered environments limits possibilities for recognizing indigenous peoples' internal diversity and cultural adaptability. Assuming such a correlation also implies that if *place* disappears, cultural *identity* does as well. By extension, it freezes indigenous cultures in time as well as space and denies indigenous individuals their rightful place as creative actors in a dynamic global system.

Rather than stripping away agency and obscuring fundamental political concerns by portraying indigenous societies as "two-dimensional victim-specimens," Ronald Niezen (2003: 110) suggests we treat indigenous people as human actors with the power—and deep desire—to shape their own destinies. Likewise, Gupta and Ferguson suggest that "too often anthropological approaches to the relation between 'the local' and something that lies beyond it . . . have taken the local as a given, without asking how perceptions of locality and community are discursively and historically constructed" (Gupta and Ferguson 1997: 6). We need, instead, to question and problematize such associations, to think of "all associations of place, people, and culture as social and historical creations to be explained, not given natural facts" (Gupta and Ferguson 1997: 4). This book responds to these calls.

Beyond its relevance for anthropologies of environment and land-scape, the story of the Grassy Narrows blockade contributes to our understanding of indigenous peoples not as marginal to the global system but as central to and constitutive of it. As the so-called core of the postmodern world fragments, people who were once viewed as peripheral now feel optimistic that they will be taken seriously by out-side observers (Friedman 1994; see also Nesper 2002). For activists at Grassy Narrows, this means that Anishinaabe people can now dare to believe in the systemic potency of their political actions.

Indigenous people share our rapidly changing world. Just as romanticizing the past can leave groups of people conceptually rele-gated to it despite irrefutable evidence to the contrary, to ignore that globalization takes place in distinctively local ways is to ignore the inventive potential of cultures and the people who create them (see Appadurai 1996; Hutchinson 1996; Englund 2002). Examples of what Marshall Sahlins (1999) calls "the indigenization of modernity"—illustrated most concretely by the implementation of introduced tech-nologies to carry out familiar subsistence activities—have become widely accepted as part and parcel of the global condition. As well, many recent works (e.g., Maybury-Lewis 1997; Ramos 1998; Niezen 2003; Sissons 2005) document the rise of movements aimed at safe-guarding indigenous peoples' natural resources, as well as their cultur-ally distinct practices and knowledge. We will return to this important topic in chapter 2.

All told, relationships between peoples and places—and the remarkable actions they inspire—must be explored and analyzed rather than taken for granted. By denaturalizing these associations, we open up a fruitful dialogue about how people come to view them-selves—and be viewed by the outside world—as rooted to place. Activism at Grassy Narrows First Nation may be about protecting the environment, but it is also about ensuring a culturally centered life, some measure of political autonomy, and a healthy homeland for gen-erations yet to come. Careful attention to how Anishinaabe activists perceive their own interests and actions reveals that the blockaders' efforts to protect their lands from industrial logging are not only cul-turally constituted, but also profoundly politically entangled. The story of the Grassy Narrows blockade demonstrates that the cultural and political context of peoples' connection to place is at least as important as the connection itself.

Research in a Contemporary First Nations Setting

A respected friend at Grassy Narrows once presented me with "a question about anthropology." Relaxing in her kitchen on a fair September morning, I was caught off guard. She repeated what an acquaintance from up north had told her: When anthropologists arrive in a community they already have in mind everything they need to know. They only visit Native people to prove they're correct. She wanted to hear my perspective. Did I think this was true? I answered, first, with a pause. I knew I could only respond openly and honestly, in a way that respected her intelligence. My reply had two parts.

The easy answer was no: I didn't feel like I had a definitive explanation for *anything*. During my time at Grassy Narrows, I was open—probably more than ever before—to any kind of knowledge or understanding I could achieve. I welcomed new directions and influences and attempted to match my intentions to fit the interests of the Anishinaabe activists and tribal leaders, elders and youth, hunters and educators I was getting to know. I learned to relax and allow things to happen and (despite the occasional relapse) I greeted insights as they arrived rather than trying to force their emergence.

Still, while my anthropological occupation did not necessarily doom me to undue preconception, it most certainly did not inoculate against conceptual baggage. I arrived in northwestern Ontario with a prefabricated theoretical and personal position. Renato Rosaldo (1989: 8) writes of the ethnographer as a positioned subject who, no matter how sensitive to cultural nuance she may be and no matter how hard he may try, is "prepared to know certain things and not others." From start to finish, I could never ignore who I was and where I came from.

Acknowledging the impossibility of objectivity in anthropology has generated productive discussion in recent decades. Claims that we could ever possess "pure knowledge" appear to have finally been put to rest. Over forty years ago, Jürgen Habermas (1968) suggested social scientists attempt to uncover and explore their biases, rather than sweeping them under a rug of unattainable neutrality. No longer can we pretend to estrange ourselves from our own interests. Similarly, the "dichotomous deadlock" between scientific and applied anthropology appears to be dissolving (Ginsburg 2004: x–xi) and it now appears that publicly engaging with political issues could be integral to American academic practice in the future (Checker and Fishman 2004: 8).

Embracing anthropology as an inescapably "interested" kind of knowledge (Harries-Jones 1991), I strove throughout my study of the Grassy Narrows blockade to be truthful about my own biases. I never claimed neutrality regarding the ongoing conflict between First Nations and the forest industry in northwestern Ontario. I was respectful and open as I sought out diverse perspectives, but I also remained honest about my fundamental support for the Grassy Narrows activists and their long-term goals of environmental protection, cultural revitalization, and political self-determination. This position was true to my own interests as a self-identified environmentalist and human rights advocate and, especially in First Nations and advocacy settings, I feel strongly that it opened many more doors than it closed.[3] As Kay Milton (1993: 13) avows:

> Whether we are concerned primarily for the future of the planet or of the people whose lives we study, whether we want to further the development of anthropology, to contribute to the growth of human wisdom, or to promote our academic careers, we are all engaged in the process of making our knowledge count. The only alternative is a role in which our knowledge counts for nothing.

The potency of an anthropology that advocates for the rights, education, and equality of peoples formerly considered ethnographic "subjects" cannot be underestimated. Indeed, it may ultimately be the only viable anthropology. Because indigenous peoples now possess the ability and the desire to control their own cultural representation, they are increasingly unlikely to involve themselves in outsiders' projects unless they intersect with their own interests. Recognizing the roles of power and history in shaping the ethnographic process, most ethnographers have made "a concerted move toward writing ethnography through the framework of dialogue" and many have begun to envision their work as a deliberately and thoroughly collaborative endeavor (Lassiter 2005: 5). Even then, the road is not always smooth.

Throughout my time in northwestern Ontario, I experienced the weighty implications of cultural and political difference, but I also tasted the fulfillment that bridging these rifts can bring. Gail Landsman comments on her strategy for research in a Native-White conflict setting: She states, "I have no doubt that not being aggressive I missed certain opportunities; I also suspect, however, that I gained many more" (1998:13). Like Landsman, I saw working toward mutual trust and respect as a more important long-term goal than the swift compilation of information. I knew and accepted that I would never be an "expert" in Anishinaabe culture. If such a thing exists at all, surely it is the Anishinaabe people who live and create their culture every day over a lifetime who fit the bill.

I first traveled to northwestern Ontario in late May of 2003 in order to learn about and lend my support to the blockade and community at Grassy Narrows First Nation. For a month, I camped at the Slant Lake blockade and fell asleep each night to a chorus of frogs and loons. The weather was Canada's finest. The days were comfortably warm, yet cool nights kept the region's ubiquitous mosquitoes and flies from becoming a serious annoyance. Perhaps the perfect spring, relieving a harsh northern winter, contributed to my sense of general delight. In any case, time at Slant Lake seemed to stand just bit stiller and the world looked just a bit dreamier than at any place I'd previously experienced. In this "safe-zone"—consciously distanced from the problems of reserve life—members of the First Nation community who visited the blockade for a day or an evening seemed to share my state of mind. I knew I would be back.

The following spring I returned to northwestern Ontario to begin eleven months of full-time fieldwork. Participant-observation and casual interaction with people active in Grassy's anti-clearcutting movement remained my most significant undertaking from start to finish. This demanded that I follow a fantastically variable schedule. I could be in the bush one day and find myself sitting in on a language preservation conference in the comparative metropolis of Winnipeg the next. For the most part, I embraced this diversity as one of the most satisfying and stimulating aspects of my work; I reminded myself regularly that indigenous people throughout the Americas are expected to constantly and effortlessly shift between what many refer to as "different worlds."

Shortly after I arrived in Canada, I realized that my project needed to be, indeed always had been, a multi-sited one. I was quickly overwhelmed by the impossibility of ever understanding everything about indigenous activism at Grassy Narrows. Accepting my inevitable limitations and stepping back to absorb a broad view of the blockade enabled me to move forward.[4] George Marcus (1998: 14) notes that "within a multi-sited research imaginary, tracing and describing the connections and relationships among sites previously thought incommensurate *is* ethnography's way of making arguments and providing its own contexts of significance." Following this dictum, viewing an understanding of relationships as contemporary anthropology's most vital and timely contribution to the world guided my sense of disciplinary purpose.

My fieldwork emerged as multi-sited in two distinct ways. First of all, my research frequently took me to diverse geographic locations. I conducted participant-observation research in Grassy Narrows, but I also attended meetings, conferences, and other relevant gatherings in Kenora and Winnipeg. Secondly, my work demanded that I also travel to many different cultural and political sites. I talked to people with diverse ethnic identifications, socioeconomic backgrounds, and ideological leanings. Although most of the people I worked with were Anishinaabe activists, I also sought out non-Native supporters as well as industry and government representatives.

In order to get a better grasp of the blockade's timeline and the events that set its stage, I also conducted ethnohistorical archival and media research. Although I was present for part of the blockade at Grassy Narrows, there was much that I missed, including the blockade's critical early months. Examining media coverage of the blockade—combined with the stories told by those present from its inception—allowed me to piece together a chronology of blockade events. I also wanted to learn more about what took place in the decades before the blockade and sought out materials in the news media and other sources that might help me trace its long-term development. Close attention to the significant changes people at Grassy Narrows experienced in their lifetimes was essential in shaping my ultimate comprehension of the issues at hand.

The Long Road

The road to Asubpeeschoseewagong winds like the tangled waterways of the English-Wabigoon River system. Or like the story of the

Anishinaabe people who live there. It winds up hills and past soaring outcroppings of Precambrian granite, down again and around a bend to reveal a vast expanse of silent lake. In the summer months, sedges and aquatic grasses ring nearly every lake, begging the attention of passing moose. In winter, when few but coniferous trees and ravens seem to look on, each lake outlines a desolate plain of ice and snow.

From the Trans-Canada Highway near Kenora, one heads north on Ontario Provincial Highway 671 and makes slow progress toward the reserve, just over fifty miles and an hour and a half (give or take) away. Past Island Lake, Silver Lake, Wild Lake, Keys Lake, and Havik Lake, to name just a few. In fading yellow paint, outdated messages on rock faces inform visitors: "Powwow 40 minutes." "Powwow 20 minutes." Of course, no one from Grassy Narrows needs any reminders of their whereabouts. They know this road and its landmarks well. Most of the travelers on Jones Road (as the highway is commonly called) are destined for Grassy, although anglers and a few campers add to the traffic in summer months and sports hunters appear in fall. The occasional flatbed truck roars perilously past, hauling granite monoliths from a privately owned quarry. There are, however, no logging trucks. For those accustomed to travel in the region, their absence is palpable.

Close to the halfway point, a tourist camp occupies the site of the former telegraph station that gave Jones Road its name. A stop sign at Jones cautions motorists of the Canadian National (CN) railroad's busy tracks and a cross with silk flowers poignantly reinforces the reminder. Margaret Land, a respected elder from Grassy, lost her life in an accident here several years ago. The stop sign went up after the tragedy. North of Jones, man-made landmarks are few and far between. Keys Lake—crystal clear and spring fed with a narrow strip of sandy beach—is treasured by tourists and First Nation residents alike. A small, steep parking area accommodates visitors' long summer days.

Several gravel roads, in various and constantly fluctuating states of repair, branch from the paved highway. As one approaches Grassy Narrows, Segise Road—recently used for logging activities and the site of several roving blockades in 2003—provides a popular route for First Nations members traveling into the bush for hunting, fishing, and berry-picking. It is also the shortest (although not always the most reliable) way for people from Grassy to reach friends and relatives at Wabauskang First Nation, located some forty miles to the

Figure I.2. A hand-painted sign points the way to the Grassy Narrows reserve and blockade.

east. Non-Native anglers and hunters occasionally use Segise Road to reach the Wabigoon River's Fifteen Foot Falls.

Only a couple more bends in the road and the highway comes to its official end. Here, one must make a choice: To the left lies the Grassy Narrows reserve, blandly designated English River #21 on most official maps. A hand-painted sign bearing the First Nation's clan-inspired insignia clearly marks the way to the reserve community. If, however, one continues to the right, past the Ontario Provincial Police (OPP) station and its glaring lights, the pavement abruptly turns to gravel. After a ten-minute drive to the north—bumpy and rutted in the summer and slightly smoothed by packed snow and ice in the winter—the Slant Lake site comes into view.

For most of the blockade's first year, a stick blocking half the road demanded closer inspection. Supported by others of its kind, the stick hovered at waist height, bedecked with reflective orange-mesh vests. A mustard-colored sign hung from the center of the stick, proclaiming in bold letters:

PUBLIC NOTICE: YOU ARE IN THE GRASSY NAR-
ROWS TRADITIONAL LAND USE AREA. THIS IS THE
ABORIGINAL TERRITORY OF THE ANISHINABE
PEOPLE OF GRASSY NARROWS FIRST NATION.

This unassuming display, more than any other single object, represented the concrete, physical blockade as it stood when I arrived in
Grassy Narrows. Yet its diminutive and impermanent presence fades
rapidly in comparison to other features of the Slant Lake site, the
activities that occurred there, and the rich meanings that underlie the
events of the blockade. As this study demonstrates, the Grassy Narrows blockade is much more than a mere roadblock.

The modest appearance of the Slant Lake blockade says a great
deal about its social and cultural significance. When activists at
Grassy Narrows make plans to head to the blockade to fish, share a
meal, enjoy a campfire, or to spend a peaceful night in the on-site
cabin, the physical barrier is not what they have in mind. No imper-
meable fortification ever stood here to stop the logging trucks. One
blockader told me that some of the Mohawk Warriors who came to

Figure I.3. The modest physical appearance of the Grassy Narrows blockade, summer
2003.

lend a hand during the blockade's exciting early weeks had quite a chuckle over the humble barricade. This was clearly not what recent Mohawk history, marked by the notorious 1990 Oka incident, had taught them to perceive as a roadblock (see York and Pindera 1991). Here at Grassy, she seemed proud to report, people are the real block-ade. Taken literally, her statement conjures images from the first night of the blockade, when Grassy Narrows youth stood in the stark glare of truck headlights with outstretched arms. But it is also true in a figu-rative sense; rather than the brief moments of confrontation por-trayed by the media, it is the steady flow of social activity at the blockade that visitors like me remember most.

And so, assuming that one stops to read the sign (as many curious non-Native anglers and hunters do), one's attention would instantly be drawn to the left. There blazes a campfire in a stone ring, perhaps tended by someone frying fresh walleye, perhaps simply enjoyed among friends and family. A pre-relocation-style log cabin—erected as part of a traditional skills youth education program—lies a bit fur-ther from the road. Children play contentedly, happy to be outdoors and surrounded by playmates. For Anishinaabe activists and their families, the places to congregate, cook, and unwind are what the blockade is all about. The blockade is much more than a physical bar-rier; it is a way of being and a site of conscious cultural revitalization.

Somewhat ironically, the Slant Lake blockade makes use of an abandoned logging camp turnaround. Vacant for at least forty years, thick brush covers two long-discarded cars from this distant era. Poplar sapling flagpoles propped in small spruce trees wave the flags of the Kanehsatake Warrior Society and Grassy Narrows First Nation. An upside-down Canadian flag—the flag of a Canada in distress—also flies. The sacred fire stands just behind, inside a tipi with a ragged appearance that bears witness to several fires.[5] The sacred fire burned steadily from December of 2002 until the fall of 2003 and is still peri-odically relit by community members.

The campfire on the outside of the turnaround serves as the main warm weather gathering and cooking area. It was around this fire, talking and—more importantly—listening, that I first journeyed into the social and cultural world of the blockade. Beyond the fire ring and past the chairs and cooking supplies that radiate from it, a path slopes downhill toward Slant Lake. Fishing for walleyes (or pickerel, as they are often called in these parts) and northern pike (also known as

jackfish), swimming, and observing the local wildlife are daily activities. A rowboat, a small canoe, and one paddle rest on shore awaiting
communal use.

A row of seven structures lines the turnaround. These one-room,
plywood "shacks" are utilized periodically for sleeping and storage. At
the south end of the Slant Lake site sits a large plywood roundhouse
with orange tarps for a roof, two functional woodstoves, and a solar
generator capable of powering lights and small appliances. The roundhouse serves as the main gathering area in winter and provides shelter
in rainy conditions. Beyond the roundhouse, a meticulously leveled
powwow ground quietly anticipates the annual traditional powwow
held there each spring since the blockade began. The blockade's three
outhouses are located across the road.

While hardly a display of physical power, the blockade is both a
symbol and an act of resistance. As geographers Steven Pile and
Michael Keith (1997: xi) write,

> The term resistance draws attention to the myriad spaces of
> political struggles, but also to the politics of everyday spaces,
> through which political identities constantly flow and fix.
> These struggles do not have to be glamorous or heroic, about
> fighting and opposition, but may subsist in enduring, in refus-
> ing to be wiped off the map of history.

To be sure, at times the blockade at Grassy Narrows *was* glamorous
and confrontational. At these moments, it attracted the kind of
media attention that thrives on such excitement. But for the most
part, the blockade quietly endured—and continues to endure—as a
symbol of the ongoing negotiations of power and identity that shape
contemporary First Nations life. At least as important as its status as a
site of overt resistance, the Grassy Narrows blockade is also a place
where Anishinaabe people resist through the simple act of living.

The concept of resistance appears to implicitly call for an oppo-
nent—for something or someone to actively resist. On the surface, it
would be easy to point to the logging corporations that operate in the
area as this necessary "enemy." And, at one level, this assessment
would be accurate; when asked about the purpose of the blockade,
most of the First Nation's activists initially cite a desire to bring the
clearcutting to a halt. But deeper issues are also at play. As subsequent

chapters describe, the story of the Grassy Narrows blockade cannot be understood as separate from the community's mutigenerational struggle to endure in the face of political, cultural, and environmental domination. As Grassy Narrows' Deputy Chief Steve Fobister once told me, "It's a long road."

Terminological and Linguistic Notes

I use the term Anishinaabe throughout to refer to the group of Native North American people who are also known as Ojibwe and Chippewa. This word is widely believed to derive from Algonquian roots meaning "original," "first," or "natural" man, although other interpretations have been proposed.[6] For the Grassy Narrows activists I worked with, Anishinaabe is the preferred term of self-reference, but Ojibwe is also heard regularly. The precise etymology of the term Ojibwe is contested. Popular explanations draw on a root verb meaning "to pucker," either in reference to a characteristically Anishinaabe style of moccasins with a puckered toe (Densmore 1979 [1929]) or to the unsavory practice of roasting enemy captives until "puckered" (Warren 1984 [1885]). It is also possible that the term was corrupted from a word meaning "those who make pictographs," in reference to the birchbark engravings of the Midewiwin society (Danziger 1979). Chippewa, frequently utilized in official documents and designations in the United States, is simply an Anglicized version of Ojibwe.

As in other cases where written language serves as a recent complement to a rich oral tradition, many different spellings exist for these terms: Anishinabe, Ojibwa, and Ojibway are the most common variations. The plural of Anishinaabe is Anishinaabeg, which also possesses plentiful alternative spellings. When citing a particular piece of literature, I use the term and spelling utilized by that author. I refer to the First Nation community that forms the center of this study interchangeably as Asubpeeschoseewagong Netum Anishinabek, Grassy Narrows First Nation, or simply (following local practice) "Grassy."

When referring specifically to an indigenous group, I use as precise a name as available. To more widely describe peoples with ancestry and roots on the North American continent, I use the terms First Nation, Native, and North American Indian interchangeably in some cases. In others, these terms carry more specific connotations. "First Nations" tends to refer to the Canadian context, while "North American Indian" is a more general term of reference. The term most frequently used by First Nations people in northwestern Ontario to describe themselves is "Native," as opposed to non-Native (and usually white) others. Following their lead, I routinely employ the word in this manner. I recognize that all of these terms are problematic and that compelling arguments for and against each term's use exist.

The term Anishinaabemowin designates the language spoken by Anishinaabe people. Terms in Anishinaabemowin used here make use of the double-vowel spelling system, unless quoting or citing a different system. Pronunciation of Anishinaabemowin terms can seem overwhelming to someone not accustomed to the language's characteristically long strings of syllables. But, generally speaking, Anishinaabemowin is actually much more phonetically rational than English. A long vowel is indicated by a double vowel, as in the word for dog: *animoosh* (a-ni-moosh). Asubpeeschoseewagong is pronounced a-sub-ee-shko-see-wa-gong. There are dozens of mutually intelligible Anishinaabemowin dialects, spoken from the eastern Great Lakes region as far west as the Rocky Mountains, which diverge most fundamentally in pronunciation. The dialect spoken at Grassy Narrows differs only slightly from that used in northern Minnesota, and the Minnesota dialect dictionary (Nichols and Nyholm 1995) is used widely in northwestern Ontario.

The grammatical structures of Anishinaabemowin are incredibly complex, and I do not claim expertise on the subject. Although I studied Anishinaabe language as extensively as possible, my conversational skills remain at a basic level. Language was a frequent line of inquiry and a topic of shared interest, and even my limited understanding allowed many insights that would have otherwise been impossible. Nevertheless, based on a combination of my limited language skills and the all-pervasiveness of English in the Grassy Narrows community, my fieldwork was conducted almost entirely in English. While elders in the First Nation community are typically fluent in Anishinaabemowin and speak it among themselves, younger band members use English as their primary language. I discuss the issue of language loss and the current status of Anishinaabemowin at Grassy Narrows in more detail in chapter 6.

One

Anishinaabe Cultural History and Land-Based Subsistence

On the Reserve

Heading north once more on the long and meandering road, the large sign pointing the way to Grassy Narrows again comes into view. The road to the left reaches the reserve in a few short minutes. The first thing one might notice about the reserve is how hilly it is. The second thing would likely be the proximity of so much water. On all sides, the reserve is surrounded by a jigsaw puzzle of clear northern lakes, most of them part of the English-Wabigoon River system. The shoreline refuses to remain straight for even an instant and the roadways' constant curves follow suit. The reserve's homes and public buildings, its water tower and heating plant, and its narrow ribbons of pavement do little to hide the region's natural beauty.

To most outsiders, the houses lining the reserve's nameless thoroughfare and meandering side lanes look reasonably well spaced and orderly. From an Anishinaabe perspective, however, the appearance of order belies the truth. The boxy houses, numbered and positioned in neat rows, show little regard for traditional conceptions of space or kinship. The reserve community is a product of 1960s relocation and government planning rather than Anishinaabe sensibilities about how and where people should live. Inside and out, houses on the reserve vary in quality and style. The majority are prefabricated and band-owned, differing mainly according to their era of construction and level of upkeep. Scattered throughout the reserve are several newer split-levels so identical that distinguishing characteristics—one has a satellite dish, another a broken window on the lower level—must be actively sought out. A few older homes with prominent logs or stucco, though, do seem truly unique. With the temporary annual exception of the week or two in April after the snow melts but before the school's Earth Day cleanup, the reserve's roadsides and public spaces are kept reasonably clean. Still, children's playthings and aged cars, kept around for their valuable spare parts, dot many yards. Dogs of all possible descriptions wander the roads or relax sedately on wooden porches.

The road goes on, up a precipitous hill and past the Gospel Believers—a small white church built by missionaries—and down into another valley. Then up again and past an overgrown cemetery, manifestly syncretizing Christian and Ojibwe beliefs. On and up past several clusters of homes until arriving at the powwow grounds and band office in "downtown" Grassy Narrows (people I met from other First Nations in the region often joked about Grassy's unusually centralized layout, with the band offices, multipurpose complex, and school all within view of one another). The band office is a nondescript, brown building with few windows and a high front counter that hides the receptionist from view. Bulletin boards and booklet racks advertise community events, employment opportunities, health information, and other news. A row of offices for the chief and twelve councilors—elected every two years—runs along the back wall. A break and meeting room with couches, cushy chairs, a sink, and a coffee maker is easily the building's most inviting room. On the other side of a shimmering bay—part of Garden Lake—looms the community's large school. The Sakatcheway Anishinabe School is an attractive modern facility, with separate elementary and high school wings, as well as a cafeteria, gymnasium, and two fully equipped computer rooms.

Driving slowly with the safety of the reserve's many pedestrians in mind, the road comes to an end in J.B.'s parking lot. The only permanent store in Grassy Narrows, J.B.'s also serves as the community's post office, gas station, and occasional social hub.[1] A rectangular blue building with one small, high window and a set of wooden stairs leading up to a heavy white door, J.B.'s looks like it should house a construction office or warehouse. A neon "open" sign gives away the building's true identity. Inside, soda coolers and displays of refrigerated and frozen foods line the back and left walls. An assortment of convenience-style packaged goods stocks the shelves in the center of the room. Since everything must be trucked up from town, prices at J.B.'s are high. Nevertheless, people pick up items as needs arise and children flock to J.B.'s to buy candy and soda pop. The store also carries a small assortment of fishing and camping supplies for the handful of tourists who drop in during the summer months. J.B.'s has one full-service gas pump and accepts all major credit cards. As the blockade at Grassy Narrows got underway, a large jar was placed on the checkout counter; its handwritten label read: "Donations for Blockade."

J.B.'s rutted parking lot, situated as it is at the end of the reserve's modest system of pavement, also functions as a turnaround. Beyond this, a gravel road intended to someday reach the Old Reserve is under construction. Anyone born at Grassy Narrows before the early 1960s spent his or her early years on the Old Reserve and invariably holds fond memories of life several miles upriver. Many Grassy Narrows residents—especially elders who lack the physical ability or means of transportation needed to reach the Old Reserve by boat, foot, or snowmobile—look forward to the road's completion. They long to physically visit the sites where countless recollections and stories have taken them so many times before.

The Boreal Forest: Climate, Topography, and Ecosystems

Grassy Narrows lies between 50° and 51° north latitude and at 94° west longitude. Like the rest of northwestern Ontario, winters are cold, long, and dark. According to data from Environment Canada, the average January temperature hovers around -18° Celsius (or -1° Fahrenheit) and snowpack reaches several feet in a typical winter. Attaining the benchmark of -40° (where the Celsius and Fahrenheit scale meet) is not a rare occurrence. Lakes freeze hard enough by late December to permit vehicular traffic and the booms of breakup are not heard until the middle of April. Residents of the region celebrate spring. By mid-April, the snow disappears and temperatures rise gradually until they reach an average of 18° Celsius (65° Fahrenheit) in July. With an annual average around twenty-three inches, precipitation is most abundant in June and July, but comes when it chooses. Pleasant by most any standards, summers here are treasured. Beginning in late August, the poplar leaves turn a dazzling shade of yellow. Snow begins to accumulate once again in late October or early November.

In the heart of the massive U-shaped Canadian Shield—the worn away roots of a Precambrian mountain range—northwestern Ontario's topography offers little direction to water on its way to the sea. Although perceptibly hilly, the overall relief is low and drainage is poor. Water moves slowly to the Arctic Ocean, spending time in numerous lakes before passing through the Wabigoon, English, and Winnipeg rivers, resting in Lake Winnipeg, and eventually flowing on to Hudson Bay by way of the Nelson River. While the granitic rock of the Shield is billions of years old, surface features are the result of recent glaciations. Glaciers left their mark on this land just nine thousand years ago, and the quantity of exposed rock testifies to their scouring power.

When the glaciers retreated, they left only a thin layer of sandy topsoil behind. This fact, combined with the brevity of the northern growing season, makes agriculture impractical. When Euro-Canadian settlers first arrived, they thus found this land relatively undesirable (a bit of luck not shared by the Anishinaabe groups living in the fertile Rainy River Valley that straddles the United States border to the south and the rich Red River Valley to the west). Due to its lack of agricultural potential, non-Native Canadians have often perceived the boreal forest as a marginal wasteland. Of course, the indigenous peoples who inhabit the region see it very differently. A rich boreal forest ecosystem, dotted with countless bogs and lakes, rises from this rocky land. Poplars and conifers—spruce, firs, and pines—dominate the uplands, while wild rice and other hydrophilic plants thrive in low-lying areas. The closed boreal forest canopy allows little sunlight to penetrate the forest floor, limiting undergrowth in most locales. Even so, the slow rate of decomposition gives the forest a gnarled, enchanted appearance (Henry 2002).

Mammalian life flourishes in the boreal forest. The multitude of tracks each animal leaves behind makes the forest seem all the more alive. Looking down on the massive footprints of a timber wolf or lynx compels one to look just a little harder into the dense trees in search of eyes. The presence of innumerable black bears—at least when not deep in hibernation—also gives pause. Richard Nelson describes how for the Koyukon of Alaska, "a person moving through nature—however wild, remote, even desolate the place may be—is never truly alone. The surroundings are aware, sensate, personified" (1983: 14). In northwestern Ontario, too, the world is a watchful, living one.

The noisiest and most visible creatures in the northern forest are birds. Although only present in summer, common loons are truly "common" here and can be so loud that they keep a light sleeper awake. The silhouettes of ravens, whiskey jacks (also known as gray jays or camp-robbers), bald eagles, and hawks hover overheard. Although few birds spend the winter here (around twenty species), the spring migration brings enough songbirds and waterfowl (around three hundred species) to make up for the seasonal lack (Henry 2002). White pelicans, great blue herons, snow and Canada geese, and white-throated sparrows are among those who make their summer residence in the boreal forest of northwestern Ontario.

Anishinaabe History: Movements in Time and Space

> The story properly told, or the song properly sung, *is* true.
> —Edward Chamberlin, *If This Is Your Land, Where Are Your Stories?*

For thousands of years, indigenous peoples have lived in the forests of northwestern Ontario, surrounded by the harsh richness of the land. Yet, exactly when groups identifiable as Anishinaabe first arrived in the area remains a matter of contention. Today, both non-Native residents of northwestern Ontario and Anishinaabeg draw on their own interpretations of history in their attempts to establish the legitimacy of their respective claims to the land. In Indian County as in academia, the struggle to control the history of Native North America has been marked by heated battles. Who is privileged to write history? And how do those fortunate few choose to write it? In essence, these are questions about power and its consequences. History, it is often said, is written by the victors. But history can also tell us when power structures are contested and changing.

If it is true that the victors write history, what does it mean when peoples formerly considered marginal or oppressed begin imagining and writing their own pasts? In this context, what to accept as historical evidence becomes a critical question. The *Delgamuukw* decision set an important legal precedent in this regard. *Delgamuukw* began in

1990, when two British Columbia First Nations (the Gitxsan and Wet'suwet'en) argued before a provincial court that they retained title to their traditional lands because they had never signed a treaty with Canada. Eventually, the case reached Canada's Supreme Court. While the Gitxsan and Wet'suwet'en did not officially win the case, the judgment passed down on December 11, 1997 solidly acknowledged First Nations' oral tradition as a valid form of history. In *Delgamuukw*, "the court indicated that oral testimony and oral tradition merited considerable attention in law and that it should be taken into account when assessing First Nations cases" (Coates 2000: 91, see also BC Treaty Commission 1999). On the surface, *Delgamuukw* was about land claims, but at a deeper level it was about the meaning and making of history (Neu and Therrien 2003).

Exploring oral tradition as a form of history is a project that some historians and anthropologists have taken seriously for several decades now. Vansina (1985), for instance, points out that what we understand as history is culturally specific. Furthermore, other societies rarely share the Western fixation with uncovering or proving "objective" historical facts and linear sequences of events (Sahlins 1985; Comaroff and Comaroff 1992). Rather than searching for a factual picture of the past, non-Western peoples' understandings of historical truth—as remembered through stories, landmarks, art, and numerous other mnemonic techniques—have more often involved translating past events to fit contemporary circumstances and meanings. In this context, oral history may be best seen "not as 'evidence' about the past but as a window on ways the past is culturally constituted and discussed" (Cruikshank 1990: 14). Rather than relegating history to the forgotten past, oral societies have found ways to keep it living and relevant. As Anishinaabe scholar Gerald Vizenor (1984: 24) poetically expounds,

> The Anishinaabeg did not have written histories; their world views were not linear narratives that started and stopped in manifest barriers. The tribal past lived as an event in visual memories and oratorical gestures; woodland identities turned on dreams and visions.

The historical consciousness Vizenor describes continues to inform how Anishinaabe people contemplate their own histories and how they make sense of the intersections between their own views of the past and those held by others.

Generally speaking, Anishinaabe and Western historical traditions agree that the people now occupying the Northwestern Great Lakes region have origins in more easterly parts of North America. The group of people today known interchangeably as Anishinaabe, Ojibwe, and Chippewa—together with closely related groups like the Potawatomi and Ottawa/Odawa—migrated from an eastern land of salt water, most probably near the mouth of the St. Lawrence River. Assigning a precise date to the commencement or completion of their westward journey remains impossible and, in any case, the movement did not occur all at once. Instead, "the migration was a process of extended-family visits to relatives, of invitations to live with more westerly groups, and of traveling in both directions many times" (Peers 1994: 28).

In both temporal and spatial terms, the journey from the east to the Lake Superior region was an extended one. Edward Benton-Banai, an Anishinaabe elder from Lac Court Oreilles, Wisconsin, shares the oral narratives he learned from his elders in *The Mishomis Book* (Benton-Banai 1988). According to Benton-Banai, the Algonquin people living along North America's eastern shores long ago received prophecies warning them to move or face destruction. In response, they began a journey that would last for hundreds of years. Several stopping points marked the travelers' route: Niagara Falls, Manitoulin Island, Sault St. Marie. The Anishinaabeg knew they were close to their final destination when the prophecy of finding wild rice ("the food that grows on the water") was fulfilled near present-day Duluth, Minnesota. From there, they traveled the short distance east along the southern shore of Lake Superior until they arrived at Madeline Island.

William Warren, a mixed-blood nineteenth-century historian, also documented the migration story. In his *History of the Ojibway People*, Warren wrote:

> Through close inquiry and study of their valued figurative traditions, we have discovered that the Ojibways have attained to their present geographical position, nearly in the centre of the North American continent, from the shores of the Atlantic Ocean, about the Gulf of the St. Lawrence River. (1984 [1885]: 76)

It is of some significance that Warren first learned of this "figurative tradition" while standing in a doorway, peering in on an initiation ceremony. Standing, as it were, in the doorway seems representative of Warren's own life. Warren was the oldest son of Mary Cadotte, an Anishinaabe and French woman, and Lyman Warren, a fur-trader of English *Mayflower* descent. He was educated at an eastern boarding school, spoke fluent Anishinaabemowin, and wrote in a way that combined aspects of Anishinaabe and Euro–North American cultural traditions. Critically, Warren respected and made use of oral history in his written work (see Schenck 2007).

Although Warren reported seeing a copper medallion carved with a notch for every "lifetime" the Anishinaabeg had lived at Madeline Island, he does not attempt to provide a precise date for when the migration took place. Instead, he states simply that an elder told him it was "many strings of lives ago" (Warren 1984 [1885]: 79). Following Warren's observation of eight notches on the medallion, and using fifty years to stand for one lifetime, Benton-Banai estimates that Madeline Island was settled around 1394 and that the first news of white contact—deduced from a figure with a hat carved on the copper disc— took place around 1544. Based on his knowledge of oral tradition as well as his consideration of what "the scholars" have to say, Benton-Banai believes that the migration started around 900 AD and took around five hundred years to complete (Benton-Banai 1988: 102).

Many non-Native scholars, on the other hand, date the Anishinaabe arrival at Madeline Island more than two hundred years later than Benton-Banai's calculation (see Danziger 1979: 26–27). Whether or not Anishinaabeg lived at Lake Superior beginning around the fifteenth century or not until the seventeenth, it is likely that their expansion west and north out of the Lake Superior area reached its peak in the eighteenth century. Danziger (1979) estimates that by the early 1840s, Anishinaabe people occupied roughly the same areas as today—stretching from the northern section of Lakes Huron and Michigan northwest to the Lake Winnipeg region, with the Lake Superior area serving as a core. It also appears based on fur trade records that Anishinaabeg were already living on both sides of Lake Winnipeg by the end of the eighteenth century and were well established in that region by the early nineteenth (Peers 1994).

Historians have often cited conflict with the Iroquois and involvement in an expanding fur trade as the most important motivating factors for Anishinaabe movement (Warren 1984 [1885]; Jenness 1977 [1923]; Hallowell 1992). Ethnohistorian Harold Hickerson (1970: 13) similarly notes the significance of Ojibwe participation in the fur trade:

> Contrary to the often expressed notion of the shrinkage of Indian groups due to European encroachment, the Chippewa in the long run, underwent great expansion through their contact with Europeans, largely due to the energetic participation in the fur trade.

As Anishinaabe people made inroads into formerly Dakota territory, warfare between the two groups escalated. Eighteenth-century conflicts in the areas that would later become Wisconsin and Minnesota are well documented. According to Nute (1941), around 1660, the Dakota were still in possession of Northern Minnesota. It was at this time that they began to be pushed out by arriving Anishinaabe groups. Long struggles over the territory followed, and the area is believed to have been under Anishinaabe control by 1750.

It is likely that Cree, rather than Dakota, bands were living in the Lake of the Woods area and the region immediately to the north prior to Anishinaabe arrival, but this displacement is scantily documented at best (Danziger 1979). According to Anishinaabeg in the region today, by the time the first white person—a seventeen-year-old Frenchman named Jacques De Noyan—arrived in the hilly lands surrounding Lake of the Woods in 1688, the Anishinaabe people were numerous and strong.

Does the date of Anishinaabe peoples' arrival in their contemporary homelands really matter? In most cases, anthropologists focus on how history—as understood and believed—shapes culture in the present day. But for some people dates matter a great deal. Some non-Natives are quick to point out that the Anishinaabe arrived in northern Minnesota and the southern parts of northwestern Ontario at roughly the same time the first white men entered the area. In a compact book entitled *The Indian Wars*, for instance, Duane R. Lund pointedly notes that white explorers were in the vicinity of northern Minnesota in 1660, 1679, and 1732 (Lund 1995). Several non-Natives I spoke to in Kenora echoed his position. When they cite the "fact" that Anishinaabe people arrived in the region around the same time as Europeans, these individuals deploy history in an attempt to validate continued non-Native control and extraction of the area's natural resources.

Traditional Culture and Ways of Life

The northwestern Ontario Anishinaabeg are part of a larger cultural and linguistic tradition. Anishinaabemowin (the language spoken by Anishinaabe people) belongs to the Algonquian language family, which includes groups as diverse as the Cree (to the north), the Mi'k-maq (on the east coast), and the Blackfoot (of the high plains to the west). Among indigenous North Americans, the Anishinaabe were historically numerous and powerful. They remain today behind only the Cherokee and Navajo in terms of population. By early historic times, Anishinaabe people controlled a vast area of northeastern North America, straddling the region later divided by the United States–Canadian border.

Traditional Anishinaabe social organization was based on an informal tribal structure, with bands of three to four hundred comprising the basic social unit (Jenness 1977 [1932]). Individual families and groups retained a significant degree of autonomy and, as leaders in times of war or peace, chiefs governed based on influence and respect rather than institutionalized coercive force. Although politically independent, bands were closely socially integrated through marriage and the clan system. An exogamous and patrilineal clan system created kinship ties based on shared *doodems* (or totems).[2] Clans were represented by familiar animals. Principal clans included crane, loon, fish, bear, marten, deer or moose, and bird (Warren 1984 [1885]; Benton-Banai 1988), but the relative prominence of each varied regionally.

Prior to European contact, the Anishinaabe lived a seminomadic lifestyle, moving according to seasonal patterns of resource availability. As a consequence of their frequent mobility, Anishinaabe material culture emphasized portability. Light yet durable and easy to locate throughout Anishinaabe territory, birchbark (*wiigwaas*) was used for baskets and other containers as well as for birchbark canoes (*wiigwaasi-jiimaan*).

Birchbark was also essential for the construction of Anishinaabe dwellings. Dome shaped wigwams (*wiigiwaaman*) were the most widespread structure. Wigwams varied in size, but were typically ten to twelve feet in diameter and of round or oval shape. Based on her 1917 fieldwork, Frances Densmore described the construction of one such lodge at White Earth, Minnesota (1979 [1929]: 23–24). In this case, fourteen ironwood poles were stuck into the ground, their ends twisted together overhead and tied with basswood bark. Additional ironwood poles horizontally encircled the structure, completing the wigwam's frame. With the exception of one doorway—later hung with a heavy blanket—the walls were lined with woven bulrush mats and the top of the lodge covered with rolls of birchbark. In the frigid months of winter, a second layer of bulrush mats was added, and along with it a layer of insulating air between the wigwam's two thin walls. A fire in the dwelling's center provided the only heat. When the time came to relocate, families packed their mats and birchbark rolls, but left the wigwam's frame standing. Difficult to transport yet easy to replace, a new frame was assembled at each location. Women, Densmore notes (1979 [1929]: 25), were in charge of wigwam construction.

In northwestern Ontario, the traditional Anishinaabe land-based seasonal subsistence cycle (or "annual round") (see Densmore 1979 [1929]; Danziger 1979) did not differ dramatically from that observed in other parts of the North American subarctic.[3] Through the chill of December, January, February, and March, Anishinaabe peoples' primary subsistence activities included ice fishing and the trapping of beaver, otter, marten, wolf, lynx, and snowshoe hare. With families dispersed for the season, a lesser amount of opportunistic large game hunting also took place in the winter. Canoes provided the preferred means of transportation during the warm seasons, but once the lakes and rivers froze, most travel took place on foot; snowshoes (*aagimag*) stand alongside the canoe as an important Anishinaabe innovation in transportation technology.

As winter relaxed its icy grip, people awaited the noisy arrival of untold numbers of ducks and geese. In late April and early May, waterfowl returning to boreal forest lakes or passing through along their migration routes to more northerly destinations offered a welcome source of food. As soon as the ice broke up, Anishinaabeg began fishing the open waters, often concentrating their earliest efforts on

rapids or known spawning zones. Birchbark was collected most intensively in the springtime, when it peeled easily and cleanly from the
tree. And, although a marginal resource in northwestern Ontario due
to the scarcity of maple trees at this latitude, the collection of maple
sap for producing maple sugar was an important spring tradition for
Anishinaabe people to the south.

From its commencement in May until the waters turned icy with
fall, open water fishing remained a dominant activity. With many
families gathered at prime fishing locations, summer was also the most
social of the seasons. Late summer was a time of particular bounty. In
August, Anishinaabeg harvested the annual crop of wild rice
(*manoomin*) and picked several varieties of berries. Both resources,
together with dried meat and fish, were processed for storage in
underground caches. With fall's arrival, hunting for migratory waterfowl once again became a central activity. Large mammals—moose,
white-tailed deer, and bear—were hunted most intensively in the fall
months. As fall gave way to winter, families once again dispersed,
resuming trapping and continuing the cycle of land-based subsistence.

Transitions: A Mixed Economy

Like many indigenous peoples of the northern forests, the Anishinaabeg of northwestern Ontario shifted gradually from an exclusively
land-based to a mixed economy over the course of many decades,
facilitated in large part by their participation in the historic fur trade.
At Grassy Narrows, these changes accelerated dramatically in the
1960s and 1970s when relocation and mercury poisoning impacted
the community. In a few short years, a mixed economy emphasizing
land-based subsistence supplemented with a small amount of wage
labor and other sources of monetary income became a mixed economy in which—at least from a strictly material point of view—the
reverse was true.

Throughout the eighteenth and nineteenth centuries, Anishinaabeg in the Canadian Shield region continued to move fluidly
according to the demands of the fur trade. Family and extended
family groups traveled with the seasons and trapping formed the heart
of economic life (Hickerson 1970). Over time, particular groups
became associated with specific trading posts operated by the Hudson

Bay Company, where they traded furs for firearms, steel traps, cloth, and other provisions each spring and often remained to fish during the summer months. One of these posts was located up the English River from present-day Grassy Narrows at Lac Seul and attracted a loose confederacy of Anishinaabe families (Shkilnyk 1985). At the time Treaty Three was signed in 1873, the Anishinaabeg gathered at Lac Seul were under the traditional hereditary leadership of Chief Sakatcheway. In the years following the treaty, the government established reserves, not to exceed one square mile for every five band members, for each group of signatory Indians. In 1882, the people associated with Lac Seul were divided into the two groups that became Grassy Narrows and the smaller Wabauskang First Nation. The two communities remain closely linked today through ties of family and friendship.

Through the first half of the twentieth century, people at Grassy Narrows sold furs and blueberries for cash and a handful participated in various types of wage labor, but the bulk of the community's subsistence still came directly from the forest. A small Hudson Bay Company store operated on the Old Reserve, but its limited variety of items and high prices meant that Grassy Narrows residents purchased only basic supplies—hunting and trapping equipment, flour, sugar, and lard—regularly. Almost every family on the Old Reserve in this period planted a small plot of corn, squash, onions, and potatoes. Still, the people of Grassy Narrows remained highly mobile and spent most of their winters out on their traplines. Contacts with non-Native Canadian society were limited to semi-annual visits from Indian Health Service doctors and ceremonial Treaty Day visits from an Indian Agent and RCMP (Royal Canadian Mounted Police) officer (Shkilnyk 1985).

In the postwar boom of the late 1940s, Barney Lamm, a businessman from Minnesota, built a luxurious lodge on Ball Lake, located several miles upriver from Grassy Narrows. From that time on, men from the First Nation community participated seasonally in the burgeoning tourism industry, working as fishing guides for wealthy anglers. The construction of Jones Road in the late 1950s and government-mandated relocation in the early 1960s ushered in more dramatic changes. Grassy Narrows residents now had access to a wide variety of desirable commodities. As chapter 3 describes in more detail, scientists detected methyl mercury in the English-Wabigoon

Figure 1.1. Anishinaabe children pose with blueberries for sale in Kenora, circa 1912. Photo by C. G. Linde. Used with permission of the Minnesota Historical Society.

River system in 1970. The impacts of relocation and mercury poisoning compounded one another. After relocation, the community's transition from a relatively independent, subsistence livelihood to participation in the wider wage labor system had accelerated quickly. Many citizens of Grassy Narrows, now working as commercial fishermen or fishing guides, depended upon the river more than ever before for their living. These economic opportunities collapsed after the discovery of mercury in the river.

By 1977, the community was economically dependent upon steadily increasing transfer payments from the Canadian government, with 37.2 percent of all income deriving from unearned sources and the government functioning as the community's principal employer (Shkilnyk 1985: 148). A report published by the University of Manitoba's Natural Resources Institute the same year (Kelly et al. 1977) similarly listed band administration as Grassy Narrows' most profitable occupation. The socioeconomic situation has improved little over the past thirty years. Unemployment, underemployment, and welfare dependency remain high.[4] On welfare "paydays," the band office bustles with activity as people claim their checks, supermarkets in Kenora regularly sell out of basic supplies, and some residents dread the disruptive drinking parties they know will follow.

From an economic standpoint, the situation at Grassy Narrows bears little resemblance to the traditional ideal, yet First Nation residents' land-based subsistence activities differ more in quantity than in quality from the pattern described here. Although fewer people today engage in land-based subsistence activities and those that do tend to engage in them less often, almost every family group includes someone who hunts, fishes, and/or traps at least occasionally. Many community members continue to gather each season's characteristic wild resources despite the social and economic upheavals of the past fifty years. Furthermore, those who are unable to participate regularly in land-based subsistence speak of the community members responsible for keeping these traditions alive with genuine respect.

At Grassy Narrows today, trapping remains the dominant cold-season subsistence activity, although fishing also takes place during the winter. Grassy Narrows trappers hold thirty-one registered traplines scattered throughout the Traditional Land Use Area that surrounds the community.[5] Travel to and within the trapline almost always occurs by snowmobile and trips are usually completed in one day, although a few trappers maintain cabins that make longer stays feasible. In addition to registered trapline holders, official "assistants" and younger relatives frequently accompany trappers in order to develop their own skills. While the majority of the community's trappers learned their skills by observing and assisting as youth, several Grassy Narrows residents have become involved in trapping more recently with help from Ontario Ministry of Natural Resources training courses.

The most commonly sought furbearers include beaver—one of the only species trapped for its fur that Grassy Narrows residents also prize as a food source—and members of the weasel family: pine marten, river otter, fisher, mink, and wolverine. Red fox, lynx, wolf, and muskrat are also trapped periodically. Trapping provides supplementary income for many men and women at Grassy. Four times a year, the North American Fur Auction comes to Kenora to purchase furs from the region's trappers. Years ago, high fur prices meant that a skilled trapper could support a family by trapping alone. During my time at Grassy Narrows, a trapper who worked hard and had a bit of luck could still secure as much, I was told, as $8,000 over the course of a winter.

Despite constant anxiety about mercury and other toxic substances in the English-Wabigoon River system, fishing is enjoyed by Grassy Narrows residents of all ages. Walleye are famously abundant in northwestern Ontario's waters. Men, women, and children alike fish with rod and reel (this usually means jigging from boats or casting from the rocky shoreline with inexpensive jigheads and rubber lures) and a few men gather to snare fish with wire during the spring spawning season. Commercial fishing remains insignificant due to restrictions in place since the mercury contamination of the 1970s, but tourism has rebounded to some degree and a few dozen men—as well as a couple women—from Grassy find seasonal work as fishing guides.

In late summer, people eagerly await the ripening of two important wild foods: wild rice and blueberries. The availability of these resources varies according to weather conditions. Additionally, wild rice remains at the mercy of the dams that now constrain the English-Wabigoon River system; if water levels are raised while the rice is still in its vulnerable floating leaf stage, an entire harvest can be damaged beyond recovery. If, however, conditions have been favorable, both crops are astoundingly rich. Harvesting wild rice requires access to a boat and considerable skill, but a handful of Grassy Narrows residents collect the aquatic grain each year and share the products of their labor widely. Abundant and accessible, hundreds of First Nation residents take part in the seasonal harvest of wild blueberries.

In the fall—and to a lesser extent throughout winter and into early spring—First Nation members hunt moose and white-tailed deer by firearm. Most frequently, two or three people set out together in the morning or evening, hunting with the aid of a boat or vehicle for transportation. Meat from these large animals is frozen for consumption throughout the year. In both fall and spring, migratory waterfowl are also harvested.

Several factors now combine to limit First Nation members' participation in land-based subsistence. Children, for one thing, must remain close to school. Although I heard of a few parents who took their children out of school for a land-based subsistence event they deemed important, on no occasion did this extend beyond a day or two. Travel into the bush also requires transportation in the form of a snowmobile, boat, or truck as well as the gas to get it there. This requires money. As a paradoxical corollary of the contemporary mixed economy, the same adults who hold regular jobs are most able to afford such travel yet are often too busy with other demands to undertake it.

Land-Based Subsistence in the Twenty-First Century: Culture, Identity, and Politics

Although foods harvested from the bush are a valued part of Grassy Narrows residents' diet, for most people they are a caloric supplement rather than a subsistence base. Today, people at Grassy purchase the majority of their provisions in the supermarkets of Kenora. Yet, it would be highly erroneous to assume that wild foods are inconsequential because they provide only a small percentage of First Nation members' caloric intake. For some families in certain parts of the year wild meat, fish, rice, and berries complete many meals. Even more important, however, is the relationship between the harvest and consumption of wild foods and Anishinaabe cultural identity. For many people at Grassy Narrows, land-based subsistence is much more than simply a source of livelihood; it is deeply symbolic of a way of life.

Land-based subsistence is the quintessential aspect of northern Natives' cultural lives. As Paul Nadasdy (2003: 63) puts it, "to First Nations people living in the Arctic and Subarctic, hunting is synonymous with life itself."[6] Kirk Dombrowski (2001: chapter 4) similarly points out that subsistence is both an identity and a livelihood; it is both a way of life and a way to live. In the past, the truth of these statements was quite literal. While economic patterns have shifted considerably, indigenous peoples in the north continue to depend—to varying degrees—on hunting for physical as well as psychological sustenance. Nadasdy (2003: 64–65) goes on to describe how for Kluane people in the southwest Yukon, "[hunting] has been *the* fundamental organizing principle of their culture, structuring and informing every aspect of their entire way of life." Despite the complex transitions of recent years, this statement rings true at Grassy Narrows.

Like other Native northerners, residents of Grassy Narrows hold wild foods—things like moose meat, venison, beaver, walleye, wild rice, and blueberries—in higher regard than the commodities available for purchase in town (see Wenzel 1991: 137–38 and

Nadasdy 2003: 75–76). Not only do they consider such items healthier, but the acts of gathering and consuming wild foods are also important markers of a contemporary Indian identity. By gathering berries and rice and by hunting, fishing, and trapping, people at Grassy Narrows connect to their Anishinaabe heritage. As respected harvester Andy "Shoon" Keewatin put it in the summer of 2004, these things "remind them who they are." For Shoon and others at Grassy, a life of land-based subsistence, the cultural identity that accompanies it, and the forest that enables it cannot be bought or sold.

Land-based subsistence helps construct an affirmative Anishinaabe identity. It gives Anishinaabe people a way to define themselves that breaks free of mainstream society's pessimistic comparisons and categorizations. The devastating poverty of Canada's First Nations has been well documented (e.g., York 1990), even if not fully grasped by the general Canadian public. Although they do lament the blatant economic disparities that divide them from their Euro-Canadian neighbors, many Anishinaabeg feel that their cultural, spiritual, and social richness far outweighs their material poverty. Keeping culturally distinct patterns of land-based subsistence alive lies at the core of this perceived wealth. For Anishinaabe people in northwestern Ontario, firsthand experience with environmental degradation—most unforgettably the discharge of mercury into the English-Wabigoon River system—instilled a harsh lesson: If the environment becomes further degraded, traditional land-based subsistence and the rich set of cultural beliefs and practices that go along with it are likely to cease.

In fact, Grassy Narrows residents' reactions to the health risks associated with toxins in the environment also highlight the symbolic significance of land-based subsistence. Mercury contamination and, more recently, the aerial spraying of herbicides (a standard step in the industrial forest regeneration process) have led many First Nation members to worry about the safety of consuming the wild foods they harvest. Judy DaSilva—a devoted anti-clearcutting activist and mother of five young children—once expressed her concerns about contaminants at a public forum. An outsider attending the event suggested a simple solution: Why, he asked, didn't they simply stop eating wild foods? Judy had been taken aback. Reflecting on this exchange, she emphatically told me, "It's not just something you quit. It's not just food for us; it's spiritual."

In addition to bolstering Grassy Narrows residents' feelings about their own culture and cultural identity, their practice of land-based subsistence also makes a strong statement to the outside world. It marks Grassy Narrows First Nation as a culturally and ethnically distinct entity, with unique practices, institutions, and associated rights. Activists at Grassy Narrows frequently speak of the need to "assert their rights." But what do they mean? How do they translate abstract political declarations into on-the-ground actions? Most often, such assertions take the form of hunting, fishing, and other land-based subsistence pursuits within the Grassy Narrows Traditional Land Use Area. Based on the guarantees of Treaty Three, Anishinaabe people have the legal right to harvest resources for their own subsistence throughout the region even when these activities may be illegal for northwestern Ontario's non-Native population. They possess, for instance, the right to hunt outside of Ontario Ministry of Natural Resources sanctioned seasons, are not required to obey bag limits, and are able to hunt and fish without a license. Natives are also permitted to use some harvesting techniques not permissible for the general public.

In recent years, the people of Grassy Narrows have been able to hunt, fish, and trap with little harassment. Throughout much of the twentieth century, however, Anishinaabeg in the Kenora district were frequently prosecuted for carrying out these activities (Phelan 2001). As Nesper (2002) explains regarding the "violating" behavior of Native people in northern Wisconsin, the denial of these basic rights led many to see land-based subsistence as a conscious declaration of the rights they possess by virtue of their distinctive indigenous cultural, historical, and legal identity.[7] Hunting, fishing, and gathering— as components of an economic mode of production—have always been cultural activities. Today, however, these practices have also become strikingly self-conscious and deeply political. For Anishinaabeg in the twenty-first century, engaging in land-based subsistence activities has become an inescapably political act.

"Culture," Justice Thomas Berger (1991: 139) writes, "must have a material basis. This gives the idea of Native self-determination and the subsistence culture on which it depends a compelling urgency among the peoples of the Arctic and sub-Arctic." For the Grassy Narrows blockaders, preserving the land has become a precondition for the preservation of Anishinaabe cultural identity; the presence of viable ecosystems with healthy plant and animal populations and a rich diversity of species is taken as a prerequisite for the survival of land-based subsistence culture. It is the natural environment of Grassy Narrows' Traditional Land Use Area that provides the First Nation's residents with the material foundation Berger prescribes. In this context, Grassy Narrows activists understand protecting the land as a *right*, closely linked to the safeguarding of their treaty and Aboriginal rights. It is to this topic that we now turn.

Two

From Aboriginal Policy
to Indigenous Empowerment

Defending their land-based subsistence tradition and the Anishinaabe cultural identity it represents is an essential part of Grassy Narrows activists' agenda. As well, the blockaders' anti-clearcutting stance cannot be considered independent from their desire to see their Aboriginal and treaty-guaranteed rights recognized by the Canadian government, timber industry, and public. But why did the blockade occur when and where it did? Why, in December of 2002, was the time finally right for First Nation members to take direct action? Tracing the political prehistory of the Grassy Narrows blockade—a blockade story of a different kind—can begin to answer these questions. At the same time, telling the story of Native North American activism challenges more dominant narratives that place indigenous victimization and oppression at their centers (Fixico 2007: 7).

As we will see, Grassy Narrows residents' decision to initiate a blockade arose from what Jerome Levi (writing about indigenous cultural politics in Mexico) terms a "unique blend of pressures and possibilities" (2002: 10). J. R. Miller's words—inspired by the conflict that shook Oka, Quebec in 1990—are also equally relevant at Grassy Narrows: First Nations communities have "experienced enough setbacks to be angered and just enough victories to be encouraged to continue their resistance" (1991a: 299).

The Nature of Native Rights

An appreciation of the multiple threads that interweave to form the fabric of American Indian life is central to the notion of "people-hood." Proposed as a constructive core assumption for future studies of American Indians and other indigenous groups, the peoplehood model considers four interrelated factors—language, sacred history, religion, and land—and holds that "no single factor is more important than the others and all necessarily support each other as well as a par-ticular group's larger sense of identity" (Holm et al. 2003: 12). Fur-thermore, united by common language, shared sacred history and ceremonial cycles, and by collective knowledge and use of a particular territory, Holm et al. argue that a "people" is an inherently sovereign entity (2003: 17). It is in this spirit that indigenous activists around the world insist that they be referred to in the plural not as *people* but as *peoples*—as distinct autonomous groups with associated rights to self-determination (see Niezen 2003: 160–65).[1] Grassy Narrows activists often defend the legitimacy of the blockade by appealing to their rights as an indigenous people. The clearcutting of Grassy Nar-rows' Traditional Land Use Area, they argue, violates their Aboriginal and treaty rights. It undermines their right to contribute to decisions that impact their traditional lands and impedes their treaty-guaran-teed ability to engage in a variety of land-based subsistence pursuits.

A basic understanding of the history of Aboriginal rights in Canada and the principles that underlie them is helpful for appreciat-ing the blockaders' position. Since Europeans set foot on the North American continent over five hundred years ago, many changes have ensued. To greater or lesser degrees, the indigenous peoples of North America have been dispossessed of their lands and resources. As a result of assimilationist projects and policies, many First Nations people internalized their diminished social status and relative lack of rights (York 1990). The situation is gradually improving; citizens in Native communities are now amassing knowledge about their rights and—although debate regarding the various dimensions of Aboriginal rights continues—the Canadian government has recognized Aborigi-nal rights as intrinsic.

Encouraging shifts in Canada's political climate initially became apparent in the early 1970s. In the landmark 1973 *Calder* case, the Canadian Supreme Court acknowledged that Aboriginal rights and title exist in law unless explicitly extinguished by the Crown.[2] Michael Asch (1984: 54) observed that the *Calder* case,

> firmly established a legal concept of singular importance: that even within the ideological orientation of English legal tradition, aboriginal peoples could be shown to have rights that originated prior to contact and that could exist without express acknowledgement by a British or Canadian sovereign. In other words, it defined for Canadian law the fundamental principle of aboriginal rights.

The issue of *certainty*—the desire on the part of developers to avoid areas with contested land rights—ensures that Aboriginal rights issues will remain prominent well into Canada's future (Blackburn 2005) and that the federal government will continue working to convert undefined Aboriginal rights into delineated treaty rights through continuing negotiations with northern First Nations.

Aboriginal rights are now entrenched in Canada's constitution. Section 35 of the 1982 Constitution Act recognizes and affirms existing Aboriginal and treaty rights held by the Aboriginal peoples of Canada (for this reason, these are sometimes called "Section 35" rights). As the Canadian Royal Commission on Aboriginal Peoples (CRCAP) states, "Aboriginal self-government can never be a gift from an 'enlightened' Canada. The right is inherent" (CRCAP 1996: 25). Still, exactly how to characterize such rights has evaded codification and considerable differences of interpretation have divided First Nations and government perspectives.[3] As Asch explains, "the problem is simple: although all parties agreed to put 'aboriginal rights' into the Act, there was no consensus regarding its meanings. Rather, as the constitution explicitly states, this meaning is to emerge through further dialogue and discourse" (Asch 1984: 1, see also Canada 1995). These complexities aside, discussions about Aboriginal rights provide Grassy Narrows activists with a broad legal context within which to position their anti-clearcutting activism.

Leaders of the blockade also point out that long before *Calder* and the Constitution Act, the Royal Proclamation of 1763 established the earliest legal precedent for Aboriginal rights. The proclamation reserved all lands west of a "Proclamation Line"—roughly drawn along the spine of the Appalachian Mountains—for Native peoples, unless or until the land was ceded to the British Crown. Additionally, the proclamation included a specific reference to the reservation of Indian hunting grounds. According to the proclamation, only the British Crown could enter into negotiations with Indian Nations or acquire Native lands, ostensibly to "prevent the abuses that characterized land sales in the coastal colonies" (Coates 2000: 80). After 1763, Indian peoples had to be dealt with at the highest governmental level before their land could be formally opened to white settlement. While the United States chose to ignore the proclamation following the Revolutionary War, it remained law in Canada.

The 1763 Proclamation continues to set the tone for contemporary Native rights struggles. While it does not formally recognize Aboriginal sovereignty—quite to the contrary, the proclamation identifies British sovereignty as paramount—the standard was set that "Aboriginal lands in areas not previously settled by Europeans were to be used for and by First Nations people until a proper treaty had been negotiated" (Coates 2000: 81). This was the motivation, then, behind the rush to secure treaties in the fertile agricultural regions of western Canada during the 1870s.

Treaty Three: Context and Contestation

Because their forefathers negotiated and signed a treaty with the British Crown, the people of Grassy Narrows (in common with other northwestern Ontario Natives) possess an assemblage of treaty-guaranteed rights. While outside observers—including government officials as well as the majority of non-Native Canadians—tend to see the 1873 signing of Treaty Three as negating the validity of its signatories' Aboriginal rights, most Anishinaabe people believe otherwise. By signing Treaty Three, they argue, their ancestors relinquished nothing. Furthermore, many Anishinaabeg view their rights as sacred gifts from the Creator. As one Grand Council Treaty Three[4] (ND a) brochure states:

> [These rights] can neither be given nor taken away by other peoples, nations or governments. Our freedom of movement arises from our traditional use and occupation of Turtle Island. This is a natural right of our people; which can be rec-

ognized, but neither created nor rescinded by a man-made document.

While they do not believe their inherent rights were extinguished by their forefathers' participation in the treaty process, activists at Grassy Narrows do acknowledge the difficulty of working within the Aboriginal rights framework that has characterized prominent cases in British Columbia and the Territories where treaties were never negotiated.

Asserting and affirming the rights guaranteed by Treaty Three of 1873 is thus central to the Grassy Narrows blockaders' objectives. Although debate surrounds the treaty's interpretation and the rights it promises, very few Anishinaabe people today complain about the treaty itself. Indeed, activists at Grassy Narrows value their treaty highly; they merely desire that their views of it and the rights it establishes be respected by all. In both Canada and the United States— joined under Great Britain until the American colonies declared independence in 1776—the relationship between Native peoples and settlers has long been an ambiguous one. In both cases, Indian peoples were—and are—recognized as marginally independent yet simultaneously subordinate groups, a position that inspired U.S. Justice John Marshall to coin the term "domestic dependent nations." Indian Nations have been perceived as sovereign enough to validate the treaties that allowed settlement by non-Natives, but rarely in recent times have they been perceived as sovereign enough to decline them or interpret them on their own terms (see Churchill 2002). For many indigenous observers, the fact that treaties—defined most fundamentally as agreements between *nations*—exist at all affirms their sovereign status.

Negotiating Treaty Three

Unlike south of the border, Euro-Canadian leaders endeavored to avoid the overt confrontation and warfare that arose as waves of non-Native settlers flowed west. From a logistical standpoint, Canada simply did not possess the financial or military strength to fight such wars. To its credit, the Canadian government rarely pretended it could seize Indian lands without prior negotiation (Miller 1991b:

412). Instead, as the Canadian nationalist project encouraged Euro-Canadians and recent European immigrants to travel west to cultivate the fertile prairies, the government negotiated a series of eleven "numbered" treaties.

The 1870s saw the peak of treaty-making in Canada; seven of the eleven numbered treaties were negotiated during this decade. These treaties eventually covered most of western Canada, with the exception of British Columbia and the far north. In the early 1870s, a newly confederated Canada sought desperately to secure a Canadian route to the rapidly growing settlement in the fertile Red River Valley, located where Winnipeg, Manitoba now stands. Although there was little potential for agriculture in the rocky landscape of northwestern Ontario, passage through its difficult terrain was unavoidable. The Anishinaabe groups positioned along the route were taken seriously as a threat to safe passage. The federal government felt it needed their cooperation if Canada, as a long-term project, was to succeed. Not surprisingly, government negotiators appear to have placed considerable pressure on the Indians to come to agreement (Dawson 1873).

The Canadian government intended Treaty Three as the first of the numbered treaties, but difficult negotiations and the distraction of the Red River Rebellion led to delay.[5] Troops on their way to squelch the rebellion passed through the Treaty Three area unscathed in 1870, yet "because the Ojibwa near the Lake of the Woods objected to the progress of troops and surveyors through their territory the government began talks with them as soon as the Red River resistance had been dealt with" (Miller 1991a: 161). A delegation of Anishinaabe leaders from the Rainy River, Lake of the Woods, and Lac Seul regions of northwestern Ontario met with representatives of the British Crown and the fall of 1873 to negotiate the third of the numbered treaties. When the negotiations commenced, approximately 1,400 Anishinaabe men, women, and children were gathered at the northwest angle of the Lake of the Woods (Daugherty 1986).

The negotiations presented many challenges. In fact, two prior attempts—in 1871 and 1872—to reach an agreement had failed. The Anishinaabeg of the area had earned a reputation as astute, skilled, and insistent negotiators and were unwilling to stray from the terms and conditions they desired. Notes taken at the negotiations clearly demonstrate Native leaders' insistence that the land in question was

Indian country and that their agenda was not to be lightly dismissed (Dawson 1873). Their skill and relative success is reflected in the treaty they eventually signed. The formal negotiation took three days and produced a six-page document. By today's standards, Treaty Three—and the negotiation process that produced it—may appear inherently inequitable, but in the context of the late nineteenth century it represented a notable achievement on the part of capable Anishinaabe negotiators. Treaty Three was the first of the numbered treaties to include hunting and fishing rights on unoccupied Crown lands. And, in comparison to previous treaties, it granted more reasonable annuities and rights to its Native signatories (see Friesen 1981; Daugherty 1986).[6]

Interpreting Treaty Three

The negotiation and signing of a treaty does not always imply common understanding. The parties to Treaty Three held different assumptions and had different objectives for entering into negotiations. As Taylor (1987: 45) points out:

> It appears that government and Indians began from different assumptions, and that there was little attempt on the part of the government either to understand the Indian viewpoint or to convey its own to the Indian people. Under these circumstances, it is hardly surprising that Indian interpretations of the treaties do not conform to those of the government, or that there are some variations in the viewpoints of Indian people themselves on the meaning of their treaties.

Just as understandings of the treaty's implications and the reasons for signing it diverged in 1873, so conflicting views continue to exist as to the treaty's original intent and how, accordingly, it can best be interpreted in the twenty-first century.

From the perspective of the Canadian government, the foremost impetus for Treaty Three was the attainment of an Anishinaabe land cession. While the government's most pressing original ambition involved securing a transportation route through northwestern Ontario, the Crown soon decided that acquiring the land itself was a preferable option (Daugherty 1986). To the government, Treaty Three—like the other numbered treaties—signified a land surrender agreement in which the Indians ceded whatever claims they had to occupy and use their traditional homelands in return for gifts and annual payments (Miller 1991b). The official written version of the treaty is consistent with this goal. The version of Treaty Three published by Canada (1966 [1871–1874]: 4) states:

> The Saulteaux Tribe of Ojibbeway Indians and all other Indians inhabiting the district hereinafter described and defined, do hereby cede, release, surrender and yield up to the Government of the Dominion of Canada for Her Majesty the Queen and Her successors forever, all their rights, titles, and privileges whatsoever, to the lands including within the following limits.

While the government's main objective was to arrange the surrender of Native lands, the Anishinaabe people of the area, in contrast, hoped to establish a relationship with the Crown that would enable their people to survive and thrive—physically and culturally—in a rapidly changing world. They saw the treaty as a way to accomplish this goal (Daugherty 1986).

The existence of unofficial versions of Treaty Three lends credence to the argument that Anishinaabe negotiators may not have possessed the same view of what they were agreeing to as government officials. The most significant among these alternative versions is known as the Paypom Treaty. Drawn from a set of notes taken at the 1873 negotiations by Joseph Nolin, a Métis man employed by one of the attendant chiefs to record the event, the Paypom Treaty shows clearly that the official version of the treaty does not perfectly reflect the 1873 discussions. In fact, research indicates that Treaty Three as published by Canada may have actually been written beforehand; government officials eager to expedite the treaty process may have based their version on the previous year's negotiations (Daugherty 1986). The Grassy Narrows blockaders believe that the Paypom Treaty better reflects the true terms and conditions of the Treaty Three agreement. Critically, the Paypom Treaty says nothing about land surrender.

Another discrepancy between the official version of Treaty Three and the Paypom Treaty concerns traditional subsistence rights. While the published version of Treaty Three provides for Anishinaabe hunting and fishing rights, it also includes caveats regarding the potential regulation and negation of these rights if and when the land became needed for non-Native settlement or resource use. The official version of Treaty Three declares:

> They, the said Indians, shall have right to pursue their avocations of hunting and fishing throughout the tract surrendered . . . subject to such regulations as may from time to time be made by Her Government of Her Dominion of Canada, and saving and excepting such tracts as may, from time to time, be required or taken up for settlement, mining, lumbering or other purposes . . . (Canada [Federal Government] 1966 [1871–1874]: 5)

The Paypom document, on the other hand, makes no mention of the exceptions and limitations contained in the government version. Rather, it states that "The Indians will be as free as by the past for their hunting and rice harvest" (Grand Council Treaty Three ND b). Both the Paypom Treaty and the published version of Treaty Three unambiguously include First Nations hunting rights, but while Paypom mentions continued rights to wild rice, the document fails to comment on any form of fishing rights. Conversely, the government's published version of Treaty Three explicitly cites fishing, but not wild rice. Ironically, timber was not a major concern at the time of the treaty because the boreal forest ecosystem produced trees then considered too small and of too poor quality to merit their profitable harvest (Daugherty 1986). Today, of course, forestry issues have moved to the forefront.

According to Anishinaabe understandings of Treaty Three, Native people in the region would permit a right-of-way through their land and allow the government to undertake specific activities in the area. In exchange, they expected fair compensation (Daugherty 1986). It remains uncertain how well the original Anishinaabe negotiators understood the government's notion of land cession.[7] Clearly, most contemporary Anishinaabeg do not see Treaty Three as a land surrender agreement. As one Anishinaabe man firmly informed me, nothing was surrendered at the signing of the treaty and there was never any surrender of rights, jurisdiction, or way of life. Anishinaabe activists at Grassy Narrows seem to share his perspective. They maintain that their forefathers saw Treaty Three as a peace and friendship agreement. As several blockaders told me, it is unimaginable that their ancestors would have agreed to give up their lands and rights. If they had fully understood the concept of land cession, they argue, the treaty would never have been signed. And if Treaty Three lands were never truly surrendered, a large portion of northwestern Ontario remains Anishinaabe land to this day.

The contemporary interpretation of historical treaties is not merely an academic matter. Not only does the view of Treaty Three as a contract of peace and friendship—rather than a surrender of Anishinaabe rights, lands, and influence—energize the debate surrounding the treaty's interpretation, but this interpretation underlies Grassy Narrows citizens' attempts to gain control over their Traditional Land Use Area. A lawsuit filed by three Grassy Narrows First Nation trappers in April of 2000 claimed that the hunting and trapping rights guaranteed by Treaty Three were federally protected under the 1982 Constitution Act and, therefore, that the Province of Ontario had no legal power to grant forestry permits to logging companies. Although complicated by Canada's federal jurisdiction over Indians and Indian lands and provincial jurisdiction over natural resources, the lawsuit was intended as a political statement. It urged members of the wider society to begin thinking of Treaty Three as a legal agreement that guarantees Anishinaabe people's continued access to natural resources and acknowledges their claims to traditional lands. This case will be discussed further in chapter 4, but its point should be well taken here: The contemporary interpretation of treaties is an arena in which First Nations communities like Grassy Narrows struggle to assert and augment their power relative to the nation-states that encompass them.

"Indian Affairs exists to keep us down"

Canada's first Indian Act was passed in 1876, only three years after the signing of Treaty Three, and has dominated Aboriginal policy ever since.[8] Asserting its exclusive legislative responsibility over Indians and lands reserved for Indians, the federal government created the Indian Act in an attempt to consolidate and simplify Canadian policies pertaining to Native peoples. While the government ostensibly intended the act to protect Indians from negative outside influences and unscrupulous dealings, the ward-guardian relationship it established quickly began to appear more coercive than protective (Miller 1991a: 192). Reflecting an increasingly restrictive and assimilationist mentality, the Indian Act was revised numerous times. The 1880 version of the Indian Act enabled the newly established Department of Indian Affairs to impose an elected band council governance system upon Native groups, even when they preferred to maintain traditional non-elected patterns of leadership (Miller 1991a). In most Canadian Native communities, this externally imposed form of governance remains in place today.

While Anishinaabe people embrace and promote the basic tenets of Treaty Three as they understand it, their feelings toward the Indian Act tend to be exceedingly negative. In dozens of conversations on the topic with Anishinaabe activists, political leaders, and ordinary citizens, I heard not one positive remark regarding the Indian Act. Indeed, many Anishinaabeg in northwestern Ontario feel that the Indian Act fails to honor the original intent of the treaties and effectively erodes the strength of Treaty Three. As one man put it, "There was never an agreement to live by the Indian Act. There was an agreement to live by the treaty, but never by the Indian Act." Unlike Treaty Three, the Indian Act was unilaterally developed and implemented by the Canadian government.

From a broad First Nations perspective, the inequality that continues to characterize Aboriginal-Canadian relations has its foundations in the Indian Act and the assimilationist attitude that lies beneath it (Mercredi and Turpel 1993). More often than not, resentment and suspicion flavor Native political leaders' and activists' dealings with the Canadian government. Although Canada's Department of Indian Affairs and Northern Development does provide numerous social and economic programs and services to communities like Grassy Narrows, many indigenous activists and advocates remain unimpressed.[9] Based on measures of education, health, income, and housing conditions, Aboriginal people have consistently been found to face the worst living conditions of any group in Canada.

Conversely, unemployment, suicide, criminal detention, and physical abuse occur within the Native population at rates much higher than those seen in Canadian society as a whole (Stavenhagen 2004). Grassy Narrows First Nation presents no exception to these statistical trends. "The government," one blockader emphatically told me as we rode together though the reserve on a dark February night, "has done *nothing* for us." She called my attention to the "paper shacks" that lined both sides of the road as evidence.

I first set foot in Grassy Narrows with a naiveté predicated upon my middle-class, Euro-American background. I knew that the governments of Canada, the United States, and other colonial nations had inflicted countless harms upon indigenous peoples, but I assumed that they had proceeded with predominantly noble intentions in mind. Certainly, government representatives and missionaries had been ignorant. They had failed to understand the consequences of their actions. Yet, they were products of historical circumstance who could not have foreseen the damage their decisions would cause. I realized quickly that the Native victims of such oversight did not share my forgiving view. At Grassy Narrows, the harsh lessons of history sowed the seeds of mistrust so prominent today.

In January of 2005, Deputy Chief Steve Fobister enlightened me regarding what he saw as the intentional breakdown of traditional Anishinaabe systems of belief and leadership at the hands of Indian Affairs and the Government of Canada. Between phone calls in his noisy office, he put it bluntly: "Indian Affairs exists to keep us down," he told me. In Steve's view, the ruination of Grassy Narrows and other First Nations communities across Canada had been shrewdly planned and deliberately executed. The "natural disasters" that impacted Grassy Narrows—the smallpox epidemic of the late nineteenth century and the influenza outbreak of 1919, hydroelectric dam–associated flooding, relocation, mercury poisoning, and now clearcutting—could not be seen as inadvertent mishaps.[10] Traditional healers and leaders had been unable to deal with such catastrophes and Indian Affairs officials knew it well when they stepped forward to convince Anishinaabe people that the government alone could solve their problems, that a Euro-Canadian way of life could make things better.

First Nations people throughout Canada critique the Indian Act as a deeply assimilationist project designed to eliminate community and cultural identity (see Erasmus and Sanders 1992; Mercredi and

Turpel 1993). Many Grassy Narrows activists express their resentment at the apparent total control the Indian Act continues to exert over Native people's lives. For the blockaders, the Indian Act represents a long-standing source of anger and a scourge to rise above. Located outside the Indian Act–instituted reserve and with adherents who recognize the legitimacy of leaders outside of the Indian Act–imposed Chief and Council system, the blockade at Slant Lake poses a fundamental challenge to the Indian Act.

Trends in the Judicial System

Quite distinct from their negative perception of the Indian Act and the Department of Indian Affairs, activist leaders at Grassy Narrows have been encouraged by a handful of decisive cases argued before Canada's Supreme Court. As individual precedents and for the trend they collectively represent, these cases are significant factors in the blockade's political prehistory. While hardly inspirational, the earliest court case in the blockaders' legal repertoire is commonly referred to as *St. Catherine's Milling*. With Canada's 1867 confederation, the British North America Act awarded jurisdiction over Indians and Indian lands to the federal government. Natural resources and the management of Crown-owned lands, however, fell to the provinces. Not surprisingly, the provinces were little inclined to pay much heed to "Indians and lands reserved for Indians," since this was an area of federal responsibility (Miller 1991b: 406).

The 1888 *St. Catherine's Milling* case was the first judicial test of this sphere of provincial power. Although it related to Aboriginal issues, no Native people were actually involved in the case. It was, instead, a debate between the Province of Ontario and the Government of Canada over forest resource management. Both parties claimed the same parcel of land in northwestern Ontario as theirs to regulate; while the federal government argued for Crown control of the area based on its coverage by Treaty Three, the province argued that Ontario should manage the natural resources in question. With a judgment asserting that "the rights of the provincial government took precedence over any outstanding or existing Aboriginal claims" (Coates 2000: 82), the Province of Ontario won the case. The precedent set by *St. Catherine's Milling* remains important because it grants Ontario the ability to license timber corporations to manage large areas of Crown land that overlie Grassy Narrows' Traditional Land Use Area. Although activists at Grassy Narrows may find the standard set by *St. Catherine's Milling* objectionable, they acknowledge its role in establishing the framework within which they must work.

Following the *St. Catherine's Milling* decision, it was to be many years before First Nations concerns again entered the court system. Since the 1960s, however, numerous Native rights cases have been argued before Canada's Supreme Court and, in many instances, First Nations interests have prevailed. Several of these court cases— *Calder*,[11] *Sparrow*,[12] *Delgamuukw*, and *Marshall*—stand out as the most celebrated and most inspiring to First Nations activists. Among the Grassy Narrows blockaders, it is the 1997 *Delgamuukw* and the 1999 *Marshall* decisions that figure most prominently.

As noted in the previous chapter, the two First Nations involved in *Delgamuukw*—the Gitxsan and Wet'suwet'en of British Columbia—had no historic treaty. On that basis, they argued that they retained title to their traditional lands in the Nass River Valley. Although the decision refrained from ruling on their land claim, *Delgamuukw* set an important precedent. *Delgamuukw* reinforced the fact that First Nation peoples' rights to land are protected by the highest law of Canada, Section 35 of Canada's Constitution. Where a First Nation's interest in a particular parcel of land can be proven to have existed to the exclusion of others before newcomers declared sovereignty over the area in question, that First Nation's right to the land is understood as inherent. *Delgamuukw* went a step further than simply affirming First Nations peoples' rights to make use of the land, suggesting that "Aboriginal Title is a right to the land itself" (BC Treaty Commission 1999: 2). The case also took steps toward defining the rights Native individuals and groups in Canada possess; included in this package of rights is the right to harvest traditional resources— even when done by modern means and for modern purposes—so long as it does not fundamentally alter the relationship between First Nations peoples and their lands.

Despite their forefathers' participation in the historic treaty process, activists at Grassy Narrows see two additional aspects of the *Delgamuukw* decision as highly relevant to their own situation. *Delgamuukw* established the obligation of the Crown to consult, in good faith, with First Nations on issues relating to their traditional lands or territories. Grassy Narrows activists frequently denounce the federal government, the Ontario Ministry of Natural Resources, and the corporations that harvest timber within their Traditional Land Use Area for their continuing failure to consult with the Native community. *Delgamuukw*'s acceptance of oral testimony and oral tradition as important considerations in First Nations cases also possesses potentially monumental implications in the northwestern Ontario context. Whether or not mainstream Canadians and non-Native governments will ever accept an Anishinaabe understanding of Treaty Three as "legitimate" hinges upon their acceptance of a historicity—a way of understanding the past—that differs considerably from typical text-centric schemes. The ways in which people think about history and what they are willing to count as a part of it have very real consequences for the people of Grassy Narrows. *Delgamuukw* dealt with non-treaty First Nations but, based on its acceptance of oral history as evidence, those who do have treaties are today able to hope that someday the agreements their forefathers negotiated and signed will be interpreted as they intended. They can now be optimistic that they or their children will someday be able to confirm that the treaties were intended to establish peace and friendship rather than the surrender of land (Cardinal ND).

Unlike *Delgamuukw*, the 1999 *Marshall* decision dealt explicitly with treaty rights and interpretation. One of the few major Native rights court cases to originate in eastern Canada, *Marshall* focused on commercial resource harvesting. In 1993, a Nova Scotia Mi'kmaq named Donald Marshall Jr. was charged with harvesting eels illegally. In his initial trial, a Nova Scotia judge ruled that the parts of the Mi'kmaq treaty of 1760 that referred to commercial allowance were no longer valid because the commercial mechanisms have drastically changed in the intervening centuries (Coates 2000). Following this unfavorable decision, Marshall took his case to the Supreme Court of Canada, where it was found that some degree of commercial harvesting was, in fact, legal for the Mi'kmaq. While no control or ownership of resources was recognized, the court declared that a moderate income from such harvesting was acceptable.

Although the *Marshall* case was about eels, its implications for other commonly harvested plant and animal species reached much further. Even more critically, *Marshall* established that the literal meanings of treaties could change over time while keeping with their original intent. Treaties—like Native people themselves—could be accepted in a modern context and still retain their authenticity and validity. In addition, the admission of oral evidence so important in *Delgamuukw* was now unequivocally extended to include treaty First Nations. This case set the precedent that "the historical context in which an agreement was made is an integral part of the consideration of the terms and conditions of the treaty" (Coates 2000: 12). Although many non-Native fishery workers in the Maritimes reacted strongly against a decision they felt threatened their livelihoods, *Marshall* was an important victory for First Nations people throughout Canada. In the spirit of the *Marshall* decision, many of the same Grassy Narrows band members who have been involved in the blockade now assert their right to harvest and sell forest products by operating a small-scale sustainable logging and cabin construction enterprise. And, as with *Delgamuukw*, the possibility that their own interpretations of their treaty may someday be given credence—and their claims to land they feel they never surrendered legitimated—continues to serve as a source of inspiration.

While impossible to determine what the future will bring, the Canadian court system, at least on a national level, has appeared increasingly supportive of First Nations rights. From oppressive and assimilationist policies like the Indian Act to recent judicial victories, the trajectory of Aboriginal policy in Canada has enabled and encouraged Grassy Narrows activists' participation in the wider movement for indigenous empowerment.

First Nations Rising

Anishinaabe activism in northwestern Ontario can be understood as a reaction against the Indian Act and the colonial mindset it embodies, but it is also a response to positive changes that have transpired in recent years. The rapid rise of the American Indian Movement (AIM) in the 1970s and the resultant growth in public awareness of Native struggles—among American Indian citizens as well as the general public—played a vital role in establishing a political climate in which residents of Grassy Narrows felt empowered to take direct action. Although its public prominence peaked in this era, American Indian activism did not simply appear unprecedented with the 1968 Occupation of Alcatraz Island, nor did it come to a close following the Longest Walk a decade later. On the contrary, Native peoples have found ways in every historical epoch to innovate, resist, and accommodate, both within their communities and in their relations with local, state, and federal governments (Cobb 2007: 58). Because the history of the Red Power Movement has been the subject of extensive study, the following is not intended as a comprehensive treatment (see Nagel 1996; Johnson et al. 1999a; and Cobb and Fowler 2007 for more on this topic). Instead, I present a more localized history that centers on the specific precedents that have been most immediately influential for Grassy Narrows residents and for the trajectory of Anishinaabe activism in northwestern Ontario.

As we will see, not only have citizens of Grassy Narrows First Nation been encouraged by local, national, and international stories of indigenous activism, but they have also crafted these precedents into valuable strategic lessons. From the directly observed occupation at Kenora's Anicinabe Park, to prominent First Nations actions across Canada, to global indigenous rights campaigns known to Grassy Narrows activists only via print and electronic media, the global rise of indigenous activism made the blockade at Grassy Narrows a realistic possibility.

The Occupation of Anicinabe Park, 1974

While by no means the largest or best-known instance of First Nations activism in Canada, the 1974 occupation of Anicinabe Park took place only fifty miles from Grassy Narrows in Kenora. This event had a monumental impact on many individuals who would later become leaders of Grassy's anti-clearcutting movement. The palpable tension underlying relations between the Anishinaabeg of northwestern Ontario and Kenora's non-Native citizens has a long history. By the mid-1960s, many Anishinaabe people living in Kenora and the surrounding district were fed up. In the fall of 1965, over four hundred Natives marched through the streets of Kenora to protest their inequitable treatment in the town's public spaces and business and their poor economic and housing conditions (Kenora Daily Miner and News 1965). It was the 1974 occupation of Kenora's Anicinabe Park, however, that introduced the region to full-fledged direct action. The occupation followed a three-day "Ojibwa Nations

Conference" held at the park from July 20th through the 22nd. The event took place only one year after the infamous siege at Wounded Knee, South Dakota and several prominent (AIM) leaders—Harvey Major, Clyde Bellecourt, and Dennis Banks—were among the conference's 250 to 300 attendees (see Kehoe 1989 and Johnson et al. 1999a regarding the 1973 standoff at Wounded Knee). Serving as the keynote speaker, Banks urged Native people to "work together for their own protection" and "called for an end to violation of Indian people everywhere" (Kenora Daily Miner and News 1974a).

Initially, the conference appeared orderly, but many non-Native Kenorans worried that even the smallest "spark" could set off confrontations between conference attendees and townspeople (Holland 1974). Their anxieties were not unfounded. After the conference's official end, approximately 150 people—including nearly eighty women and children—refused to leave Anicinabe Park, thereby becoming "occupiers." Some of the Indians involved were Anishinaabeg from the area; others had traveled across North America to attend the conference.[13] Included among the occupiers were many of the visiting AIM leaders as well as a handful of Grassy Narrows and Whitedog residents. Some leaders of the Anicinabe Park occupation played on non-Native fears; the occupiers did not refute assumptions that the Indians were heavily armed and Harvey Major told a local reporter, "If just one of our Indian people is hit by a bullet Kenora will go up in smoke" (Kenora Daily Miner and News 1974b).

As the occupation stretched to fill days and then weeks, the situation grew increasingly tense. The occupiers erected barricades at the park's entrances and closed the park to all media personnel. An ad hoc Indian security force patrolled the park and its boundaries. Meanwhile, over one hundred police officers called in to deal with the potentially dangerous situation maintained a twenty-four-hour presence just outside the park's perimeter. On August 11th, a non-Native building contractor removing materials from a nearby construction site reported bullets, presumably fired by an Indian sentry, whizzing over his head (Kenora Daily Miner and News 1974e).

Inside the park, Indians made Molotov cocktails, participated in traditional drumming, and went about the routine business of constructing shelters, tending large open fires, and preparing meals (Hutchison and Wallace 1977). Located alongside a sheltered Lake of the Woods bay, people fished and cooked onsite throughout the occupation. By August, the occupiers had made their mark on the park; the following words were scrawled across the campground office's wall:

> This piece of land
> we stand on, is our
> Flesh n' blood
> Bone n' marrow
> Of our bodies, This
> is why we choose to die here at
> Anishinabe Park.[14]

In addition to their complaints about the noisy drumming, townspeople were dismayed when the Indians cut down several of the park's trees.

Kenora's mayor at the time, Jim Davidson, was sympathetic to the plight of Native people in northwestern Ontario. Publicly expressing a view that cost him reelection, he commented that the occupation had "succeeded in turning the eyes of Canada to conditions here" (quoted in Holland and Ralko 1974). In late July, federal and provincial negotiators arrived to begin the dispute resolution process. Davidson played a key role in the negotiations that peacefully ended the occupation on August 18th (Kenora Daily Miner and News 1974f). Steve Fobister of Grassy Narrows was among those selected by the occupiers to represent their interests in these negotiations (Kenora Daily Miner and News 1974c).

On the surface, the Anicinabe Park dispute appeared to revolve around the legality of Kenora's ownership of the park. In 1929, a non-Native owner had sold the land that was to become Anicinabe Park to the Department of Indian Affairs. At the time, Indian Affairs purchased the parcel for the specific purpose of establishing an "urban reserve" for the region's large Indian population. The land was intended to be used by Native families who wished to remain close to a hospitalized relative or had other business to conduct in town. With the surge in tourism that followed World War II, the parcel was sold to the town of Kenora and converted into a public campground in 1959. In 1974, the park's Native occupiers justified their actions by citing the illegitimacy of Kenora's ownership; they argued that title to the park should rightly be in Anishinaabe hands.

The occupation's deeper motives, however, can be traced to many of the same issues—the unremitting injustices faced by Native people and the widespread loss of indigenous lands and ways of life—that enraged American Indian activists across North America in the late 1960s and 1970s. In the early days of the occupation, an unnamed Indian spokesman stated, "If the Ojibwa Nation is to survive it must start gaining back some parts of what it has lost. We have decided to start with Anicinabe Park" (Kenora Daily Miner and News 1974b). In addition, a hard-hitting Grand Council Treaty Three report called *While People Sleep* (Grand Council Treaty Three 1974) had recently detailed grim statistics on the disproportionate occurrence of violent death among Native people in Kenora and the surrounding area. This report contributed to conference attendees' sense that justice was not being served in the region. Some local First Nations people suggested in hindsight that perhaps the occupation could have been prevented if non-Native town leaders had taken the report more seriously (Holland and Ralko 1974).

While successful in turning Kenorans' immediate attention to Native issues, the public prominence that resulted from the occupation seemed to fade as quickly as it had risen. In the weeks following the occupation, a group of non-Native townspeople called the Kenora Citizens Committee formed in order to examine the complaints that provoked the occupation. Their investigations of the park's disputed title led to no change in ownership. Today, the events of 1974 barely permeate Kenorans' collective memory; among non-Native residents, only active supporters of Native rights and amateur historians recall the occupation as a meaningful chapter in the history of their town. The modern campground at Anicinabe Park, likewise, offers no clue that it was once the site of an occupation. Although many of the Anishinaabe activists involved concede that Kenora's non-Native population gradually disregarded the occupation's objectives with the passage of time, some lasting gains did result. Following the occupation, concerned volunteers organized a Native Street Patrol which, more than thirty years later, still works to ensure that First Nations people in need receive treatment rather than abuse.

While all but forgotten by non-Native Kenorans, Grassy Narrows residents—elected band leaders and blockaders alike—remember the occupation of Anicinabe Park well; even people too young to have any direct memory of the event have usually heard it described by others. In several ways, the Anicinabe Park occupation shaped Grassy Narrows activists' attitudes and strategic approach. First, the event set a valuable precedent of collaborative cooperation that was recognized even as the occupation unfolded. As Louis Cameron of Whitedog First Nation commented to a reporter in 1974, "There has been little unity shown among our people for a long time and this occupation shows it can be done" (Dusang 1974). When anti-clearcutting activism became a reality at Grassy Narrows, the movement's leaders recognized the importance of involving Grand Council Treaty Three and other local First Nations communities from the outset.

Second, the 1974 occupiers saw direct radical action as a last resort; according to participants, they believed that a physical stand was the only way to get the government and the public to take their concerns seriously. Using aggressive tactics, the occupation of Anicinabe Park successfully brought issues of Native injustice and land rights into Euro-Canadian consciousness, however temporarily. Although hesitant to blockade in the early years of their anti-clearcutting campaign, Grassy Narrows activists were similarly prepared for confrontation when they felt they had exhausted all other options. Third, and most importantly, the occupation at Anicinabe Park placed direct action firmly within Grassy Narrows activists' realm of possibility. Experienced first-hand by some band members and known to many more, direct action became a realistic tool for bringing lofty goals within reach.

Precedents and Possibilities: First Nations Activism from Coast to Coast

As well-read chapters in Canada's recent history, accounts of Native activism from across the country have also influenced the Grassy Narrows blockaders' outlook and approach. Local or distant, subtle or striking, the First Nations activism of recent decades did not cause the Grassy Narrows blockade; rather, the precedents it set made the blockade possible. While specific instances of Native North American activism can be studied singularly as manifestations of indigenous empowerment in action, such events have also played key roles in shaping indigenous activism as a process. Melissa Checker describes how, for African American Environmental Justice activists in Hyde

Park, Georgia, "a civil rights legacy provides a foundation from which activists think about and struggle with environmental problems" (Checker 2005: 9). Likewise, Anishinaabe anti-clearcutting activism must be regarded as a recent development framed by a long-term historical trajectory; the wider context of First Nations activism has been vital in creating a political and cultural atmosphere in which grassroots activists in small indigenous communities like Grassy Narrows feel empowered to step forward to fight for their rights, lands, and futures.

Individual activists at Grassy Narrows have taken inspiration from a variety of unique personal experiences. Judy DaSilva, the dedicated campaigner introduced in the last chapter, was barely a teenager when the 1974 Anicinabe Park occupation took place. Judy did not participate in the occupation, though she does recall hearing about the excitement unfolding in town. Not long after, Judy moved to Winnipeg to further her education. There, she got involved with a group of Native residents working to improve living conditions in the city's North End slums. During her time in Winnipeg, Judy met prominent First Nations activists from across Canada and appears to have taken long-term, life-shaping inspiration from these encounters. Recounting the story of how she became the devoted activist she is today, Judy recalled the time Milton Born With a Tooth—a respected Native rights leader from Alberta—asked her when she planned to return to Grassy Narrows: "There is still a fight at home," he advised her. This remark influenced Judy's eventual decision to return to Grassy Narrows and her ultimate leadership in her community's anti-clearcutting movement.

Kitty, a young Grassy Narrows activist central to the blockade since its inception, traces her personal motivation to an event that took place in Winnipeg more than a decade later. As for Judy, the awareness, perspective, and determination to fight for change acquired in the city followed Kitty home. While not the first instance of direct First Nations protest in Canada, few would dispute that the confrontation that shook Oka, Quebec in the summer of 1990 was among the most influential. As a troubled preteen, Kitty ran away from her parents' home on the reserve that summer. After traveling to Winnipeg, Kitty inadvertently found herself at a rally in support of the Mohawk protesters. In hindsight, she sees this rally as a defining moment in her life. This, she explained, was where she first became inspired to take a stand for her own people and for Grassy Narrows.

Cree/Métis writer Kim Anderson points out that, like Kitty, many First Nations people in Canada "refer to Oka as a turning point in their lives. . . . It was a call to consciousness for many Native people about identity, as it renewed our awareness and resistance to the way in which Aboriginal people are treated in Canada" (Anderson 2000: 125). The incident began as a protest against the non-Native municipality of Oka's planned golf course expansion, but the immediate conflict over land rights told only part of the story. In addition to their complaint that Kanehsatake title to the golf course (which included a traditional burial ground and a sacred grove of pine trees) was being disregarded, Mohawk Warriors and their supporters were enraged by what they saw as the unreasonable and unrelenting overpolicing of Mohawk communities (Miller 1991a). In response, dozens of Natives—from Kanehsatake itself as well as from the nearby Akwesasne and Kahnawake Mohawk reserves—set up blockades and occupied the golf course for over six months. The Canadian media paid rapt attention when the protest turned violent on July 10th, leaving one police officer dead. York and Pindera (1991) tell the story of Oka well. They also describe the event's important legacy:

> For most of Canada's aboriginal people, the lessons of Oka were simple. For hundreds of years, peaceful negotiations and polite discussions have led nowhere. When they followed the rules imposed by the federal government, Indians relegated themselves to a position of insignificance. Their land claims have taken decades to settle or been dismissed on technicalities. By refusing to obey the rules, however, they finally gained the attention of the nation. (York and Pindera 1991: 286)

First Nations people throughout Canada identified with the Mohawks' challenges and goals. While their enactment of the blockade strategy differed considerably from the fortified barrier that stood at Oka, Kitty and other Grassy Narrows First Nation activists appear to have learned Oka's key lesson well: Direct action speaks louder than any words.

Though less prominent than Oka, several other episodes of First Nations activism in Canada—at Ipperwash, Ontario; Gustafsen Lake,

British Columbia; and in Nova Scotia—also made lasting impressions on the Grassy Narrows blockaders. In 1995, approximately thirty residents of Stoney Point First Nation moved into Ipperwash Provincial Park to protest the federal government's failure to return land it expropriated for a military base during World War II. Their stand ended in tragedy; an Ontario Provincial Police officer fired his weapon at the protestors, fatally striking an Anishinaabe man named Dudley George (CBC 2004). The shooting served to intensify already existing tensions and the lengthy public inquiry into George's death stretched into the first decade of the new millennium.[15] The same year, an armed standoff occurred at Gustafson Lake, located in the British Columbia interior. Led by a sixty-five-year-old organic farmer known as Wolverine, local Shuswap and Secwepemp people attempted to defend sacred and unceded Sun Dance grounds from ranching expansion (MacKinnon 1995; Samuel 1996). Following failed negotiations, the Royal Canadian Mounted Police (RCMP) commenced a military-style siege in an attempt to bring the month-long occupation to an end. One unarmed Native woman was shot and eighteen people were charged for their role in the standoff, including Wolverine himself. Like the events at Ipperwash and Gustafson Lake, the fallout from the 1999 *Marshall* Supreme Court decision, described earlier, highlighted for both First Nations and non-Native Canadians the antagonistic nature of race relations in Canadian society. As Mi'kmaq fishermen asserted their newly affirmed right to the commercial fishery, non-Native Maritimers at Burnt Church and other Nova Scotia villages who depended on the same fishery for their own livelihoods expressed their fear through violence against Native people and their property (Coates 2000).

Taken together, these protest events imparted several valuable lessons to Anishinaabe activists in northwestern Ontario. Some of the lessons of Oka, Ipperwash, Gustafson Lake, and Burnt Church overlapped those taken from the Anicinabe Park occupation. These events underscored the value of generating allies in other First Nations communities as well as among non-Native supporters. The events' widespread media coverage also made the value of the media as a tool for reaching potential allies clear. Again paralleling the lessons of Anicinabe Park, these more recent protests affirmed direct action as a sure way—sometimes the only way—to bring attention to their cause. But from the tragedies at Oka, Ipperwash, Gustafson

Lake, and Burnt Church, Grassy Narrows activists also learned what *not* to do. From the outset, they have been adamant about leaving violence and weapons out of their protest activities. Now that they are positioned to serve as role models for other First Nations activists, they advocate an unambiguous policy of nonviolence.

Over and above their consciousness of the recent history of Canadian First Nations activism, leaders of the Grassy Narrows blockade pay close attention to ongoing and emerging indigenous struggles taking place across North America and around the world. Even when their direct involvement is unfeasible, they enthusiastically scan media coverage of current events and often maintain personal contacts among those closer to the action. As we will see, activists at Grassy Narrows see themselves as participants in a network that extends far beyond their fluid territorial and cultural boundaries and even farther beyond Canada's permeable national borders.

Indigenism: Global Contexts and Connections

I spent the afternoon of July 19th, 2004 at the beach. A cool, clear spring-fed lake, Keys Lake is one of the most popular stops along Jones Road. Only fifteen minutes south of Grassy Narrows, the lake gets its share of visitors from the reserve as well as scores of high season tourists. Its strip of coarse sand is long and narrow and its beach slopes gently into refreshing water. The stark outline of a mature boreal forest lines the lake's wide bay. The day was warm and the sun hot against our skin. Dee and Annika (both non-Native blockade supporters who had arrived in June and decided to stay on for the summer) relaxed on a large cotton blanket with Kitty and me while Kitty's three-year-old daughter and five-year-old nephew played in the shallows. As we soaked in the afternoon's beauty, Kitty and Dee made plans to travel to British Columbia that August. Kitty was especially eager to make the trip and shared her motivation with the rest of us. She had a vision, she declared, of a strong network connecting all the First Nations. She wanted to help others understand the ties she felt so powerfully. Kitty paused for a second, looked out over the lake's sparkling surface, and went on to explain how indigenous communities around the world—people as far away as Australia and New Zealand—are all part of the same interconnected web.

That Grassy Narrows First Nation and the people who live there qualify as part of the indigenous world goes unquestioned by community members and outsiders alike. Although Grassy Narrows residents more routinely refer to themselves as Indian or Native, Anishinaabe or Ojibwe, "indigenous" stands as an established alternative term of self-designation as well as an accepted external descriptor. Native studies classes offered by Grassy's Sakatcheway Anishinabe School, for instance, are run by a department called the Indigenous Learning Centre (ILC). And when, in May of 2003, a representative from the United Nations visited Grassy Narrows, that person was the UN's Special Rapporteur on Indigenous Human Rights (Barrera 2003a). Several of the groups the blockaders have partnered with—the Indigenous Peoples Solidarity Movement (IPSM) and Indigenous Environmental Network (IEN)—prominently feature the word "indigenous" in their names. Judy DaSilva's words have been published in *Indigenous Woman Magazine* and activists from Grassy have participated in numerous conferences—and been invited to many more—geared toward the collective indigenous struggle. Furthermore, as one Kenora-based journalist told me, Grassy Narrows has succeeded in making itself a symbol of "indigenous people standing up to big-business."

But what does all of this imply? Ronald Niezen defines *indigenism* as a new phase in Native activism, an "emerging form of political resistance" fueled by the growth of worldwide communication networks and the consciousness of shared situations and goals that have arisen from such networks (Niezen 2003: 16). Founded—somewhat paradoxically—on the notion of a collective indigenous identity and on visions of enduring cultural rootedness and connection to the land, indigenism offers a twenty-first-century model for resisting state marginalization and domination.[16] Regarding the "unique blend of pressures and possibilities" Levi (2002: 10) describes, indigenism figures prominently on the latter side of the equation. Activists at Grassy Narrows draw much of their inspiration and their will to endure from the resistance of other indigenous communities, from the interest of supportive outsiders, and from the knowledge that they, in turn, may serve to inspire and influence others. They are both active members and co-creators of this emerging global movement.

An estimated 370 million indigenous people live in seventy different counties (United Nations Permanent Forum on Indigenous

Issues 2005) and comprise roughly 5 percent of the world's population (Maybury-Lewis 1997: 11). For decades, the United Nations has acknowledged that indigenous issues go far beyond straightforward domestic politics (Warren 1998: 6).[17] In 2000, the UN formally marked its increasing attention to indigenous concerns with the creation of a Permanent Forum on Indigenous Issues (UNPFII). As well, we have recently emerged from the official International Decade of the World's Indigenous Peoples, which spanned the years 1995 to 2004. Not only have indigenous issues gained legitimacy and notoriety within the world governmental agenda, but "indigenous" as a conceptual category has also entered the global popular mindset. Today, "field guides" to indigenous groups (e.g., Hughes 2003) sell well, indigenous cultural tourism is a booming business, and major corporations have lucratively converted indigenous peoples and themes into marketing strategies. An outpouring of support for indigenous causes and the possibility of new alliances have accompanied these trends. As it becomes increasingly accepted and advantageous, people who can legitimately declare an indigenous identity are often eager to do so because of the perceived benefits such associations can offer.[18] Consequently, more and more people are claiming—or reclaiming— indigenous identities and historically marginalized groups are now "becoming" indigenous at a rapid rate (Hodgson 2002: 1037; see also Conklin and Graham 1995; Gupta 1998).

Still, defining just what "indigenous" means—and determining who should or should not qualify for categorical inclusion—has proven difficult (Kuper 2003; Tsing 2007). The picture is complicated by cultural and ethnic diversity within the global indigenous community and by the fact that the sociopolitical contexts and challenges faced by indigenous peoples are extremely diverse. Still, geographically and culturally distant groups frequently share patterns of historical domination and ongoing marginalization, as well as fundamental concerns and ultimate objectives—struggles for land, recognition, and rights—in common. Based on these commonalities, the United Nations, nongovernmental organizations, and a majority of scholars and activists working on the subject appear to agree on a few essential characteristics.

According to the United Nations Office of the High Commissioner on Human Rights (UNOHCHR),

Indigenous or aboriginal peoples are so-called because they were living on their lands before settlers came from elsewhere; they are the descendants . . . of those who inhabited a country or a geographical region at the time when people of different cultures or ethnic origins arrived, the new arrivals later becoming dominant through conquest, occupation, settlement or other means. (UNOHCHR 1995: 1)

Anthropologist David Maybury-Lewis has also proposed a comprehensive definition of the term:

Indigenous peoples claim their lands because they were there first or have occupied them since time immemorial. They are also groups that have been conquered by peoples racially, ethnically or culturally different from themselves. They have thus been subordinated by or incorporated in alien states which treat them as outsiders and, usually, as inferiors. . . . The salient characteristic of indigenous peoples, then, is that they are marginal to or dominated by the states that claim jurisdiction over them. (Maybury-Lewis 1997: 8)

As these definitions suggest, the rhetoric and reality of shared stories—coupled with an accordingly politicized collective consciousness—underlie both the indigenous concept and the movement founded upon it. Indigenous peoples have, by definition, faced colonization and external domination and have often come to define themselves in consequently oppositional terms based on their ongoing struggles against foreign cultural powers (Sissons 2005: 13). In more than a few cases, they have also survived episodes of genocide or ethnocide (Maybury-Lewis 1997). Indigenous peoples have been forced to cope with the loss of homelands and lifeways; they have endured attempts at forced assimilation and concurrent devaluation of their own cultural practices and beliefs. The colonial past, seen through indigenous eyes, cannot simply be relegated to the pages of history; fundamentally unaltered power-structural inequalities continue to contour indigenous people's daily lives, communities, and sensibilities. As an evolving social project, indigenism represents a cooperative effort by socially, politically, and economically disadvantaged groups to challenge—and ultimately change—the circumstances of their lives.

Indigenous peoples' recent histories often include tales of environmental as well as sociopolitical manifestations of inequality. Today, many of those within the indigenous "imagined community" (Anderson 1991) feel a sense of unification against what they see as the conjoined enemies of state oppression and industrial resource development. Niezen (2003: 9), in fact, sees the indigenous movement as arising from marginalized groups' common experience of negative impacts resulting from resource extraction and economic modernization. Indigenous activists around the world work to prevent hydroelectric dams from flooding their homelands, to stop mines from stripping their hillsides and poisoning their waters, and to protect the last remnants of the old-growth forests that sustain their land-based cultural lives. The story of environmental change at Grassy Narrows First Nation, told in the following chapter, can be read as a paradigmatic example of the indigenous experience of environmental injustice.

L ife intervened, and Kitty never made it to British Columbia that summer. Her vision, though, remained as strong as ever. Other activist leaders at Grassy Narrows share Kitty's farsighted view and her determination to fight for their collective future. Though the blockade itself is a recent development, the blockaders' political discontent is anything but. What *is* new, what enabled the Grassy Narrows blockade to become a reality in December of 2002 is the steadily increasing sense of empowerment Native communities have experienced over the past thirty years. Education about Native history and rights, political and judicial victories, and the existence of abundant role models—offset by anger at the inequities indigenous peoples continue to confront—have given rise to the political activist stance so widespread in First Nations communities today. Inspired by changes in political climate, models of First Nations activism from across Canada, and the emerging global indigenous movement, Anishinaabeg in northwestern Ontario now feel empowered to take a stand against injustices that have frustrated them for decades. The people of Grassy Narrows now dare to hope that when they speak out they will be heard.

Three

A World Transformed

The discontent that led citizens of Grassy Narrows First Nation to initiate the Slant Lake blockade in December of 2002 did not arise in a vacuum. As we have seen, delving into Grassy Narrows' past is essential to understanding community members' present-day actions, motivations, and inspirations. The previous two chapters explored the cultural and political factors that coalesced to make the blockade possible. But addressing why the blockade took place when and where it did also means considering the environmental and ensuing social changes that helped lay the groundwork for anti-clearcutting activism at Grassy Narrows.

Over the past eighty years, dramatic anthropogenic changes to the immediate environment—flooding, relocation, mercury poisoning, and clearcutting—have adversely affected Grassy Narrows residents' health and subsistence practices. Critically, First Nation members' perceptions of the natural world and their place within it have also been transformed. The history of environmental degradation at Grassy Narrows is heartrending, but it is also much more. For the community's activists, it is a symptom of enduring injustice and a source of rage. Based on the collected memories of individuals within the Grassy Narrows community, this chapter tells this important story.[1]

Environmental and Social Change at Grassy Narrows First Nation

Through the first quarter of the twentieth century, the people of Grassy Narrows made their homes on the secluded peninsulas and islands of the winding English-Wabigoon River system. As chapter 1 describes, they derived their living primarily and directly from the land; despite Anishinaabe peoples' long-term participation in the fur trade, they continued to live a seasonally mobile life of hunting, fishing, gathering, and trapping with comparatively minor intrusions from the outside world.

1920s: Flooding

In the late 1920s, wider Canadian policies and practices directly impacted the community's immediate physical environment for the first time when the construction of hydroelectric dams—upstream at Ear Falls and downstream at Caribou Falls—raised water levels and flooded near-shore portions of the Grassy Narrows homeland (Kenora Miner and News Staff and the Canadian Press 1984).

Many Grassy Narrows residents still bitterly resent the careless flooding of their traditional burial grounds. With the hindsight of eighty years, the community's activists view the construction of the dams—and the lack of communication about the project with Anishinaabeg living along the river—as an initial example of environmental injustice. Deputy Chief Steve Fobister, for example, pointedly contrasted the public's widespread ignorance of the flooding of hundreds of Anishinaabe gravesites that resulted from hydroelectric development with the rage and public outcry that ensued when, in 1998, several non-Native graves at Kenora's Lake of the Woods Cemetery were vandalized. To this day, wild rice crops remain at the mercy of the dams; crops often fail dismally when dam managers raise water levels at a sensitive time for the young aquatic plants. It is this sort of injustice—visible in its most recent manifestation as the large-scale industrial clearcutting now ravaging the Grassy Narrows Traditional Land Use Area—that the blockaders hope to ultimately overcome.

1960s: Relocation

The disruption caused by hydroelectric development paled in comparison to the changes future decades would bring. Prior to 1963, Grassy

Narrows was inaccessible by road. Before this time it was a "fly-in" community, like a majority of reserves further north remain today. People old enough to recall life before relocation remember it fondly. The use of dog sleds in the winter, long journeys on foot, canoes or small motorboats for water-based transportation in the warmer months, and a seasonal pattern of movement still live within the memory of the elders and middle-aged people who recounted tales of their youth for my benefit. Most of the active hunters and trappers at Grassy Narrows today learned their rich set of bush skills as children, when their families moved seasonally to utilize distant parts of their traditional territory.

In the early 1960s, the Canadian government persuaded Grassy Narrows' elected leaders to move their community several miles to the south. A new logging road—known as Jones Road after the telegraph station situated halfway between Kenora and Grassy Narrows—had been constructed in the late 1950s. By linking Grassy Narrows to this road, the move would expedite the delivery of government services and the establishment of educational facilities. Citing the technical difficulties of road construction on the narrow peninsulas of the Old Reserve (Shkilnyk 1985; Vecsey 1987), the government found it preferable to relocate—and thereby consolidate—Grassy Narrows' entire population rather than extend the road five extra miles.

Besides the attractive promise of a school, the government agreed to provide electrical power and indoor plumbing systems to the New Reserve; it took many years, but both these services are present in most homes today. Still, many community members opposed the move; people told me that several households resisted relocation as long as possible. Even forty years later, memories of relocation seemed too painful for some people to talk about. The government hypothesized that relocation would facilitate the delivery of services to the First Nation while simultaneously smoothing Anishinaabe people's incorporation into Canadian society. In reality, its consequences were disastrous.

Geographically speaking, Grassy Narrows' move was only a stone's throw, but relocation dramatically altered the community's social landscape. Homes on the Old Reserve had been widely spaced. Spread across the tangled channels of the English-Wabigoon River, their layout reflected extended family or clan groupings. On the New Reserve, homes were arranged in tidy Euro-Canadian style "subdivisions" with prefabricated structures and densely packed conditions.

Rather than living in extended clan-based configurations, people chose—or were assigned—residence sites at random. Not surprisingly, the community's most fundamental systems of social organization were seriously disrupted; it was now imaginable for individuals to disregard norms and obligations formerly monitored by close kin.

People I spoke to remember very little involvement with drugs or alcohol prior to relocation. All of this changed rapidly after the move. Shkilnyk (1985) reports that the widespread pathological use of alcohol began in the mid-1960s and that Grassy's first recorded cases of infant death due to alcohol-related neglect took place in the 1969–1970 term. Criminal justice system involvement in the First Nation's affairs was minimal prior to relocation, but by the late 1960s the crime rate had risen considerably. Likewise, the incidence of suicide and violence—especially among young people—increased dramatically following relocation. Despondent New Reserve residents referred to their new home as a "concentration camp" (Shkilnyk 1985) and a "cage" (Erikson and Vecsey 1980).[2] Countless times, I asked friends at Grassy Narrows if they felt the move was worth it. Countless times, the answer was a vehement no.

Even before the 1960s, the people of Grassy Narrows were part of a global economic system. Anishinaabe people's active participation in the fur trade provides the clearest historic example. Yet, as Niezen argues based on the James Bay Cree context, the fur trade did not undermine Native groups' forest-based lifestyle. Instead, "the forest way of life has a long history of accommodation and innovation resulting from outside influence," with technologies and ideas adapted to suit local needs (Niezen 1998: 7, 39). Infrequent but predictable contact with Indian agents and the local presence of the Hudson Bay Company had also been ubiquitous elements of pre-relocation life at Grassy Narrows. Once the move took place, however, the recently constructed Jones Road connected Grassy Narrows to the small city of Kenora, just over fifty miles to the southeast. By extension, the road also linked Grassy Narrows to the rest of the world with a new and intense immediacy. Literally and symbolically, relocation repositioned the community at the global-local interface, at the end of the newly expanded road system.

The changes of the 1960s had lasting impacts. Following relocation, First Nation members became increasingly familiar with non-Native ways of seeing the world. By choice or by necessity, the people of Grassy Narrows developed a rich fluency in Euro–North American culture. The school built on the New Reserve meant that non-Native teachers now lived within the Grassy Narrows community, resulting in daily interaction between Anishinaabeg and outsiders. After relocation, regular trips to town also became feasible. A few families found ways to purchase their own vehicles and many more relied on hired taxis. Roughly corresponding to Grassy's relocation, Canadian Indian policy shifted its emphasis to the provision of social assistance; with welfare, unemployment insurance, family benefit, and other transfer payment checks in hand, Indian people in northwestern Ontario now had significant amounts of money to spend (Shkilnyk 1985: 125). Most frequently, they chose to spend it in the non-Native owned businesses of Kenora.

When electricity finally reached Grassy Narrows in 1975, the arrival of television opened up new channels for First Nation residents' exposure to outside ways of life, mainstream social attitudes, and popular cultural movements. Simultaneously, with fewer people spending less time harvesting forest resources, community members' sense of direct familiarity with the immediate natural world began to decline. This, coupled with a rapidly expanding global awareness, led to transformed understandings of the environment that paved the way for the anti-clearcutting activism of future decades. The environment had always been the tangible setting for Anishinaabe daily life. It now took on an additional role. The environment became an abstraction, a conceptual category capable of evoking new symbolic meanings. It became "the environment," set aside from human experience as a potential arena of widespread concern.

1970s: Mercury

Already struggling to cope with the impacts of relocation, the Grassy Narrows community faced even more troubling times in the 1970s. In March of 1970, scientists announced the discovery of methyl mercury in the English-Wabigoon River system. The mercury originated in effluent released by a chemical and pulp mill located in far upstream Dryden, Ontario. From 1962 to 1970, roughly 20,000 pounds of the substance entered the river and followed its gradual northwesterly course (Troyer 1977; Erickson and Vecsey 1980; Shkilnyk 1985). As the water flowed on, anaerobic bacteria in the riverbed transformed the mercury from the comparatively benign inorganic compound released by the plant into a deadly bioaccumulating form. Mercury contamination was a major blow for downstream First Nations' health, economy, and psychological well-being.

It was the work of a University of Western Ontario graduate student named Norvald Fimreite that drew public attention to the ecological disaster unfolding in northwestern Ontario. As a part of his doctoral research, Fimreite was studying the effects of mercury-treated grain on upland birds and of industrial mercury discharge on fish. His results showed high levels of mercury in fish from waters downstream of chlor-alkali plants like the one located in Dryden. Ontario's Water Resources Commission, pressed into action by Fimreite's findings, undertook studies of the English-Wabigoon River in 1969. On March 3rd of 1970, laboratory results confirmed their suspicions. On March 26th, George Kerr, the province's minister of energy and resource management, ordered the Dryden plant to stop all discharge of mercury into the river (Troyer 1977).

Anishinaabe fishermen and their families did not need scientific training to notice disturbing changes taking place in the river. Well before the official announcement of mercury contamination, people at Grassy Narrows noticed subtle changes in the water, in the discernable health of the fish they caught, and in their own health. People especially recall an unusual number of infant deaths and children with health problems in the years before the mercury was first scientifically documented (McDonald and Isogai 2001). The fact that many of the amalgamated symptoms of mercury poisoning—numbness of extremities, joint pain and cramps, tremors, tunnel vision, loss of balance, and hearing and speech impairment, among others—often have other causes makes diagnosis in hindsight impossible (Harada et al. 2005). Throughout the region, however, people reflect back with feelings of certainty that many of those who died in the 1950s and 1960s of what then appeared to be Parkinson's or other diseases were actually mercury poisoning's earliest victims.

At Grassy Narrows, the economic changes of the previous decade meant that in addition to the fish directly consumed by community members, dozens of Grassy Narrows residents working as commercial fishermen or as fishing guides for the tourist industry also depended on the river more indirectly for their livelihood. By the spring of 1970, fish from ten lakes within the English-Wabigoon River system—including Clay, Ball, Indian, and Grassy Narrows Lakes—were deemed unsafe for consumption. In May of that year, commercial fishing on the river was banned and lodge owners received letters urging their guests to "fish for fun" (Troyer 1977).[3] Fearing fiscal losses, most of the region's lodge owners attempted to downplay or even conceal the problem from tourists, but Barney and Marion Lamm—the owners of the Ball Lake Lodge and employers of dozens of Grassy Narrows residents—opted for integrity. Fearing for the health of their customers and guides, they closed their business (Hutchison and Wallace 1977). Almost overnight, unemployment at Grassy Narrows jumped from 20 to 80 percent due to mercury related job losses (Troyer 1977) and an estimated 90 percent of men in the community were out of work (Erikson and Vecsey 1980). The welfare economy introduced in the 1960s tightened its grip on the people of Grassy Narrows.

Despite their early suspicions that something was wrong with the river, people at Grassy Narrows were having trouble coming to terms with the enormity of the crisis they faced. Most Grassy Narrows residents continued doing what they had always done—eating fish—even after learning of its potential toxicity. Few people I spoke to about the initial announcement of mercury, in fact, recalled the community's reaction as a dramatic one. Several factors help explain their seeming disregard. The river's large and plentiful walleye had long been a favored source of protein. Additionally, fish were one the most accessible remaining sources of wild food on the New Reserve. By consuming fish, people at Grassy were able to maintain the culturally distinct Anishinaabe identity reflected in their memories of life on the Old Reserve. Compounding these factors, First Nation residents observed as tourists continued to eat their catch with no adverse effects (Hutchison and Wallace 1977).

Over time, however, the health problems Grassy Narrows residents observed appeared to worsen. Gradually people began to link the symptoms exhibited by their friends, relatives, or themselves to the presence of mercury and came to fear the now-toxic fish. In the fall of 1972, Tom Strong, a forty-two-year-old trapper and fishing guide, died suddenly (Hutchison and Wallace 1977). Though Tom had always been healthy, he began experiencing slurred speech, weight loss, and chest pains in the summer of that year. He was camped with his family harvesting the annual crop of wild rice when he died of an apparent massive heart attack. In the same year, a boy was born to a fishing guide and his wife with what looked like a full-blown case of acute mercury poisoning. It was not lost on Grassy Narrow residents that, in both cases, the victims and their families were heavy consumers of fish.

In 1975, a delegation of Grassy Narrows and Whitedog First Nation members visited Minamata, Japan. Between 1932 and 1968, the Chisso Chemical Corporation dumped approximately twenty-seven tons of mercury into Minamata Bay, the primary source of food for residents of the southern Japan town. By the late 1950s and early 1960s, acute mercury poisoning had impacted thousands. In Japan, the Canadian group met with individuals and families that had been severely impacted by mercury poisoning. After learning about the tragedy at Minamata first hand, Bill Fobister commented:

> It seems to me we are in the same position. They are polluting our livelihood and destroying our economy. So we have the same problem and we should work together to try to show the government, the polluters, that we are the ones suffering, not them. (Quoted in Hutchison and Wallace 1977: 117)

Bill and his fellow travelers returned to northwestern Ontario determined to prevent further deterioration in their own situation.

The Grassy Narrows community reeled from mercury poisoning throughout the 1970s and into the 1980s. The trend toward increasing alcohol abuse and violence that began in the 1960s spiraled out of control, resulting in what Shkilnyk—working at Grassy Narrows in the late 1970s—perceived as "a community destroyed." In 1978, she reported, 66 percent of Grassy Narrows residents could be considered "heavy" or "very heavy" drinkers. And, in 1977–1978 alone there were twenty-six recorded suicide attempts by people between eleven and nineteen years of age—almost one-fifth of this age group. Three of these attempts were successful (Shkilnyk 1985).

Yet, even when extensive medical sampling of Grassy Narrows residents' hair and blood revealed mercury levels significantly higher than those of the general public, the government remained reluctant to admit that mercury was to blame for the community's tragic situation (Troyer 1977: 130). It took a decade and a half, but a compensa-

tion fund finally became a reality in 1986, when parliament negotiated a settlement agreement requiring the corporation that released
the mercury to pay $16.6 million to the Grassy Narrows and White-
dog bands, including $2 million to be devoted to those impacted by
the long-term health effects of mercury poisoning (Canada 1986;
Kenora Daily Miner and News 1986).

Environmental Health, Environmental Vulnerability, Environmental Injustice

Worldwide, the psychosocial effects of environmental degradation
and environmental risk on indigenous communities have been enormous. Stuart Kirsch (2006: 200), for instance, describes the horrific
impacts of the Ok Tedi Mine on the Yonggom people of New Guinea:
"Their landscape," he writes, "is no longer a site of productivity, but a
scene of loss. Instead of providing them with security, it confronts
them with new, indecipherable risks." Likewise, the economic and
health impacts of mercury poisoning at Grassy Narrows intertwined to
produce important changes in First Nation residents' views of the natural world. These changes ultimately set the stage for the community's
anti-clearcutting campaign.

Erikson and Vecsey (1980: 159) made the following observations
regarding mercury poisoning at Grassy Narrows:

> The discovery of mercury in the local waters has presented a
> psychological and perhaps even spiritual problem, for the
> apprehensions and uncertainties that follow such a discovery
> can affect the mind as surely as the poison itself can affect the
> body. This process is a subtle one and difficult to document,
> but it takes the form of a pervasive fear that the world of
> nature and the world of men are now contaminated and can
> no longer be trusted in the old way.

Niezen (1998: 88) describes comparable Cree reactions to the discovery of mercury in the James Bay region by pointing out that "such dramatic changes to the land as flooding and contamination of fish can
only lead to a sense of sorrow or spiritual malaise among those accustomed to a careful scrutiny of human relationships with animals and

the environment." Although the origin of mercury contamination in the James Bay region differed from the English-Wabigoon River's industrial pollution, the anxiety and sense of vulnerability that resulted from the substance's presence did not.[4]

Although the fundamental cultural ties that bind Grassy Narrows residents to their homeland remain strong, several important changes have taken place. In the wake of mercury poisoning, human and environmental health have become irrevocably linked in the minds of many First Nation residents. Judy DaSilva once eloquently expressed this point of view: Our bodies, she told me, are a kind of an internal environment; what we put into them and how we treat them reflects how we treat the land. Former Treaty Three grand chief and supporter of the Grassy Narrows blockade Leon Jourdain (2003: 3–4) has also called attention to the links between Anishinaabe and environmental health:

> When the land is sick, our people get sick. When the land is abused, our people are abused . . . personal health results from social health and, for Anishinaabe people, social health depends heavily on cultural relationships to the land, including the forest.

Critically, many Grassy Narrows activists now feel that the positive, sustaining nature of their environment can no longer be unreservedly trusted. They struggle to reconcile their desire to retain their land-based way of life with the risks inherent in eating the products of their labor. They take stock of the deluge of health problems they and their neighbors face and feel they have valid reasons to suspect the environment—or, more accurately, the distant industrial system that contaminated it—as a root cause.

As the most tangible intersection of the external environment and the human body, environmental health concerns are a vital component of Grassy Narrows activists' agenda. Hunters and trappers from the community have expressed concerns that something seems amiss with the animals; they cite spots on moose livers and external sores afflicting many species as evidence. Highly sensitized to the potentially negative impacts of environmental degradation on human and animal health, activists at Grassy Narrows worry that eating wild foods regularly may lead to a disproportionately high risk of contamination-related illness. Over and above their continuing anxieties about mercury in the environment, the herbicides sprayed each summer as part of the industrial forest regeneration process lead them to suspect even more chemical contamination.[5] Each summer, as the spraying season approaches, blockaders discuss strategies—posting large signs, camping in anticipated spray zones—to stop it from taking place.

Witnessing the defenselessness of the river in the face of anthropogenic devastation also led to shifts in the way people at Grassy Narrows comprehend their relationship to the environment. Scholars of Algonquian cultures recognize a complex set of reciprocal social associations between humans and more powerful "other-than-human-persons" as a central and definitive component of the Anishinaabe human-environment relationship (see Hallowell 1975, 1992). Mercury poisoning complicated this perspective. It shifted the balance of power and introduced a conceptual environment increasingly vulnerable to human destruction. Mercury contamination also shifted the balance of responsibility: The natural world came to be seen as more in need of human protection than ever before. While activists at Grassy Narrows today continue to conceive of the environment as "powerful" and to position themselves humbly within it, they are simultaneously—and without any apparent incongruity—able to envision themselves in the role of environmental defenders. As an environmentally protective movement with environmentalist allies and supporters, the blockade would have been inconceivable in the absence of this outlook.

For the blockaders, finally, taking action to protect the environment has become a deeply political project. The Grassy Narrows environment has become an actual and potential site of sociopolitical inequality—a place where injustice is enacted, revealed, and written on the landscape. Scarred by hydroelectric dams and mercury contamination, the river now reminds them of the systemic inequities and disparities their community confronts. Over the past several decades, links between social and environmental forms of injustice have gradually come to the forefront. Inspired by the profoundly negative impacts of the Ok Tedi Mine on the Yonggom people of New Guinea, Stuart Kirsch's (2006: 25) characterization of pollution as a kind of social relationship is equally pertinent in northwestern Ontario. An analogously politicized perspective colors how activists at Grassy Narrows make sense of their past and present. Based on events that took place decades ago, wild rice crops continue to be ruined and people continue to be sick. And, these days, many community members perceive clearcutting as the most recent environmental manifestation of injustice. From their perspective, the blockaders emphasize, the same fundamental inequity underlies mercury poisoning and clearcutting; the same corporate and government mentality that "no one lives up there" justifies carelessness and abuse.

All told, the environment surrounding Grassy Narrows is a different place, materially and conceptually, than it was only a few generations ago. Most First Nation members today make their living in ways quite unlike those of their grandparents. Their river is polluted and will remain so well into the future. In addition, clearcutting now threatens many of the land-based subsistence activities that remain. Enmeshed more than ever before in a global economic system, people at Grassy today depend less directly on the immediate environment, yet they also appreciate the links between the environment and their own health more concretely than ever before. The ability of the land to provide and sustain, though by no means less valued, is now trusted less freely. The environment has become a vulnerable space, susceptible to anthropogenic destruction and in need of human protection. Perhaps most significantly, it has also become a politically charged landscape, a potential site for injustice and a battleground in the wider struggle to overcome it.

As a consequence of the changes described in this chapter, when Grassy Narrows residents saw clearcutting within their traditional territory accelerate in the 1990s many of them understood it simultaneously as an instance of an extensive global environmental crisis, as a potential health hazard, as a threat to Native rights and traditional land-based subsistence culture, and as a manifestation of systemic injustice. This outlook ensured that, at least as significant as any ecological or conservation goals Grassy Narrows activists proposed, challenging their subordinate political position—manifested in assimilationist policies like the Indian Act, in their community's ongoing economic and social hardships, and in the disproportionately distributed impacts of environmental degradation—would be central to the blockade and its long-term ambitions.

The Grassy Narrows Blockade

By the 1990s, most of the building blocks for anti-clearcutting activism at Grassy Narrows First Nation had fallen into place. In order to follow the trajectory of the blockade, I find it helpful to identify four discernable, if somewhat overlapping, phases. Phase One (chapter 4) corresponds to the period of increasing awareness and anger directed at clearcutting in the region that characterized the decade leading up to the blockade. Beginning in the 1990s, a core group of community activists stepped forward to challenge threats to their traditional homeland, way of life, and legally guaranteed rights. Over the course of several years, protest actions escalated and a growing number of First Nation residents got involved in Grassy's emerging anti-clearcutting campaign.

Along with the blockade itself, Phase Two began in December of 2002 (chapters 5 and 6). This phase was an exhilarating time for participants and observers alike. Accompanied by a handful of dedicated supporters from outside the First Nation, Grassy Narrows activists resided at the blockade full-time from its inception until the fall of 2003. In the blockade's frigid early months, rented portable trailers and a generator system made their uninterrupted presence at the Slant Lake site possible. A vigilantly tended sacred fire—lit in the blockade's initial hours—burned constantly throughout this period. By spring, volunteers were constructing plywood cabins to house anticipated visitors, high school teachers were holding daily Native studies classes on site, and visiting supporters and media personnel were arriving almost daily. Outside support groups—including the Winnipeg-based Friends of Grassy Narrows—organized in response to Grassy's calls for public support. During this period, groups of Grassy Narrows activists repeatedly staged roving blockades in more distant parts of their Traditional Land Use Area and apprehended logging contractors on a regular basis.

With the arrival of another winter, the blockade entered Phase Three (chapter 7). It had become too costly—monetarily and personally—to maintain a full-time presence at Slant Lake. In addition, it had now been months since logging trucks had traveled through the Slant Lake site; they opted instead to haul their loads to the Kenora mill via a longer and more costly, but less potentially confrontational route to the east. Yet even when their constant presence at the blockade was no longer a necessity, some members of the Grassy Narrows community continued to spend time at the blockade site. There, they shared potluck style meals with family and friends, rekindled the sacred fire, or simply spent a peaceful evening away from the reserve. It was also during this third phase that the formally elected band leadership entered into a series of talks involving Abitibi-Consolidated—the multinational paper corporation holding the forest management license for the bulk of Grassy Narrows' traditional territory—and the Ontario Ministry of Natural Resources.

Meanwhile, the blockaders' network of external supporters continued to expand. By the fall of 2004, members of other First Nations communities intent on standing up to protect their homelands and rights increasingly began to look to activists at Grassy Narrows as role models, thus ushering in Phase Four of the Grassy Narrows blockade (chapter 8).

four

Beginnings

In the years before Grassy Narrows residents first publicly protested clearcutting in their traditional territory, at least a few community members already possessed a keen interest in cleaning up their immediate environment. On the heels of the tumultuous 1970s and 1980s, some people felt the need to "do something" about the reserve's garbage problem. They had witnessed firsthand the adverse impacts of mercury poisoning in their community and, by the mid-1990s, they were determined to take control of their environmental situation. Significantly, activists I spoke to about the blockade movement's local roots cited these efforts as an initial instance of organized action at Grassy Narrows.

Grassy Narrows is not the only northern First Nation to hold an outdoor clean-up each spring, but in the 1990s people at Grassy began to explicitly link their actions to a wider "environmental" cause. Simple but effective, they timed this yearly event to correspond to North American environmentalists' celebration of Earth Day each April 22nd. More than a decade later, it seems that their efforts were successful: An annual Earth Day clean-up conveniently follows the spring snowmelt each year. Today, the event is organized by the community's Sakatcheway Anishinabe School and students armed with trash bags play a proud role in keeping their community clean. First Nation residents' observation of "Earth Day" reflects an awareness of and willingness to adopt, adapt, and "indigenize" (Sahlins 1999) some

85

of the ideas and strategies of the wider environmental movement. This became a critical factor later on when Grassy Narrows activists sought outside support for their anti-clearcutting campaign. Along the same lines, the inclusion of the word "environmental" in the soon-to-be-formed Grassy Narrows Environmental Group's name would prove to resonate well with potential allies.

The Grassy Narrows Environmental Group

The formation of the Grassy Narrows Environmental Group (GNEG) also predates public anti-clearcutting activism.[1] GNEG initially organized in 1996 in reaction to proposals circulating at the time to store nuclear waste in the geologically stable Canadian Shield region near Grassy Narrows. An influential GNEG member who worked to defeat the nuclear waste proposal before her later role in the fight against clearcutting, Judy DaSilva told me that she and the other founders of GNEG felt the health risks to future generations were not worth the impressive sums of money nuclear waste storage could bring. Judy also mentioned that she first met Winona LaDuke, an Anishinaabe activist and former United States vice presidential candidate from White Earth, Minnesota, while opposing the nuclear waste storage proposal.[2] Like Judy, the other early members of GNEG went on to become central to the Grassy Narrows blockade. The networking and community organizing skills they learned in the mid-1990s appear to have played an important role in the anti-clearcutting activism that followed.

GNEG is a loosely structured, informal association. Although several core members—many of them siblings or extended family members—form GNEG's consistent center, the unofficial nature of membership allows people to move fluidly in and out of the group. For this reason, estimating the number of people involved in GNEG is difficult. Depending on timing and the level of involvement deemed necessary for inclusion, the figure ranges from around fifteen to well over one hundred. At least four people involved with GNEG have filled positions within Grassy Narrows' formal band leadership in the past decade. Yet, while a degree of overlap exists between GNEG and Grassy Narrows First Nation's Chief and Council, the two function according to very different schemes of organization and leadership.

The Chief and Council is a formally elected body with structure, power, and authority determined by Canada's Indian Act (see chapter 2). As is the case for other Canadian First Nations, Grassy's Chief and Council possesses a limited degree of federally recognized sovereignty. Financed by Canada's Department of Indian and Northern Affairs (DIAND), the Chief and Council regulates and distributes funding, subject to federal approval, for community infrastructure and social services. In addition, band governance provides a significant number of jobs—both directly and indirectly through Grassy's school, day care, and other community operations—in an atmosphere of employment scarcity.

Conversely, GNEG's loose structure more closely parallels ethnohistorically documented patterns of Anishinaabe leadership. Based on his 1930s studies of the Ojibwe living along Manitoba's Berens River, Hallowell (1992) described Anishinaabe leadership prior to the development of arrangements with the Canadian government as unstructured and localized in nature. Customary Anishinaabe leaders held no coercive authority over others and political structures were egalitarian, local, and informal, with individual Anishinaabe families and villages enjoying considerable autonomy (Hallowell 1992, see also Danziger 1979: 23). "Chiefs" and "bands," Hallowell points out, "were devices introduced by the government as a convenient means of dealing with Indians whose native culture did not function through persons whose role it was to represent them in transactions with outsiders" (Hallowell 1992: 35). In addition, even though successful and lasting leadership depended upon one's personal abilities and characteristics, customary Anishinaabe leadership followed hereditary lines (Warren 1984 [1885]; Kohl 1985 [1860]; Densmore 1979 [1929]). Mirroring these customary patterns, GNEG operates according to informal, egalitarian principles. While several particularly articulate individuals have gained recognition as prominent spokespersons, GNEG possesses no officially designated leaders. Fittingly, based on the widely known fact that his great-great-grandfather was Grassy's last hereditary chief, some Grassy Narrows citizens also acknowledge one of the group's respected core members as a top contender for the role of customary chief.

GNEG's pattern of leadership allows its advocates to claim close ties to a "traditional" Anishinaabe cultural past. Significantly, they feel that it also allows them to step outside the constraints of the

Indian Act, an option not available to those working within the Indian Act imposed Chief and Council system. While members of GNEG tend to see this as a positive political step, GNEG's independence from the formal band leadership means that the federal and provincial governments—along with most mainstream Canadians—do not recognize its power as legitimate. When government personnel, industry representatives, journalists, and most other members of the general public wish to communicate with "the people of Grassy Narrows," regarding blockade-related matters, they almost invariably approach the band's Chief and Council rather than GNEG, despite the fact that GNEG acted autonomously in initiating and maintaining the blockade. And, when negotiations commenced between Grassy Narrows First Nation, Abitibi-Consolidated, and Ontario's Ministry of Natural Resources late in 2003, it was the Chief and Council rather than the core members of GNEG who enjoyed the ability to speak for the First Nation.

Logging History, Logging Heritage

Commercial logging in the region surrounding Grassy Narrows began in the 1920s, when northwestern Ontario's forest industry shifted and expanded to meet U.S. and Canadian consumers' growing demand for newsprint (Lake of the Woods Museum 1999). In contrast to today's year-round harvest, logging in the early days was a seasonal affair, typically taking place only in the winter months when the ground was frozen and the construction of temporary "ice-roads" possible. Logging operations in the first half of the twentieth century were comparatively small-scale; they employed crews of men instead of massive machines and relied on horse-drawn sleds for transportation. People at Grassy Narrows with whom I spoke about the history of logging in their region tend to regard this type of logging as relatively undisruptive to the boreal ecosystem. By the 1960s, however, horse-powered logging was a thing of the past. Following relocation, people from Grassy recall the ubiquitous presence of slow-moving logging trucks as they hauled their loads on the then-gravel route to town.

Kenora's pulp and paper mill began operating in 1924. With numerous upgrades and expansions, the mill remained one of the town's most important industries into the early years of the twenty-first century. Many of Kenora's residents view logging not only as economically central, but also as an important part of their town's heritage (Lake of the Woods Museum 1999). From its modest origins as a fur trading post called Rat Portage, the town grew rapidly in the 1880s and 1890s with the construction of the trans-Canadian railroad. Logging was a significant factor in the town's expansion and success. In 1905, when a local grain company refused to have "Rat Portage" printed on their packaging, the three conjoined towns on the north shore of Lake of the Woods—Keewatin, Norman, and Rat Portage—combined the first syllables of their names to produce the pleasant sounding Kenora. A First Nations community to Kenora's immediate east retains the Rat Portage (*Washashk Onigum*) designation. In the 1990s, Kenora's three major mills—Abitibi-Consolidated, Trus Joist (a subsidiary of Weyerhaeuser), and Kenora Forest Products—consistently employed several hundred in a town of just under 16,000. While tourism plays an increasing role in the region's economy, the forest industry remains highly significant.

As the main zone of cultural and social interaction between Anishinaabeg from twenty-eight First Nations communities in the Treaty Three area, fly-in communities further to the north, and non-Native Canadian society, Kenora possesses a well-documented history of racial tension. In the late 1970s, one journalist wrote of Kenora's "Indian Problem" as the town's claim to fame (Newton 1979) and Kenora has long been dubbed the "Mississippi of Canada." Many Natives and Euro-Canadians I spoke to feel this reputation remains well deserved today. They cite subtle mistreatment of First Nations people in stores and restaurants and overt attacks on Native youth by a group calling itself the "K.I.B." (Kenora Indian Bashers) as indicators of the ongoing pervasiveness of racism in their town.

For anti-clearcutting activists from Grassy, the general perception of Kenora as a logging town—combined with its history of racial tension—resulted in a view of Kenora as "enemy territory." When Grassy Narrows activists decided to speak out against logging, some concerned Kenorans worried that their actions might amplify the already high tensions between the First Nations community and non-Natives. Given the economic and cultural significance of the industry to many Kenora residents, these concerns were legitimate. It also seems that Kenora's close ties to the forest industry put a damper on the amount of support the blockaders received from people in town. Based on his conversations with acquaintances in town, one Grassy Narrows trapper hypothesized that many Kenorans silently supported GNEG's cause but remained unwilling to admit it publicly because their friends or family members worked at the mill.

The 1999–2019 Whiskey Jack Forest Management Plan

Logging has been an established component of northwestern Ontario's economy for many decades. It has existed, in some form, in the Grassy Narrows region for the past ninety years. Why, then, was it only so recently that visible protest ensued? What finally caused Grassy Narrows residents' to take action? Annual logging rates in Canada's boreal forests increased from 1.6 million acres in 1970 to 2.5 million in 2001 (Knudson 2001). The forests of northwestern Ontario have been extensively impacted by this trend. Significant expansion in the region's forest industry took place in the 1990s, even as jobs in the sector decreased due to mechanization and consolidation (ForestEthics ND). Throughout the 1990s, residents of Grassy Narrows observed as the pace and intensity of logging in their Traditional Land Use Area accelerated. First Nation residents regularly utilize the region's network of logging roads to access sites for hunting, trapping, and gathering. Plainly visible from these roads, enormous clearcuts began appearing "almost overnight" (Phelan 1999a). Kitty, a young Grassy Narrows activist and mother, expressed her distress in a 1999 public statement:

> Every year my mother has taken me out to pick the berries and each time I notice the forest disappears more and more. This year it was only a 15-minute ride before it began to look like a desert. I felt this emptiness inside me. It was like it wasn't only the trees being chopped away, it was also my culture.[3]

In addition, large cuts overlapping portions of some First Nations members' traplines prompted many Grassy Narrows residents to take serious notice. First Nation citizens' growing awareness of Aboriginal and treaty rights and their increasing confidence in the efficacy of indigenous political actions (see chapter 2) were also significant factors. The most immediate catalyst, however, was Abitibi-Consolidated's 1999–2019 Whiskey Jack Forest Management Plan.

Abitibi-Consolidated Incorporated was a leading global manufacturer of newsprint from 1997 to 2007. In 2007, Abitibi-Consolidated—itself the product of a 1997 merger of Abitibi-Price and Stone-Consolidated—merged with Bowater to form AbitibiBowater. Despite these changes in corporate structure, the firm was known simply as "Abitibi" during the most active years of Grassy's anti-clearcutting campaign. Even before its merger with Bowater, Abitibi was a multinational corporation that conducted business in more than seventy countries and employed a workforce of approximately fifteen thousand. In 2004, Abitibi operated twenty-one sawmills and twenty-seven paper mills and was responsible for the management of 17.5 million hectares of Canadian forest. Included among the numerous forestry areas managed by Abitibi was northwestern Ontario's Whiskey Jack Forest. The Whiskey Jack—a designation created by the forest industry for use in the management planning process—covers over ten thousand square kilometers (6,200 square miles). Significantly, three-quarters of the Whiskey Jack Forest overlaps Grassy Narrows First Nation's traditional territory.

In order to retain its license to manage the Whiskey Jack, the Ontario Ministry of Natural Resources (OMNR) required Abitibi to submit a new twenty-year Forest Management Plan (FMP) for provincial and public approval every five years. While Forest Management Plans must include long-range planning for a twenty-year term, they are revised and resubmitted every five years; for this reason, projected harvests for the first five years of a given plan typically generate the most interest. Abitibi-Consolidated's 1999–2019 Whiskey Jack FMP proposed the harvest of 3.9 million cubic meters of wood fiber in the first five years of the plan, 1999–2004.[4] Even more critically, the FMP also included a proposed cut-block directly south of the Grassy Narrows community, in plain sight across the waters of Grassy Lake. Judy DaSilva highlighted the significance of this development: The immediacy of the threat made many community members angry enough to take action. While people could forget what was happening farther away, she said, seeing an old-growth area so close to home in jeopardy prompted Grassy Narrows residents to speak out.

Up to this point, a handful of concerned First Nation residents had written letters to the OMNR and to Abitibi-Consolidated voicing their objections to the FMP but felt that they had received little response. On December 28th of 1998, a group of approximately fifteen core GNEG members headed to Kenora to protest Abitibi's

1999–2019 Whiskey Jack Forest Management Plan. Although they timed their protest to correspond to the FMP's official due date, they arrived to find the OMNR's local office still closed for the Christmas holiday. Nevertheless, the protestors draped their vehicles with banners, held up anti-clearcutting signs in the parking lot, and alerted the media. In addition to expressing their outrage about the proximity of clearcutting to their community, GNEG members voiced more general objections to the forest industry's practice of extensive clearcutting, scarification, and the use of herbicides (employed by forest managers to retard the growth of "undesirable" tree species in recently clearcut areas) (Bland 1998).[5] Citing a decline in trapping yields and income due to the clearcuts (Phelan 1999a), they also condemned clearcutting's impact on Anishinaabe people's ability to practice their land-based subsistence culture.

Stepping into his role as the protestors' primary public spokesperson, J. B. Fobister quickly found ways to draw public attention to several interrelated concerns he and other GNEG members saw as paramount. J. B. discussed the emotional impact of the clearcuts: "It is devastating to see the land after clearcutting," he commented, "I share sadness with a lot of my people" (Phelan 1999a). And, as he bluntly put it, "This amounts to nothing less than cultural genocide" (Bland 1998). J. B. also voiced the protestors' frustration over their inability to influence decisions pertinent to the land surrounding their community. As he explained, "This is the Grassy Narrows traditional land use area, yet we're not able to stop anything that goes on there" (Phelan 1999a). This position foreshadowed arguments that would become more explicit in the years ahead as Grassy Narrows activists increasingly drew on the precedent established by the 1997 *Delgamuukw* decision to call attention to the fact that they had not been adequately consulted.

A press statement released by GNEG in conjunction with the protest declared that the logging taking place in the region was "just another case of a huge multinational corporation displacing the indigenous population in order to extract natural resources . . . no wonder Canada is being called 'Brazil of the North'" (Bland 1998). Similarly, GNEG's January 1, 1999 letter to the *Washington Post* (a major purchaser of Abitibi's newsprint) stated that the ongoing clearcutting was "comparable in every way with the pattern prevalent in the Brazilian rainforest. This is a pattern of cultural genocide against the native people and of irreversible damage to the bio-diversity of the natural forest."[6] Activists at Grassy were familiar with the challenges faced by indigenous groups in Brazil and recognized many similarities to their own situation. In fact, a delegation of Kayapo activists from Brazil had visited Grassy Narrows the previous summer and had a chance to tour some of the clearcuts in the vicinity.[7] Clearly, activists at Grassy Narrows were inspired by the encounter.

The Kayapo case has been thoroughly documented, especially regarding the importance some Kayapo activists have placed on collaborating with non-indigenous supporters and speaking in an "environmental" language attractive to potential allies (Turner 1991; Conklin and Graham 1995). These strategies played important roles as Grassy Narrows activists' anti-clearcutting campaign escalated. Additionally, from the Kayapo—who wore traditional dress for at least part of their time in northwestern Ontario—activists at Grassy may have gained a greater appreciation of the rhetorical power of "indigenous" cultural self-representation and imagery (Conklin 1997). In the years ahead, GNEG members regularly made use of contemporary Native North American symbolism: Medicine wheels, eagle feathers, and hand drums consistently appeared at GNEG's public marches, protests, and gatherings.

In the weeks that followed, Grassy Narrows residents continued to protest Abitibi's 1999–2019 Forest Management Plan. Judy DaSilva and her older sister, Roberta Keesick, both spoke publicly of taking things to a higher level, perhaps by organizing a national or international boycott of Abitibi's paper products (Phelan 1999b). Several First Nation members asked the Ontario Ministry of Environment (OMOE) to conduct an environmental assessment on Abitibi's FMP. Their request was denied. Grassy Narrows' Chief and Council sent a letter, dated January 8th, 1999, to top officials in the province's Ministries of Natural Resources and Environment outlining the OMNR's failure to respond to First Nation members' concerns or even return their phone calls. GNEG also organized a second public protest of the FMP and industrial forestry practices more generally on January 16th. Approximately fifty people from Grassy Narrows, along with a smaller number of environmentalist supporters, gathered in front of Kenora's Kenricia Hotel, where the Canadian Forestry Association was presenting its annual "Forest Capital of Canada" award for

1999 to the city's mayor. Attendees of the award ceremony reportedly paid the protestors little mind (Bland 1999a).

In mid-March, a somewhat alarmist headline reading "Threats to Blockade at Grassy Narrows" (Bland 1999b) appeared in the *Kenora Daily Miner and News*. With the new FMP scheduled to go into effect on April 1st, members of GNEG seriously considered erecting a blockade to correspond to that date. The chief at the time, Bill Fobister, supported GNEG's anti-clearcutting campaign and wrote letters to the OMNR, OMOE, and to the federal Department of Indian Affairs articulating the First Nation's principal demands, including the recognition of Grassy Narrows' 2,500 square mile traditional land base by all levels of government and the protection of Anishinaabe culture which, the letter pointed out, both originates from and depends upon that land base.[8] GNEG ultimately decided against blockading in 1999, Judy DaSilva later told me, because its members felt that public opinion was unlikely to be on their side at that time.

Although they did not block roads, neither did Grassy Narrows Environmental Group members quietly surrender their fight once Abitibi's 1999–2019 FMP went into effect. In April of 1999, GNEG formulated a concise position paper communicating their views on logging. The one-page position paper inventoried, in capital lettering, GNEG's desires:

–OFFICIAL RECOGNITION OF TLUA BY ALL PARTIES
–NO CLEARCUTTING
–WE HAVE ABORIGINAL AND TREATY RIGHTS—
HUNTING, FISHING, RICE PICKING, BLUEBERRY
PICKING
WE ARE NOT ABLE TO ENJOY AND EXCERCISE
THESE RIGHTS TO THE FULL EXTENT DUE TO
CLEARCUTTING
CLEARCUTTING INFRINGES ON OUR ABORIGINAL
AND TREATY RIGHTS
–THE HARVEST OF ANY PRESENTLY APPROVED
BLOCKS WITHIN THE TLUA MUST DIRECTLY BENE-
FIT BAND MEMBERS IE. CONTRACTS
–*TREEPLANTING ACCEPTABLE UNDER CERTAIN
CIRCUMSTANCES
–THERE MUST BE NO SPRAYING

–THERE MUST BE NO MORE ROADS BUILT
–THERE MUST BE NO SCARIFICATION
–*NO FURTHER DEVELOPMENT/DESTRUCTION
WITHIN THE TRADITIONAL LAND USE AREA
–REFORESTATION PROGRAM MUST REFLECT
VALUES OF GRASSY NARROWS FIRST NATION FOR
THEIR USE
*THESE ACTIVITIES MUST NOT PROCEED UNTIL
THE MEDIATION [CONSULTATION] PROCESS
REACHES AN ACCEPTABLE AGREEMENT

The position paper called, first and foremost, for a cessation of all clearcutting within Grassy Narrows' Traditional Land Use Area (TLUA).

As Anishinaabe people and signatories of Treaty Three of 1873, GNEG's statement argued, members of Grassy Narrows First Nation possess Aboriginal and treaty-guaranteed rights to hunt, fish, and gather. Because of the damage clearcutting inflicts on the environment, the people of Grassy Narrows have been unable "to enjoy and exercise these rights to the full extent." Clearcutting thus infringes on their Aboriginal and treaty rights. Although frankly opposed to the practice of clearcutting, the position paper leaves open the possibility of alternative methods of logging, especially if First Nation members carry out and benefit from the resulting contracts. And, although the position paper is unequivocal on GNEG's intolerance of herbicidal spraying, service road construction, and scarification, it suggests that reforestation and tree planting programs may take place under the condition that these activities "reflect the values of Grassy Narrows First Nation." While difficult to define, these values include the upholding of Aboriginal and treaty rights, the ability to maintain Anishinaabe land-based subsistence culture and, perhaps most importantly, the right of the First Nation and its members to make decisions regarding future land use and management.

The same core group who composed this position paper later became the leaders of the Grassy Narrows blockade. The fundamental goals they articulated in 1999 seem to have changed little in the intervening years. Reflecting on these objectives from the perspective of 2003–2005, activists at Grassy Narrows told me they want to be able to pick blueberries without the fear of herbicides being sprayed nearby. They want their children to someday feel safe as their families catch and eat local fish. They do not want to look over an entire trapline in one barren glance. Grassy Narrows activists see the trees, wildlife, and medicines of their homeland as vital to their way of life. They feel that clearcutting within their Traditional Land Use Area presents a serious threat to the land and their existence as a people. And, echoing their 1999 declaration, they want it to stop.

In September of 1999, GNEG hosted its first Environmental Gathering on the Grassy Narrows reserve. The event featured former Assembly of First Nations chief Ovide Mercredi as a keynote speaker and offered workshops on Aboriginal and treaty rights. Although it was small in scale and did not attract media attention, the gathering set an important precedent. With its focus on Aboriginal and treaty rights, the 1999 Environmental Gathering hinted at GNEG members' emerging community education focus. Environmental Gatherings have since become annual events at Grassy Narrows. Building on the educational objectives established in 1999, later Environmental Gatherings shifted their emphasis from adult education to youth. Held at the Slant Lake blockade site each year since 2003, these annual gatherings have enabled GNEG members to share their concerns, strategies, and knowledge with others. As well, they have allowed activists at Grassy Narrows to build rewarding relationships with other Native communities facing comparable challenges and with non-Native supporters.

The Grassy Narrows Traditional Land Use Area: Drawing a Political Landscape

"Sovereignty is not something you ask for. It's something you do." That's how Grassy Narrows band member, trapper, business owner, and GNEG spokesperson J. B. Fobister put it one November afternoon in 2004 during an intense conversation in the back of his small convenience store. J. B. was not the first make this point: Six Nations chief Oren Lyons once declared, "If a nation feels like a nation, acts like a nation, then you will be a nation" (Quoted in Niezen 2003: 171). Similarly, according to one of Gail Landsman's (1988: 60) Mohawk informants, "one does not ask for or fight for sovereignty; one lives it."

Although stopping the clearcutting that continues to ravage their homeland may be Grassy Narrows activists' most basic, immediate, and externally visible objective, the achievement of political and cultural self-determination is their most significant long-term goal. Critically, the very first demand listed in GNEG's 1999 position paper speaks to the group's desire that the federal and provincial governments—along with lower levels of government, industrial representatives, and the public—officially recognize the Grassy Narrows Traditional Land Use Area. But what is this area? And, why is it so significant?

In May of 1979, Grassy Narrows chief Simon Fobister addressed a panel of representatives from the province of Ontario, the Canadian federal government, Grassy Narrows and Whitedog First Nations, Ontario Hydro, Lake of the Woods Water Control Board, and Reed Limited. The ad hoc panel had been created to explore potential solutions for the problems then plaguing the First Nation community and to address the possibility of compensation for damages related to flooding, relocation, and mercury poisoning. In his presentation, Fobister talked about the need for education among Grassy's youth. He emphasized that land, not money, was the key to Grassy Narrows' future. Petitioning for control over important traditional resources, Fobister asked the government,

> to return to the people of Grassy Narrows the exclusive use of, or the control over access to, land and resources that have traditionally been relied on for food or barter, on which a substantial portion of the population still depends for a livelihood, and which are the key resources for the future economic and social development of the community. (Grassy Narrows Band 1979, cited in Vecsey 1987: 298)

And, for the first time, he introduced the Grassy Narrows Traditional Land Use Area (GNTLUA). The GNTLUA described in 1979 paralleled the over two-thousand-square-mile area held by Grassy Narrows families as registered traplines.

In 1984, the Ontario Ministry of Natural Resources produced maps that included a delineated GNTLUA. The boundaries of the GNTLUA resembled unpublished maps drawn by Peter Usher in 1981 based on what elders had told him about where they used to

hunt, fish, and trap (Vecsey 1987). But the OMNR maps also designated numerous plots of land already leased or promised for timber,
mining, recreational canoe routes, and other competing non-Native
uses superimposed over the GNTLUA (Vecsey 1987). As the OMNR
maps clearly illustrated, Grassy Narrows First Nation and Ontario
were making conflicting claims to same area. Ultimately, Ontario
chose merely to consider band members' access to lands and resources
instead of recognizing Grassy Narrows' self-governing authority over
the GNTLUA.

When they began to overtly oppose Abitibi's clearcutting practices in the late 1990s, activists at Grassy Narrows immediately perceived the need for an official-sounding term of reference to describe
their customary homeland to the general public and the media. They
returned to the GNTLUA designation. Concurrent with their initial
public protests, GNEG members began using the term regularly. By
the time the blockade began, the GNTLUA had become both a strategy and a symbol for Grassy Narrows activists' intertwined political,
environmental, and cultural goals.

For generations, the people of Asubpeeschoseewagong have lived
upon and utilized the area now termed the GNTLUA. Long before
Grassy Narrows became a "Canadian" First Nation and even longer
before the province of Ontario came into being, Anishinaabeg traveled unimpeded throughout the area, partaking in a seasonal cycle of
subsistence. Only fifty years ago, elders recall, fluid mobility throughout the region was still commonplace. Thus, while the GNTLUA—as
a region consistently used and valued by a particular group of people—
has clearly existed for a long stretch of time, it has only recently been
described in codified, bounded terms. As a phenomenon of the late
twentieth century, the GNTLUA designation is one way that activists
at Grassy Narrows have chosen to "do" their sovereignty.

Pile and Keith (1997: 30) point out that "in one sense, power is
the power to have control over space. . . . In another sense, power can
be mobilized through the reterritorialization—the resymbolisation—of
space." In its present utilization by the Grassy Narrows blockaders, the
GNTLUA designation makes a symbolic political statement about
control—or, at least, desired control—over a particular piece of land.
Grassy Narrows activists see attaining decision-making power within
the GNTLUA as a potential path toward making political and cultural
self-determination a reality. They see environmental protection within

the GNTLUA as inextricably bound to cultural preservation; they want to stop the clearcutting so that they and others in their community can continue the land-based subsistence practices that form the enduring heart of contemporary Anishinaabe cultural life.

Grassy Narrows is far from alone among indigenous communities that have chosen to delineate a spatial boundary in recent years. For them, Colin Scott (2001: 7) observes,

> Political survival demands a dual, seemingly contradictory strategy. On the one hand, First Nations are impelled to enlighten and persuade outsiders about the character and meaning, in Aboriginal terms, of their relationship to homelands and waters. On the other hand, in order to create legal and constitutional space for the defense of and autonomous development of their territories, they are forced to negotiate Aboriginal cultural and political landscapes in relation to Euro-Canadian concepts of property and jurisdiction.

And so, Native peoples today frequently "borrow" this modular form of the nation-state even as they seek to assert their difference from it and challenge its power (Biolsi 2005; see also Ramos 1998). As protest escalated at Grassy Narrows, the Traditional Land Use Area designation became a powerful political device; it allowed activists in the First Nation to assert their claim to the land in a "language of property" already accepted within the wider context of the modern nation-state (Nadasdy 2003: 236).

From 1998 onward, Grassy's activists and elected leaders employed the term to describe the region of contestation. When the blockade was erected in the winter of 2002–2003, a prominent sign referenced the GNTLUA designation. GNEG members frequently used the term casually and naturally, as though the GNTLUA had existed forever. Non-Native supporters and media personnel followed suit by accepting the TLUA's existence unquestioningly. In some senses, of course, for Grassy Narrows residents their TLUA *has* existed forever—or at least since the proverbial "time immemorial." With hundreds of years of local history, they perceive their presence in the region as enduring and established, in stark contrast to the territorial claims made by relatively recent non-Native newcomers. One reason, then, that the GNTLUA became so significant for anti-clearcutting activists lies in its ability to quickly communicate a conception of Grassy Narrows and its people as a deeply rooted "traditional" part of the northwestern Ontario landscape.

The GNTLUA establishes the First Nation's rhetorical legitimacy in a landscape filled with competing designations and meanings. In the context of Native land rights disputes, "who owns the land?" is a common question. It is this kind of contestation that makes a formal designation like the GNTLUA indispensable for First Nations activists working to assert their land-based rights. Those unfamiliar with the Grassy Narrows case often ask me who "owns" the land people at Grassy fight to protect. Always, they receive a multifaceted answer. Who really owns the GNTLUA depends on whom you ask. For the governments of Canada and Ontario, as for a majority of non-Native Canadians, the answer is straightforward. They think of this land as Crown Land, owned by the federal government and managed by the province and licensed corporate interests. Anishinaabe activists, on the other hand, see their TLUA as Aboriginal land. Based on their understanding that the territory was never ceded (see chapter 2), many people at Grassy Narrows conceive of themselves as the proper owners of their traditional territory. As deputy chief and anti-clearcutting campaigner Steve Fobister declared at a 2004 First Nation Forestry Assembly, "we're *supposed* to be landowners."

2000–2002

Over the next two years, activists at Grassy Narrows continued to voice their objections to the clearcutting that continued unabated throughout the GNTLUA. On March 13th of 2000, GNEG members released a statement to the press. The release noted that the Ontario Ministry of Environment (OMOE) had responded to Grassy Narrows residents' earlier calls for environmental assessment by pledging that the corporation would put forward its "best efforts to understand and deal with" the First Nation's concerns. In the eyes of activists at Grassy, however, this had not taken place; despite their Aboriginal legal status and rights, OMOE's response struck them as identical to what any special interest citizens group might receive. Their release called specific attention to the corporation's lack of consultation by stating, "Abitibi-Consolidated has made no efforts to understand and deal with the concerns of the Grassy Narrows First Nation."

The press release went on to describe OMNR's failure to respond the band's requests for the 1999–2000 Annual Work Schedule, which designated specific parcels of land intended for harvest, tending, and renewal activities. It pointed out that "The First Nation has not even been given an opportunity to carefully examine the plans that will lead to the clear-cutting of much of its Traditional Land Use Area." Based on these factors, the release concluded with a strong statement:

> It is the opinion of the Grassy Narrows First Nation that any logging activities carried out after April 1, 2000, will be carried out illegally. Logging operations infringe on our Treaty and Aboriginal rights and we are committed to protect the land and these rights.

The release listed J. B. Fobister as the First Nation's contact person.

On April 5th, J. B.—along with two other trappers from Grassy—filed a lawsuit against Abitibi-Consolidated. A press release issued the same day outlined their case. Their suit argued that because Abitibi-Consolidated's forest operations infringed upon First Nation members' constitutionally protected rights to hunt and trap, Ontario had no legal power under Treaty Three—signed thirty-nine years before it became a province—to grant forestry permits to Abitibi, nor to any other logging company. As Sierra Legal Defense lawyer Elizabeth Christie explained, "the land became part of Ontario in 1912 on the condition that the province recognize the rights of aboriginal inhabitants, [which it] has failed to do" (Mittelstaedt 2000). As a challenge to Ontario's authority to license the forest operations impacting Aboriginal peoples' subsistence rights, the lawsuit was a potentially important and far-reaching First Nations rights case. With the assistance of the Sierra Legal Defense Fund, the three Grassy Narrows trappers petitioned the Ontario Superior Court of Justice for a judicial review. While a judicial review would have put Grassy Narrows' fight against clearcutting on the legal fast-track, this route was denied. On July 17th of 2003, Justice Edward Then cited the case's complexity as the basis of his decision to deny the judicial review application, leaving an expensive court trial as the only option (Barrera 2003b).[9]

In the months that followed, protest activity at Grassy Narrows appeared to decelerate. Abitibi's Forest Management Plan was now approved and in effect. In 2001, members of GNEG commenced work on a Wild Meat Containment Study. With financial support from the North American Fund for Environmental Cooperation and Health Canada, Judy and Roberta began collecting samples of various wild meats to be tested for mercury and other contaminants. In common with GNEG's public anti-clearcutting protests, the study was a reaction to concerns about the environment where First Nation members hunted, fished, trapped, and gathered wild resources. Clearly linked to Grassy's past experience with mercury contamination, the potential impact of contaminants on community members' health was a central focus of the study. In addition to the mercury they knew was present, many people were worried that the herbicides used in the industrial forest regeneration process could also be harming animal and human health.

Meanwhile, clearcutting throughout the GNTLUA continued. Though little protest surfaced publicly, this period was the calm before the storm. GNEG activists had turned their attentions inward. Frustrated by the failures of their previous efforts and by their inability to stop the clearcutting, they succeeded in drumming up support within the Grassy Narrows community. In the months leading up to the initiation of the blockade, J. B. and Judy visited Grassy's school. There, they spoke about the clearcutting that surrounded their community and challenged students to consider the best course of action. Their efforts to motivate teachers, students, and school administrators to join the fight against clearcutting were successful; the youth and educators of Sakatcheway Anishinabe School would play a major role in the blockade.

Once the blockade began in earnest, Grassy Narrows activists frequently pointed out that they had attempted to combat the clearcutting in their region through conventional channels for years. They had written numerous letters, called for an environmental assessment, and conducted peaceful demonstrations in Kenora, all to no avail. Repeatedly, activists at Grassy told me that their decision to take direct action was a last resort. A blockade, it seemed, was the only way to get their point across.

Five

The Blockade

On December 3rd of 2002, residents of Grassy Narrows First Nation erected a blockade at Slant Lake. Located about five miles north of the community, the blockade was intended as a peaceful but potent protest of the clearcutting taking place throughout Grassy Narrows' Traditional Land Use Area. Dozens of youth, teachers, and Grassy Narrows Environmental Group members had gathered at the site by the time three young First Nation members placed logs in the active logging road, effectively blocking the expected trucks' passage. Almost two years later Kitty reflected on her actions:

> I remember an elder once told me on my healing journey I should start with myself, my family, my community, and then our nation. I never understood that until the day my sister, another young man and I went to lay logs over the road. We did it because we were sick and tired of watching our lives slowly disappear.[1]

Judy DaSilva was also present at Slant Lake that December day. She voiced her fears that her children would never be able to use the land in the traditional Anishinaabe way if the clearcutting continued (Godin 2002a).

People from Grassy anticipated a lengthy struggle. Preparing to remain on site for an indefinite amount of time, the blockaders promptly began to establish a base camp. Right away, they dug several fire pits and set up a tipi. Soon followed the first solid building at Slant Lake—a portable plywood trapper's shack with a clear tarpaulin cover and a small but effective woodstove. On the first afternoon of the blockade, one contractor traveling north to pick up a load of logs was turned back by the group of protestors. Aggravated that the incident was causing him to lose money, he suggested the blockaders take their complaints to Abitibi's head office instead (Godin 2002a). But after years of publicly objecting to clearcutting, Grassy Narrows activists felt that following these sanctioned routes to express their frustration had only led to disappointment. Their blockade would stand.

Assisted by other Grassy residents who made the drive from the reserve to the blockade with supplies, news, and companionship, the blockaders sustained a twenty-four-hour-a-day presence at Slant Lake in the days that followed. A sacred fire was tended in a round-the-clock vigil. Leon Jourdain, then chief of the Grand Council Treaty Three regional organization, declared his support of the blockaders' actions, emphasizing that Anishinaabe peoples' land and rights have not been protected or respected by the provincial and federal governments (Godin 2002b). In response to the protestors' presence, logging trucks began to bypass the Slant Lake blockade by taking a short detour down Segise Road—which intersected with Jones Road just two miles south of the reserve community—on their way to town.

On December 11th—eight days after the blockade began—Grassy Narrows activists responded to this development with the following public notice:

> As pursuant to the hunting rights guaranteed in Treaty #3, the Anishinabek of Grassy Narrows wish to inform the public that a hunt will commence at 8:00 am, Friday December 13, 2002, and will terminate at 4:00 pm, Sunday December 15, 2002. For safety purposes, all traffic will be temporarily halted or turned back as of 8:00 pm Thursday December 12, 2002 within the affected area for the duration of the hunt. This action is a peaceful demonstration of our will to assert out rights within the area of contention.

The notice went on to describe the specific sites in question and identify its intended audience:

This notice applies to all logging trucks, and machine opera-tors. All other users of this area will be subject to a quick briefing about the hunt, and the safety issues therein, but will be otherwise allowed to pass through.[2]

Grassy Narrows activists were well aware that the practice of land-based subsistence—so central to their culture and cultural identity—could also become an effective political statement. In expressing concerns for public safety, their notice assumed the rhetoric of state sovereignty. And, by strategically evoking the treaty-guaranteed rights that protect and enable Anishinaabe subsistence, the public notice posed a direct challenge to the clearcutting they saw as destroying the land and making land-based subsistence activities increasingly impracticable.

By mid-December, between ten and thirty blockaders were consis-tently camped at the Slant Lake site. Several high school teachers had begun holding daily ecology and Native studies classes at the blockade, and students were responding favorably. The community's school bus drove them to the blockade and back each day and stu-dents arrived prepared with food and warm clothing. The principal of the community's school at the time, Sister Irene Freeman, was sup-portive of students' involvement in the ongoing protest. She cele-brated the fact that the blockade had helped students learn about treaty rights and had given adults at Grassy a new sense of pride in their young people (Clement 2003).

In anticipation of a Treaty Three area chief's meeting to be held at the Slant Lake site in January, the blockaders built a large round-house to host the event. This roundhouse, with its plywood walls and floor, orange tarpaulin roof, and two aged woodstoves, provided a rea-sonably warm place for blockaders to pass the time and remained a popular gathering place as the blockade progressed. Steadily, First Nations activists—including several members of the Mohawk and Ojibwe Warrior Societies—and non-Native supporters from across Canada began arriving to assist with the blockade. As word spread about the events unfolding at Grassy Narrows, donated provisions and letters of support began to reach their destination.

Also on site in the blockade's first days were two members of Christian Peacemaker Teams (CPT), a faith-based group committed, according to their brochure, "to active non-violence." CPT has its foundations in the Mennonite and Quaker peace churches, although the group also welcomes volunteer team members from other Christian denominations. Funded primarily by private donations, CPT works in locations worldwide where they see a need for violence reduction. The group has been active for over ten years and has teams stationed in Colombia, Iraq, and Hebron. Key among their methods—as their "Getting in the Way" motto indicates—are nonviolent techniques of witnessing, documentation, and mediation. CPT was involved in the blockade from its early days; when the blockade began, activists in the Grassy Narrows community invited the group to come help prevent and, if necessary, document any potential violence.

Although CPT's members aimed to influence the First Nation community as little as possible, their presence had a significant and lasting impact on the blockade. For over a year, alternating team members camped out at the Slant Lake blockade site, typically two or three at a time, working to reduce not only the possibility of physical violence at blockade confrontations, but also to address the structural violence to Asubpeeschoseewagong treaty rights that clearcutting of their lands implied (CPT ND). Members of CPT were quietly present at the majority of blockade actions and events as well as nearly all of GNEG's offsite protest activities. CPT's constant presence and calm consistency served as a steady source of moral support. In addition, CPT members frequently assisted First Nations activists in event planning and media communications. Although the team moved to Kenora in the fall of 2004 to continue their work on structural racism at a more regional level and officially dissolved their northwestern Ontario project in the spring of 2005, some CPT members continued to maintain informal relationships with activists at Grassy long after.

Winter at Slant Lake: The Early Months of the Grassy Narrows Blockade

A brief article in the *Kenora Daily Miner and News* marked the end of the blockade's first full month. Judy DaSilva commented for the paper on the blockade's emerging significance as a sacred site, adding that the blockade "is like a vigil—we have what we call a sacred fire at the site and can't let that burn out until we finish" (Godin 2003a). Meanwhile, as letters of support and a constant stream of visitors energized the blockaders, logging trucks continued taking their short detour around the blockade.

Among the visitors who traveled to Grassy in the early weeks of 2003 were three activists from Winnipeg, Manitoba. They hoped to learn more about what was taking place a few short hours from their home and were eager to offer their assistance. Recognizing the need for wider support, they founded Friends of Grassy Narrows (FGN), a Winnipeg-based group composed primarily of socially and environmentally conscious non-Natives from diverse walks of life. FGN began to meet regularly in the city and developed a strong core membership of about fifteen university students, independent activists, nongovernmental organization employees, and educators. Several dozen others were more casually involved.

When I referred to Friends of Grassy Narrows as an "organization" two of the group's founding members responded by explaining that they prefer to think of their group and the work it does more along the lines of a "friendship" than a formal institution. Notably, this philosophy signifies their implicit rejection of Canadian society's hierarchical structure. Many of FGN's members initially became interested in the Grassy Narrows case because of its clear intersection of environmental and human rights issues. One FGN founder told me he was drawn to this particular struggle because in it he saw "a whole bunch of issues converging all at once." While many FGN members have been attracted by the tangible, direct action philosophy of the blockade, those who visited Grassy in January of 2003 told me they were initially most impressed by the warm atmosphere at Slant Lake. After their visit they felt eager to return and motivated to coordinate further support.

Friends of Grassy Narrows became instrumental in raising funds and collecting donations for the blockaders at Slant Lake. Their fundraising efforts financed the rental of four heated trailers and a generator in the first winter of the blockade, making a sustained presence at the site a realistic possibility. In addition to their fundraising role, FGN members facilitated educational events in Winnipeg about the blockade and participated in several protest actions in Kenora. FGN also filled a critical communicatory role by maintaining a listserv and an informative website.

By mid-January, Ontario's Ministry of Natural Resources offered to step in to mediate the dispute between Grassy Narrows First

Nation and Abitibi-Consolidated (Godin 2003b). While the OMNR and Abitibi seemed eager to find a solution, people at Grassy Narrows—both the blockaders and the First Nation's Chief and Council—felt that the treaty and Aboriginal rights issues at hand were not something that could be solved quickly or locally. With the blockade attracting widespread media attention, Grand Council Treaty Three also saw fit to get involved in the events unfolding within its territory.

Chiefs from the Treaty Three area gathered in a packed roundhouse at Slant Lake on January 16th in order to discuss the blockade's future. Following this meeting, the chiefs' official decision to continue the blockade echoed the protestors' conviction that they were in for a long haul. Treaty Three's official endorsement of the blockade lent GNEG's actions an air of legitimacy and led to even more publicity. Despite the fact that GNEG members and youth rather than the community's elected leaders had been most physically present at the blockade, Grassy's Chief and Council and the blockaders appeared to be on the same page at this point in time. As Simon Fobister (who'd resumed duty as the First Nation's chief in the year 2000) commented, "These issues have been talked about since the treaty was signed in 1873—these are issues that the local Ministry of Natural Resources cannot resolve—it has to be resolved by a higher level of government" (Godin 2003c). Many blockaders shared this outlook and informed me in the months ahead that a solution to this disagreement would only be reached at a "nation-to-nation" level.

"Be Careful with Abitibi"

Although logs had ceased flowing past the Slant Lake blockade, Grassy's protestors were frustrated by the continuing passage of logging trucks via the Segise Road detour, just south of the reserve. In response, they adopted a strategy of periodic "roving" blockades beginning in February of 2003. Although spared the outright violence that cast a dark shadow over incidents at Oka (in 1990) and Ipperwash (in 1995) (see chapter 2), these roving blockades brought about tense moments when Grassy Narrows activists informed logging company personnel that they would not be permitted to pass with their load of logs or would be unable to return to their work sites.

A particularly heated standoff took place on February 6th when a logging truck, slasher machine, and two pickups attempting to travel south to Kenora encountered a group of twenty blockaders at the intersection of Jones and Segise roads. Several of the blockaders had parked their vehicles in the road to create a physical barrier. The Ontario Provincial Police (OPP) arrived quickly to arbitrate, although for some Grassy Narrows residents the community's troubled relationship with the OPP contributed to the scene's tension.[3] Kenora's *Miner and News* described the fourteen-hour standoff as coming to a peaceful end when the loggers agreed to go back the way they came (Godin 2003d). Reaching Kenora now meant detouring all the way to Red Lake Road, over an hour to the east, and south through Vermillion Bay. Needless to say, loggers operating in the area were annoyed by the extra cost. In the months ahead this lengthy detour became their standard route.

The blockaders soon drew attention to their campaign with a protest of a different type. An OMNR sign warning anyone heading north on Jones Road against the careless use of fire had long stood as a relatively overlooked part of the scenery. White with red lettering, the sign read: "Our future depends on forests. Don't destroy it. Be careful with Fire!" In neatly matched lettering, someone decided to substitute the word "Abitibi" for "Fire." The sign now warned its readers to "Be Careful with Abitibi!" The sign's new message alluded to the disagreement that triggered the blockade. Grassy Narrows residents, provincial resource managers, and forest industry representatives all concurred that their future did indeed depend on the forest; they all claimed the forest as central to their livelihood and way of life. Where they diverged, as the sign's new message affirmed, was over how the forest should be used, what it should look like, and who should have the power to make such decisions.

The altered sign's message also subtly critiqued one of Abitibi's often-repeated defenses of its clearcutting practices. Along with OMNR, the forest industry urged the public to prevent forest fires for the health of the forest, yet the corporation's foresters frequently argued that clearcutting is not ecologically damaging because it mimics the natural conditions of forest fires. Abitibi's 2004 Sustainable Forest Management Plan, for instance, cites emulation of natural disturbances during harvesting operations as a desirable strategy

(Abitibi-Consolidated 2004a: 40).[4] According to Charlotte Caron, a regional forester for Abitibi's Kenora Division, clearcutting is actually beneficial for the forest, "otherwise the trees get old and die off and it's harder for them to come back. Forest management promotes a healthy forest as opposed to one full of disease and insects" (Phelan 1999a).

Conservation ecologists (Henry 2002) and industrial foresters agree that fire is an important factor in boreal forest ecology. But, as ecologists point out and Grassy Narrows activists often reiterate, clearcutting is very different from a natural forest fire since, "unlike clearcutting, which removes almost all of the trees—and their nutrients—from a site, natural disturbances like fire leave many standing live and dead trees" (CPAWS ND). These remaining trees provide critical habitat for many animal species.

Days of Action

As time went on, the blockade drew increasing attention from other First Nations communities. Grand Council Treaty Three and Nishnawbe Aski Nation designated February 12th a "day of support" for the Grassy Narrows blockaders.[5] Responding to this call, several northwestern Ontario First Nations took action to convey their solidarity with the protestors at Grassy. Members of Aroland and Constance Lake First Nations set up a blockade on Provincial Highway 643. Hornepayne, Moose Cree, Cat Lake, and Mishkeegogamang First Nations held similar local events.

The network of solidarity between First Nations activists was already starting to play an important role in the blockade's trajectory. While face-to-face meetings between widely scattered activists were often unfeasible, the moral support of this "imagined community" (Anderson 1991) invigorated the blockade movement. Many blockaders at Grassy told me that just knowing so many people supported their cause gave them the strength to continue. In the later phases of the blockade, Grassy Narrows activists assumed a central position in this network's processual development as members of other Native communities inspired by the blockaders' stand began to seek out their expertise.

Residents of Grassy Narrows also protested on February 12th. A handful of blockaders set up a temporary roving blockade at the junction of Segise and Oak Lake roads—close to a large and active cut block—but found that logging at the site had already ceased (Godin 2003e). Other community members took their protest to Kenora. Over a dozen people from Grassy spent the afternoon in front of the OMNR's offices, holding up signs and passing out information to pedestrians. In the evening, a spaghetti dinner was served in Grassy's Sakatcheway Anishinabe School gymnasium. Along with approximately 150 Grassy Narrows residents, First Nations leaders from all over northwestern Ontario attended the fundraiser. Following the dinner, Billy Joe Green, a regionally renowned blues musician originally from Shoal Lake First Nation (just west of Kenora) performed a benefit concert.

The following week, Grassy Narrows activists returned to Kenora. On the afternoon of Wednesday, February 19th around twenty of the First Nation's youth, Environmental Group members, and teachers protested in front of the Abitibi mill. The protestors held up anti-clearcutting signs, waved to passing motorists, and cheered as some drivers honked their horns in support (Power 2003a). Film taken at the event (Clement 2003) featured Kitty on the megaphone, leading the group in a song-and-response chant:

Abitibi out of the Whiskey Jack Forest.
Stop the raping of the Whiskey Jack Forest.

Another young mother from Grassy Narrows accompanied on a traditional style hand drum. At one point, two high school students gathered their courage and knocked on the mill office's front door. No one answered.

As the afternoon wore on, the group marched through Kenora's streets, headed to the downtown office of Bob Nault, local member of Parliament (MP) for the Kenora and Rainy River district as well as minister of Indian and Northern Affairs. As several students and GNEG members filed into the office, Nault's receptionist and staff stiffened with palpable tension (Clement 2003). Informed that Nault was out of town, the protestors made their case anyway. GNEG members pointed out that Abitibi's clearcutting was infringing on their treaty rights. Not only were the people of Grassy Narrows Nault's constituents, they declared, but he was also supposed to represent their interests in his role as minister of DIAND. The protestors felt Nault should, at the very least, listen to their concerns. Outside, Kitty's chant continued:

Bob Nault is not our leader. Our true leaders are our children.

Nault's office never responded to the visit.

As it gained prominence, the blockade attracted the attention of national Aboriginal leaders. On February 27th, Assembly of First Nations (AFN) national chief Matthew Coon-Come spent the afternoon touring the Grassy Narrows community and the Slant Lake blockade site (Godin 2003g; Power 2003b). In addition to speaking with community elders and blockaders, Coon-Come met with Grassy Narrows Chief Simon Fobister and Leon Jourdain of Treaty Three. Concurrent with Coon-Come's visit, Grassy Narrows' Chief and Council signed an official declaration of support for the blockaders (Godin 2003f).

During his brief visit, Coon-Come encouraged the blockader's efforts, specifically praising Grassy's youth for their leadership role. Coon-Come pledged to help take their story to the public. As he commented to reporters, "We have a treaty here that recognizes aboriginal title and the government is ignoring those treaty rights" (Power 2003b) and "it's time to send a signal to the government" (Godin 2003g). For the protestors at Grassy Narrows, Coon-Come's visit signaled the far-reaching significance of their actions. Knowing that their blockade was now viewed as an important precedent with broad implications for First Nations rights bolstered the blockaders' determination to persevere.

Inspired by these encouraging developments, Grassy Narrows activists continued working to communicate their position and expand their base of external support. In mid-March, close to forty Grassy Narrows residents traveled by bus from northwestern Ontario to Toronto, hoping to raise public awareness and personally deliver their message to top OMNR officials. The group included Deputy Chief Steve Fobister, former chief and current Director of Education Bill Fobister, J. B., Kitty, and over a dozen high school students. On March 16th, the delegation protested in front of the OMNR's main office in Toronto. Eager to get the ear of Minister Jerry Ouellete, they were frustrated to find him unwilling to talk. Earthroots, a Toronto-based environmental group, had helped organize the protest event and around three hundred attendees—many of them urban environmentalists concerned about the clearcutting devastating parts of their own province—listened as the visitors from Grassy Narrows addressed the crowd (Godin 2003h).

Video of the protest (Clement 2003) recorded the speakers' words. Steve notified the group:

> We've come here to tell the citizens and the people of Toronto that the propaganda of this government [is] making the people believe in Ontario that the forests and the land in Ontario is fine and well—but it's *not*.

Kitty also addressed the gathering, at one point fighting tears:

> I'm so frustrated as a youth of Grassy Narrows. I'm sick and tired of everything these people do to our community. Our people are sick. And they can't even come out here and face us, but we're still gonna be there as long as the rivers flow and the sweet grass grows and the sun shines. Miigwetch.

Her declaration was met with loud cheers.

Meanwhile, other First Nations members held signs in the background, proclaiming: "Clearcuts Break the Cycle!" and "Stop Clearcutting Grassy Narrows!" Several non-Native supporters carried similar signs. At the Toronto event, it became apparent that the blockaders' network of support stretched well beyond its base in northwestern Ontario and southern Manitoba. Bill Fobister commented on how glad he was to see such an outpouring of support in Toronto, since, as he saw it, their fight was not only for Grassy Narrows First Nation, but for all Canadians. Others central to GNEG and the blockade shared his view.[6] As the Toronto event confirmed, activists at Grassy Narrows had embraced constructing a "middle ground" (White 1991; Conklin and Graham 1995) upon which they could communicate and join together with supportive non-Natives as critical to the blockade's long-term success.

The Whiskey Jack Forest Management Plan: Take Two

In the spring of 2003, Abitibi and the OMNR once again began the public consultation process, this time with respect to Abitibi's 2004–2024 Whiskey Jack Forest Management Plan, scheduled to go into effect in April of 2004. As with the 1999–2019 planning process, the first five years of the plan received the most attention. Between 2004 and 2009, Abitibi proposed a total harvest of 29,778 hectares (5,956 hectares per year), to produce 3,839,825 cubic meters of wood fiber (Abitibi–Consolidated 2004b). This harvest figure was similar to that of the previous five-year term.

On March 31st, around thirty protestors from Grassy Narrows were joined by a handful of non-Native supporters at an open house at Kenora's Lakeside Inn. Sponsored jointly by Abitibi and the OMNR, the event was intended to provide the general public with information about the new FMP and to give interested parties an opportunity to comment before the planning process moved into its final stages. At the open house, the protestors voiced their dissatisfaction with ongoing clearcutting in Grassy Narrows' Traditional Land Use Area. Chanting "Who's land—our land, who's rights—our rights, who's future—our future" (Godin 2003k), several activists from Grassy carried handmade anti-clearcutting signs. As in previous years, many of their complaints targeted clearcutting's impacts on the environment and on Anishinaabe ways of life. One protestor's sign read "Keep Our Forest Green. Stop Clearcutting." Likewise, J. B. and Andy "Shoon" Keewatin both spoke to media personnel at the event about the detrimental effects of logging on Grassy Narrows residents' trapping and hunting activities (Clayton 2003b).

More than ever before, Grassy Narrows activists now also aimed their critique at the consultation process itself. Among the signs raised by First Nation members, one read: "This Consultation??? CONTEMPT of Supreme Court Decisions" (Godin 2003k).[7] Another placard's rough lettering read, "The Con in Consultation" (Clayton 2003b). While the OMNR had offered to hold an informational session on Abitibi's FMP at Grassy Narrows, the First Nation rejected the offer, citing the consultation process's "lack of real meaning." Feeling they had made an honest effort to consult with the First Nation community, government and industry representatives perceived their rejected offer as satisfying consultation requirements. As

OMNR spokesperson Shawn Stevenson said, "The community has chosen not to interact with us" (Clayton 2003a).

Activists at Grassy Narrows felt differently. Their refusal to participate in the consultation process stemmed from their belief that the process itself was deeply flawed. They were discouraged (though not surprised) when government and industry officials interpreted their lack of participation as a green light to continue with business as usual. In his role as GNEG's spokesperson, J. B. Fobister responded to the OMNR offer by publicly declaring that until there was serious discussion—something he and other community activists perceived to be sorely lacking—they did not want to be involved (Godin 2003i). He also pointed out that First Nation residents had gone through the consultation process before and it hadn't worked; the cutting continued regardless of what they said (Godin 2003k). In the early stages of the Forest Management Planning process, J. B. explained in 2005, people from Grassy had spent hours and hours attempting to communicate their concerns to Abitibi and the OMNR, yet only one cursory paragraph in the entire FMP mentioned the presence of Native people who hunted and trapped on the land.

Others at Grassy shared J. B.'s lack of faith in the consultation process. Judy DaSilva put it bluntly when she said, "they call it consultation but it's just a word; it doesn't really mean anything" (Clement 2003). Rather than the empowering processes consultation would seem to imply, many First Nations people feel that consultation too often merely replicates the power imbalance intrinsic to modern Canadian society. Problematically, opportunities for Aboriginal participation and consultation are "being offered on the terms set by government authorities and the corporate sector" (Feit and Beaulieu 2001: 119; see also Nadasdy 2003). Even further, it appears that Grassy Narrows activists' belief that consultation lacks true meaning—or, at least, means something very different to government and industry than it does to them—often extends to a wider suspicion of the consultation process and the government that oversees it.

In several instances, I noticed Anishinaabe individuals' reluctance to participate in privately sponsored workshops based on fears that their presence at such a meeting could somehow be construed as "consultation," thus satisfying legal requirements and constituting permission to destroy their land. In December of 2005, as we waited for an informational session sponsored by the Canadian Parks and

Wilderness Society (a nonprofit conservation group) to begin, the anti-clearcutting activist and Sakatcheway Anishinabe School teacher seated to my right leaned over to ask me if we were being "consulted." He declined to sign the attendance sheet at the door and, in the question-and-answer session following the presentation, asked the presenters if this was a form of consultation. He received a negative answer, yet many First Nations citizens remain so suspicious of the consultation process that they fear their mere presence at an event like this one could be counted as "consultation." Anishinaabe people view their reluctance to participate in such workshops not as paranoia, but as a necessary degree of caution.

In the same week as the open house, Abitibi's work schedule for 2003 was made public. In an apparent attempt to move toward conflict-resolution, the annual harvest plan included a 299 hectare area to be cut by a "yet to be determined" licensee from Grassy Narrows First Nation and a 258 hectare block to be cut by a contractor from Wabauskang First Nation (Godin 2003j). While some at Grassy Narrows—including several of the band's elected councilors—welcomed Abitibi's offers of employment and economic development, members of GNEG viewed hiring people from the First Nation as a deliberate divide and conquer strategy. In the years that followed, Abitibi's efforts to hire Grassy Narrows band members seemed to increase. Even as Abitibi promoted its offers as beneficial economic development and collaboration, Grassy's activists spoke angrily of the corporation's practice of targeting young people for impermanent and low-paying positions.

While I was unable to locate—nor did I ever hear about—any Grassy Narrows citizens logging for Abitibi in the years that followed, a dozen or so people from the First Nation have recently been employed by Abitibi in other capacities: removing nuisance beavers, working in tree-planting operations, or maintaining the region's vast network of logging roads. At the 2004 Environmental Youth Gathering, one young man from Grassy told me he'd spent a few summers as a tree planter, placing black spruce seedlings in neat rows in several of the clearcuts north of Grassy. His take on working for the logging industry was matter-of-fact and he perceived no apparent disconnect between his participation in blockade events and his former employment. If you're good at planting trees, he shrugged, you can make pretty decent money this way. In contrast, one woman told me about her husband's road maintenance contract with Abitibi. Although she believed he supported the blockade in principle, he had decided against participating because of his job. Like a majority of the First Nation residents, he chose to remain a passive supporter.

The Roving Blockades of June 2003

By the spring of 2003, logging trucks were routinely detouring east of the blockade at Slant Lake and further direct confrontations with logging contractors appeared unlikely. The Mohawk and Ojibwe Warrior Society members took their leave. No longer needed, the rented trailers and generator were removed from the Slant Lake site. Yet with the arrival of good weather, more visitors were arriving than ever before. Encouraged by the outpouring of support and by the return of warm weather and plentiful sunlight, Grassy Narrows Environmental Group members and their families continued to spend each day at Slant Lake, alternately staying the night or returning to their homes on the reserve. Visitors and Grassy residents alike set up camp in tents and cabins, and a compact trailer that had served as a meat locker all winter now became a temporary residence. As the days lengthened into summer, a wave of renewed activity swept over the Grassy Narrows blockade.

In the first days of June, Grassy Narrows First Nation members traveling the gravel roads east of their community discovered that a contractor was logging a large area just north of the junction of Segise and Stewart Lake roads. Operations appeared to be in full swing and a complete array of logging equipment was present at the site. Many trees had already been cut. Although no roving blockades had taken place since February, Grassy Narrows activists felt the time was right to step up their anti-clearcutting campaign. The contractor and his crew were given two days to pull out.

On the afternoon of June 4th, packed vehicles began making the bumpy forty-five-minute trip from the reserve. By evening about thirty blockaders—several high school students, two teachers, most of GNEG's core members, and close to a dozen other Grassy Narrows residents—had arrived at the junction. The two CPT members currently stationed at Grassy Narrows also came to witness and document the event. As night fell, the group gradually diminished in size.

Figure 5.1. Bonfire at the Stewart Lake Road roving blockade, June 2003.

By midnight, all was calm at the roving blockade, but those remaining could hear the distant rumble of heavy machinery as around-the-clock logging operations continued.

The roving blockade's location had been chosen strategically. Aware that an impassible washout to the north would prevent travel in that direction, the blockaders set up at the junction of Segise and Stewart Lake roads—the loggers' only way in and out of their work-site. A large bonfire in the road burned throughout the blockade. Simultaneously adding to the symbolic barrier and creating makeshift benches, the protestors also moved several fallen logs into the road. Around two o'clock in the morning, another carload of blockaders arrived. The fresh presence of Kitty and her sister, their mother, and two members of the Ojibwe Warrior Society breathed new energy into those tiring from the long hours of waiting. The arrival of logging trucks was anticipated first thing in the morning. Almost everyone stayed up all night sipping Red Rose tea, talking, and singing songs around the fire. Several "blockade songs" had become popular among Grassy's protestors and the idea of compiling them on a CD was often contemplated. A five-bar blues number entitled "Blockade Blues," written by one of the high school teachers at Sakatcheway Anishinabe School, never failed to produce smiles with its catchy refrain: "There's a blockade goin' on, down on Highway 671."

A penetrating folk song by a Manitoba songwriter called "Where Are You Warriors?" was also a perennial favorite. Adding to the song's significance was the fact that the term "warrior" had taken on multiple meanings in the context of the Grassy Narrows blockade. Most formally, it referred to the members of the Mohawk and Ojibwe Warrior Societies who had been present at the blockade earlier in the year. Although both these groups had long since departed, several of the *ogitchidaa*—as the Ojibwe Warriors are also known—returned immediately when they learned of Grassy's roving blockades.[8] As the Grassy Narrows blockade got underway, the term *ogitchidaa*—literally translated to mean one who is "big hearted" or "courageous"—also took on a broader connotation. Nesper (2002: 125) describes how, in the context of spearfishing in northern Wisconsin, "*Ogitchidaa* became equated with individual Indian people who fought for the preservation of Ojibwe distinctiveness and rights to self-determination." Similarly, many at Grassy Narrows considered the men, women, and young people active in the blockade movement as *ogitchidaa* in their own right. In both senses, the warriors were at the roving blockade, waiting for the logging trucks to arrive.

Finally, around nine o'clock in the morning, a pickup truck carrying three loggers appeared from the direction of the active cut block. As soon as the men noticed the blockade, the truck Y-turned and headed back toward the worksite. Several minutes later, two additional pickups approached the junction. Likely notified of the blockaders' presence, the drivers seemed calm as they drew near. Kitty rose to meet the drivers. Through the open passenger-side window, the driver of the first truck asked if he could pass. "Yes, but you know you can't come back," Kitty replied. In apparent grudging agreement to these terms, the truck sped off in the direction of Kenora, followed silently by the second pickup. The expected logging trucks never arrived; the blockaders figured they'd been contacted by radio and turned back before reaching the site. Although the loggers' equipment was still on site, there was no one left to operate it; the night shift had departed and the blockaders had prevented the day shift's arrival. For the first time, the blockaders had put a logging operation temporarily out of business.

Later that day, a busload of students arrived at the roving block-ade. Close to twenty young people in grades seven and higher were accompanied by four of their teachers. As the sky threatened rain and then made good on its promise with a stormy downpour, many of the students walked two miles to reach the now deserted logging site. The self-guided tour offered them a chance to see what the cut looked like and, for some, it also provided an opportunity to participate in what one person termed "some civil disobedience." When they came to a pile of cut logs ready for transport to the mill, some of the students unstacked the neat piles, rolling and tossing the logs into the road like giant pick-up sticks. According to a later media report, a water truck at the logging site was also vandalized during the roving blockade (Barrera 2003d).

The roving blockade had now been in place for twenty-four hours. As time passed, disagreement arose over the best course of action. J. B. and Steve Fobister, each with fifty years of life experi-ence, wanted everyone still at the site to pack up and head home. This type of action, they stressed, was meant to make a statement, not become a permanent presence. Additionally, they feared a court injunction and potential arrests if the protestors lingered. Others—mostly younger blockaders and Warrior Society members—refused to back down.[9] They were adamant about continuing their stand at Stewart Lake Road. By the following morning, it appeared that J. B. and Steve had won the argument. The roving blockade was over.

Three more roving blockades took place the following week. On June 10th, last-minute preparations were underway for a Treaty Three National Assembly to be held at Grassy Narrows over the next two days. At the Slant Lake blockade, this meant the hasty construction of plywood sheds to house some of the visiting chiefs. Amid the com-motion, the young men working on the construction project and others at Slant Lake paused to share a small feast for dinner. Later in the evening, a handful of First Nation residents decided to set up a roving blockade at the junction of Segise and Deer Lake roads, twenty minutes east of the previous week's events and in the path of trucks hauling logs from cut blocks further north.

Four core GNEG members, several of their children and grand-children, and a handful of elders built a fire in the wide, sandy inter-section. A public statement issued by the band drew attention to the fact that this blockade had been the initiative of elders, women, and youth. Echoing earlier statements to the press, the release also described the purpose of the latest blockade:

> This is an assertion of our treaty rights. Our right to hunt, fish, and trap on our traditional land use area. The logging is infringing on these treaty rights and threatening the survival of future generations (Quoted in *Kenora Daily Miner and News* 2003).

In the early morning hours, the small group peacefully turned back one logging truck before heading home.

The following day, the National Assembly filled the Sakatcheway Anishinabe School gymnasium. Held at Grassy Narrows to mark Treaty Three's support of the blockade, several First Nation citizens spoke of the assembly as a historic event. Speakers were scheduled throughout the day and attendees came and went casually from bleacher seating. Most of the discussion focused on issues of Anishinaabe governance and sovereignty. Both during his term as Treaty Three grand chief and after, Leon Jourdain supported the blockaders' assertion of Anishinaabe rights within the Grassy Narrows Traditional Land Use Area as a positive precedent for the larger Anishinaabe Nation. "What you see here," Jourdain stressed on the afternoon of June 11th, "is a *nation* being built." Fluently code-switching between Anishinaabemowin and English, other presenters at the assembly focused on more specific interests, including the roles of women and elders in First Nations governance.

Early in the morning on June 12th, several loaded logging trucks were spotted heading south on Jones Road. In response, about thirty people blockaded at the junction of Segise and Stewart Lake roads once again. In addition to GNEG members and young people from Grassy Narrows, many of those in attendance this time around were visitors from other northwestern Ontario First Nations taking a break from the second afternoon of the National Assembly to partake in the action. Although the logging contractor and several of his crew members were present at the worksite, they were in the process of pulling out. Apparently, the logging trucks sighted that morning had been the contractor's attempt to get his harvest to the mill and cut his financial losses. The OPP quickly arrived on the scene. Wearing his trademark "Native Pride" cap, J. B. conversed pleasantly with the officers.

Together, they negotiated an agreement for the contractor to access his former worksite in order to remove valuable equipment. The following day, protestors staged another roving blockade at the same site in the early morning hours—prime logging truck time—but no trucks appeared.

June of 2003 was an exciting chapter in the history of the Grassy Narrows blockade. The First Nation's activists demonstrated that they remained as determined as ever to fight for their cause and had no plans to surrender in the immediate future. As J. B. told me that June, the blockade would continue until the government agreed to talk about the decades of environmental abuses Grassy Narrows had faced in the context of treaty rights. Roberta Keesick made a similar statement: "We are not going to stop until [the blockades] produce the results we want which is no more clearcutting, no more infringing on aboriginal treaty rights" (Barrera 2003f).

Blockade, Response

The escalation of Grassy's campaign resulted in a multidirectional expansion of the web of tensions surrounding the blockade. Conflict between the First Nation community and loggers—especially those driven from the area just north of the Stewart Lake Road roving blockades—intensified. One blockader reported that several of the out of work loggers showed up at the band office along with their wives in mid-June. Bills in hand, they had asked, "who will pay these now?"

A TVO documentary on the Grassy Narrows blockade aired on the evening of June 4th also fanned the flames of the dispute.[10] One clip from the program gained infamy among activists at Grassy. It showed the very contractor they were blockading at the time laughing brazenly on camera when asked if he thought he could learn anything from the Natives. Many First Nation members were deeply insulted by his response and talked about it for weeks afterward. The contractor's comments also pointed to deep disagreements about the meaning and proper use of the boreal forest environment. In the program, he pragmatically stated, "The boreal forest means my living. It has to be managed like a crop." But what loggers and industrial foresters understand as a "renewal area" the Grassy Narrows blockaders disdainfully regard as a "tree farm." Looking at the tidy, single-species rows of trees

Figure 5.2. "A tree farm is not a forest"

that the logging companies sometimes plant in clearcuts, they frequently point out that a tree farm is not the same thing as a forest. The forest, Judy DaSilva once remarked, does a pretty good job of managing itself.

Early in the morning at the June 5th roving blockade, Kitty had hit on the heart of the matter. Lounging on a tan blanket spread over the road's gravel surface, she meditated on the contractor's comments and on why she had become so dedicated to her community's anti-clearcutting movement. "They say that they need to cut these trees to have a future," Kitty said, "but we need it for the future too." Both Grassy Narrows activists and loggers, as proclaimed by both versions of the OMNR sign discussed in the previous chapter, see the forest as vital to their futures. On the one hand, people at Grassy Narrows depend on a healthy—meaning *not* clearcut—GNTLUA if they are to survive as a culturally and politically distinct community. According to the blockaders, clearcutting precludes their continued use of the land. Furthermore, it threatens their ability to live in a way that is consistent with their self-defined vision of an Anishinaabe cultural identity. Conversely, loggers feel they need access to the Whiskey

Jack Forest for their families' financial survival. In many cases, they see clearcutting as their only lucrative option. From the loggers' perspective, Grassy's blockade was keeping them from their jobs. In the summer of 2003, these uses of the forest appeared mutually exclusive to both parties.

"Geographical landscapes," according to Keith Basso (1996:75), "are never culturally vacant." Further, different people from different cultural worlds imbue places with meaning in dramatically different ways, a concept Margaret Rodman (2003) terms "multilocality." In the contested landscape of northwestern Ontario's boreal forest, both First Nation residents and non-Native loggers struggle to position their meanings and uses of the forest as paramount. In their attempts to establish control over the GNTLUA/Whiskey Jack environment, both groups work to communicate the superior legitimacy of their own claims to the forest. In addition to frequent evocation of their treaty-guaranteed rights, First Nations activists draw upon their long history in the region and upon the close connections between their way of life and the boreal forest environment to validate their claims. Yet, at least some loggers also feel a sense of connection to the land and attempt to establish their authentic attachment to place—what Satterfield (2002: chapter 6) calls their "rootedness"—in a comparable manner. The contractor featured in the TVO program, for one, feels very deeply that this forest is his home. Both in the documentary and in an earlier conversation I witnessed, he was proud to point out that he was *born* at Slant Lake, back in the days when it was a logging camp. With his family alongside, his father had been stationed at the very site where the blockade now stood.

The Grassy Narrows blockaders' clash with the Abitibi-Consolidated mill in Kenora and the Ontario Ministry of Natural Resources also grew more heated as a result of the roving blockades. Before June's flurry of activity, the blockaders had forced truck drivers to take longer routes to the mill, but had not seriously impacted the flow of logs. Now, for the first time, the blockaders had successfully halted a logging operation. The roving blockade at Segise and Stewart Lake roads had obstructed the only access to twelve thousand cubic meters of timber, worth approximately $500,000 (Barrera 2003d) and the contractor had abandoned the worksite. Charlotte Caron, a forester and spokesperson for Abitibi, told the media, "The wood we'd be expecting from that operation is not coming" (Barrera 2003c).

Representatives from the corporation and the OMNR vented their frustration as they searched unsuccessfully for a solution to the dispute. Referring to his office's offer to mediate the previous January, an OMNR spokesperson said they had been waiting for months for the First Nation to sit down and talk, but had received no response (Barrera 2003e). Unclear as to what the protesters wanted, provincial officials felt powerless to resolve the conflict (Barrera 2003f). And, like the loggers, Abitibi employees in Kenora now worried that their livelihoods might be in jeopardy. A *Kenora Daily Miner and News* article pointed out that "the blockades are starting to worry some who fear it may cause area mills to close due to wood supply issues" (Barrera 2003f). In a town historically dependent upon the forest industry, the blockade now appeared to be a genuine threat.

Reacting to the local media's coverage of recent events, some people at Grassy Narrows grew increasingly concerned about the public's perception of the blockade. GNEG members suggested that the *Kenora Miner and News*—with headlines like "Grassy Narrows Strikes Again" (*News* 2003) and "Grassy Band Throws Up Another Blockade" (Barrera 2003b)—was making them look like impulsive troublemakers, when what they were really doing was defending what was rightfully theirs.

Despite the rising tensions at the regional level, however, support for the Grassy Narrows blockade continued to soar as environmentalists and Native rights activists from across Canada and the United States learned of events in northwestern Ontario by word of mouth and through electronic news networks. On May 6th, Rodolfo Stavenhagen (the United Nations' Special Rapporteur on Indigenous Human Rights) had stopped at Grassy Narrows as a part of his tour of Canadian First Nations (Barrera 2003a). Stavenhagen's visit was a response to Amnesty International's attempt to draw international attention to the marginalization of Canada's Aboriginal population. Although brief, the UN representative's visit demonstrated the blockade's expansive reach, augmented Grassy Narrows activists' sense of community with indigenous peoples worldwide, and substantiated the importance of their work.

The week of June 23rd, an Environmental Youth Gathering and Powwow took place at the Slant Lake blockade. Organized by Grassy's youth, the gathering's main events included daily workshops, a tour of some of the GNTLUA's clearcuts, and a keynote address from environmental celebrity tree-sitter Julia Butterfly Hill.[11] The people I talked to following the 2003 Environmental Youth Gathering considered it a success. When dozens of indigenous activists and non-Native environmentalists from across North America turned out take part in the event, Grassy Narrows' abstract network of supporters became a tangible reality for the first time.

The blockade initiated at Slant Lake in December of 2002 must be understood as the dramatic culmination of a long-term process of activism at Grassy Narrows. Starting small and expanding in response to the immediate threat of industrial clearcutting, the Grassy Narrows Environmental Group eventually launched its public campaign. Environmental, cultural, and political concerns were inseparable in the minds of the First Nation's activists from their earliest days of protest. As they negotiated their place in a complex global system, Grassy Narrows activists worked to communicate a set of densely interwoven objectives that included stopping the clearcutting destroying their forests, ensuring the continuity of land-based subsistence so important to Anishinaabe culture, and asserting their Aboriginal and treaty-guaranteed rights to their land and its resources.

By the time the Slant Lake blockade got underway, activists at Grassy Narrows had already learned to value the media as a tool and to condense their heartfelt ideas into rhetorically appealing verbal packages intended to draw outside supporters to their cause. As time went on, they gained knowledge through experience and attracted allies to a diverse and expanding network of support. They increasingly came to comprehend individual actions as part of a much larger struggle. In the months ahead, as members of GNEG and Grassy Narrows' elected Chief and Council attempted to make sense of the complexity within their community, they also faced the challenge of presenting a cohesive message to government, industry, and the public.

Six

Blockade Life

The remainder of the summer passed relatively uneventfully. The contractor working closest to the Grassy Narrows community had pulled out. The fact that they had been able to stop the clearcutting in one key part of the GNTLUA filled many First Nations activists with a new sense of accomplishment. Even after the excitement of June's roving blockades subsided, the constant presence at Slant Lake continued throughout the summer. While certainly less dramatic, what took place on these countless calm days reveals a lot about the complex meanings and motives of the Grassy Narrows blockade. Although no logging trucks had attempted to slip past the Slant Lake site since late December, Grassy Narrows activists and their families continued to spend considerable amounts of time at the site. Given that their presence was no longer necessary from a strategic standpoint, why did so many people remain dedicated not only to their community's anti-clearcutting campaign, but also to Slant Lake as a physical place? What else was going on at Slant Lake that continued to attract so many? Drawn from my time at Slant Lake in the late spring and early summer of 2003, the following composite narrative begins to answer these questions by describing a typical day at the blockade.

Slant Lake Days

The chorus of wood frogs fades as the first hint of dawn touches the eastern sky. Down on Slant Lake, loon song pierces the crepuscular haze. Coals from last night's waning campfire glow silently as a lone figure moves slowly through the dim of early morning, placing another thick log on the sacred fire before returning to the plywood shack and the serenity of slumber. Northern latitudes make for long days this time of year; it is not yet four o'clock. As the sun rises to pierce the thick pine trees to the east, a cacophony of birdsong fills the air. When the sun ascends to shine brightly above the trees, daylight reveals a site still sleeping. Smoke from the scared fire rises steadily from the tipi.

As people begin to stir, Shoon pulls up in his bright blue pickup truck. Four teenage boys riding in the back jump out and head for a half-built log cabin. This is their project. Construction began several months earlier, with snow still on the ground. When school was in session and classes were being held daily at Slant Lake, the cabin had been part of the curriculum. Several students stayed on when summer vacation arrived, welcoming the chance to learn what many at Grassy regard as an important traditional skill. Built in the style of the homes occupied on the Old Reserve in the community's pre-relocation days, the cabin at Slant Lake has sentimental value; middle-aged people like Shoon and elders at Grassy Narrows grew up in cabins that looked a lot like this one. And, while not representative of precontact Anishinaabe material culture, the cabin evokes the highly valued traditionality of days past, when contemporary First Nation residents' grandparents were still able to live out on the land in relative cultural and political autonomy. At the Slant Lake blockade, reimagined traditional pasts are reenacted in the context of the present.

With the help of his young assistants or alone, Shoon comes to Slant Lake almost every day to work on the cabin. Today, he and the boys will cut several pine trees from the nearby bush and drag them back to the construction site. There, they will strip the logs' bark (although it's getting a bit late in the season for this; in spring, Shoon says, they peel "like ripe bananas") and lift them into their designated places. The cabin is progressing well. Shoon plans to use his chainsaw to cut an opening for the door (facing the road in an easterly direction) and a window (facing west toward the lake) in the next day or two. In the coming weeks, the cabin's plywood floor and ceiling will be added. Eventually, the entire one-room structure will be chinked to insulate against the cold of winter.

As work on the cabin gets underway, the two current members of CPT emerge from their A-frame structure near the lake. CPT built the A-frame in early spring, as soon as the weather permitted. Simple and functional, it is painted light yellow and furnished with two plywood sleeping bunks. An orange tarp serves as the structure's peaked roof and the woodstove inside puts out a surprising amount of heat. About thirty feet away stands a small cabin built by Barbara—an anti-clearcutting activist and grandmother in her early fifties—and her husband. Their family uses the cabin two or three times each week when they decide to sleep at Slant Lake instead of at home on the reserve. The CPTers climb the hill from their A-frame up to the campfire to cook an impressive breakfast of eggs and toast. As others who spent the night at Slant Lake—a family from Grassy, a young couple from Winnipeg spending the season as blockaders, and a few interested non-Natives from further afield—gradually appear around the fire, the CPT members head to Kenora for a day of shopping and other errands.

Time passes slowly at Slant Lake. The leisurely pace allows ample opportunity to converse, read a book, play cards, or simply contemplate the surroundings. The day warms slowly. Dragonflies and yellow swallowtail butterflies begin, respectively, to dart and flutter overhead. Ravens and eagles soar higher above the blockade. Far from the hum of electricity or steady traffic, vehicles heading toward Slant Lake are audible several minutes before their arrival. Once or twice an hour, a tourist pulling a boat on a trailer bumps loudly down the gravel road. Some of the tourists stop to read the mustard-colored sign and discover that they are within Grassy Narrows First Nation's Traditional Land Use Area before continuing north to their fishing destinations.

As the sun rises in the eastern sky, Judy and her oldest daughter arrive in their gray minivan to drop off several jugs of water. Every day or two, water from the reserve is hauled to the blockade in these large blue containers. Although not hydrologically connected to the mercury-laden waters of the English-Wabigoon River system, few choose to boil and drink the water from muck-bottomed Slant Lake. Judy nonchalantly invites some of the visitors to take a ride with her to see both the worst of the GNTLUA's clearcuts and some of the last remaining stands of old growth in the region. It is important, Judy later tells me, for visitors to see firsthand the devastation caused by clearcutting as well as the forest that people at Grassy are trying so hard to protect. Having arrived only days before, I eagerly accept her offer.

Before our tour departs, Judy—dressed in her standard blue ribbon-trimmed skirt, t-shirt, and brown sandals—checks on the sacred fire. She adds a log and lingers for a few moments.[1] As a center of neotraditional Anishinaabe spirituality, the fire is held in reverence—although usually of a lighthearted variety. Adults remind children and visitors not to throw trash into this fire and natural kindling materials are preferred over paper and gas when the fire needs a boost. When Judy emerges from the tipi that encloses the fire and climbs behind the wheel of her van, another young woman—an environmentalist from Toronto—and I join her and her ten-year-old daughter for the ride.

Steering carefully around ruts and partial washouts, we rattle north along the empty logging road, still called Jones Road this far north. For close to forty-five minutes we chat and take in the scenery as Judy drives. We progress slowly past lakes, bogs, and the Wabigoon River, which, Judy informs us, gets its unhealthy brown color from pollution originating at Dryden's paper mill.[2] Then, abruptly, the forest ends. All four of us get out to take a closer look at the immense clearcut spread over the hills to our right. Further on, we stop to explore an even larger cut off of Portal Lake Road. Both of these areas were cut in the past five years and have seen little in the way of regrowth.

The clearcuts look as brown as the forest we just emerged from did green. Slash and debris piles covering the ground make walking a challenge. What is most stunning is the clearcuts' size. Abitibi's Whiskey Jack Forest Management Plan lists 908 hectares as the average size of clearcuts in the region (Abitibi-Consolidated 2004b). But on the ground, estimating their extent is difficult. Judy's daughter runs up the road to provide scale for a photograph. A lone "habitat" tree—a large poplar snag left by contractors in accordance with provincial regulations—stands in the distance. This ghost of the former forest provides both a sense of scale and a sense of loss. For years, GNEG members have publicly expressed the distress they feel upon entering the clearcuts that dot the GNTLUA. Now, standing in one of the largest of the cuts, Judy's mood seems gloomy yet matter-of-fact. She says very little. The following day, with a similar detached composure, Shoon tells me that two-thirds of his trapline—inherited from his father and the site of a significant portion of his childhood—has been similarly clearcut.

To say that activists at Grassy Narrows view the clearcuts within their TLUA negatively would be an understatement. Yet I was surprised to find that they seldom described the clearcuts in conversation with one another or with outside supporters. Like other northern Natives, Anishinaabe people tend to value and emphasize experiential modes of knowledge acquisition above secondhand descriptive instruction (see Goulet 1998). Rather than merely tell visitors about the clearcuts, activists at Grassy choose to take them there. Clearcut tours were a regular occurrence in 2003 and 2004 and filled prominent slots on the agendas of the Environmental Youth Gatherings held at Slant Lake in those years. Highlighting the most tangible and translatable dimension of the blockaders' struggle, these clearcut tours helped activists at Grassy Narrows inspire visiting environmentalists' continued support.

On the way home, we stop briefly to investigate one of the old-growth areas. Covering a steep hill and dotted with mossy granite protrusions, the dense forest feels sheltered and moist after the dry heat of the clearcuts. In contrast to their perceptions of the cuts, many citizens of Grassy Narrows take pride in the natural beauty that remains of their homeland. On the way back to Slant Lake, we spot a beaver, a red fox, and a female black bear trailed by two cubs. Judy stops the van to leave a small tobacco offering for the bears. Several times, she notes slightly green, slow-burning poplar along the roadside that would be ideal for the sacred fire.

Back at Slant Lake, wispy white clouds materialize in the afternoon sky. People continue to arrive from the reserve. Some are seeking not only their own peace and quiet, but also a place for their children to play away from the dangerous traffic of the reserve. While adults converse around the campfire, some young children explore the nearby bush and the lakeshore just down the hill. Others endlessly circle the blockade on bikes. Several preteens run up to ask permission to take a walk on Barbara's trail. Stretching from the blockade site to the north shore of Slant Lake, the newly cleared hiking path is,

Barbara told me, a place where members of the community can come to walk, think, and heal.

Not only is Slant Lake perceived as a zone of relative safety for children, but many teens and adults also think of the blockade as a healing place. Residents of Grassy Narrows often talk about spending time in the bush as a path to spiritual and mental healing. Trappers like J. B. and Shoon are able to travel deep into the wilderness with some regularity. They treasure the sense of well-being they experience out on their traplines. For those who lack such opportunities, Slant Lake fills this important role. The blockade's unequivocal status as an alcohol- and drug-free zone also contributes to Grassy Narrows residents' perception of Slant Lake as a place for healing. Many northwestern Ontario Natives view the avoidance of alcohol and personal healing as closely related endeavors. During my time at Grassy Narrows, several First Nation members told their intensely personal stories of hardship and healing to help me understand how these links resonate within the Grassy Narrows community. While most adult GNEG members choose to avoid alcohol and drugs at this point in their lives, many members of the Grassy Narrows community continue to struggle with substance abuse. Especially on payday weekends—typically the last of the month—when many people receive government checks, the reserve can become a noisy and stressful place. Visiting the blockade is a way to remove oneself from temptation.

As the youngsters head down the hill to start their hike, a father prepares to take his four-year-old son fishing from the Slant Lake shore. I follow the activity down to the water. Immediately, I spot the dark form of moose on the distant shoreline and sprint up the hill to report the sighting. Done with his day's work on the cabin, Shoon suggests we row out to take a closer look. The two of us climb into the old rowboat that seems a permanent part of the blockade's scenery and push off through the murky water. As he rows, Shoon is eager to tell me about moose hunting. He hunts for moose every year and usually gets at least one. Some non-Natives think Indians kill moose all year long, he says, but this simply isn't true. People at Grassy normally hunt moose from August through December; in the spring and summer their meat and hides are of poor quality and, besides, no one wants to contend with the ticks that cover moose this time of year. When a group of mergansers fly over, Shoon tells me their Ojibwe name. *Kokoshiib*—fish duck. A great blue heron passes overhead, then three goldeneyes. We approach within fifty feet of the shore and the moose serenely retreats from the reeds that ring the lake, disappearing into the dense forest beyond.

When we return, father and son are proudly showing off a small northern pike. Caught on an inexpensive kiddy rod, the fish is the little boy's first. Encouraged by the preschooler's success, one of the older boys heads down to the lake to try his luck. While Slant Lake can't really be considered a favored fishing spot, kids from Grassy are always eager to cast from the smooth rocks just north of the blockade, and the lake has yielded a number of impressive walleye and northern pike. Especially for youth, elders, and adults with physical or vehicular limitations, Slant Lake offers an accessible yet symbolically equivalent microcosm of land-based subsistence in the wider Grassy Narrows Traditional Land Use Area. The scrubby forest surrounding the blockade site also gives adults a chance to learn skills they missed out on as children; after completing a government-sponsored trappers education class in the winter months that followed, Barbara set up a short trapline—and soon harvested her first pine marten—along her Slant Lake trail.

As afternoon becomes evening, some people head back to the reserve. The two CPTers return from town with enough groceries for several days. Tourists and their boats start heading south for the day, bumping back down the gravel road toward town. From the same direction, Barbara's thirty-year-old daughter and eleven-year-old grandson stop by to drop off a borrowed fishing rod. For the past few hours they'd been at the Wabigoon River, fishing from the same bridge Judy drove over during our earlier clearcut tour. I ask how the fishing had been. Although they caught four fish, Barbara's grandson tells me, they didn't keep any "cuz the water's polluted."

More than three decades after its discovery in the English-Wabigoon River system, mercury remains a frequent topic of conversation and a serious health concern at Grassy Narrows. Many people from Grassy know offhand the parts per billion (ppb) of mercury in their own bodies, and on several occasions I heard the matter discussed casually over dinner. Among those who have come to enjoy the campfire at Slant Lake is Deputy Chief Steve Fobister. Quite seriously affected by mercury himself, Steve jokes ironically about how to remove the toxin from fish: You just have to hang them upside down in the freezer, wait until the mercury falls, and then cut their heads off. Although the majority of First Nation residents continue to consume fish from local waters, a few people are concerned enough to limit their intake, especially if they already have a high ppb level. But no fish tonight. Barbara's daughter says she'll return shortly with burgers to cook over the fire.

Balancing an iron grate on the rocks that surround the campfire, Judy begins to boil water for tea. As one of the CPT members attends to a large skillet filled with cut potatoes and onions, one elderly woman reminisces. Watching the young woman cook like this over the fire reminds her of her younger days. When Barbara's daughter returns, she carries a stack of preformed "no-name" brand burgers, buns, and a couple bags of chips to share with the score of people still at Slant Lake. Others also contribute to the dinner: One woman mixes soft dough in her hands and carefully wraps it around hot dogs to roast "bannock dogs" over the fire.

A few more people depart after dinner, but at least a dozen remain at the blockade. All day, the sacred fire has been tended, with a fresh log added every hour or two. The vigil to maintain the fire has not ceased since the blockade began last December. Supporters and First Nation residents who spend the night at Slant Lake take turns rising in the darkness to ensure that the fire stays lit. Sometimes Grassy Narrows activists drive from the reserve to Slant Lake seemingly for the sole purpose of checking on the fire. Several of the GNEG men collaborate to ensure a constant supply of chopped wood. This evening, Judy calls her four children over as she unhurriedly rises and heads for the tipi. She wants to show them how to offer tobacco. In the center of the twelve-foot diameter structure, the sacred fire glows hot. Tobacco ties of yellow, red, blue, and white are mounted on three-foot wooden poles at each of the four cardinal directions. A small cloth bag, also containing tobacco, hangs from one of the tipi's support poles so that anyone who desires to make an offering is able.

The use of tobacco—*asema*, as it is known in the Ojibwe language—in ceremonial contexts is widespread among neotraditional Anishinaabeg in northwestern Ontario. Some sources suggest that tobacco was unknown to Natives this far north prior to European contact. Hallowell (1992: 25), for example, wrote in the early twentieth century that "although tobacco was of New World origin it was not known to the northern Indians [of the Berens River region, just northwest of Grassy Narrows] until introduced by the British and French after it had become widely known in Europe in the 17th century." Anishinaabeg today, however, tend to view their use of tobacco as a traditional custom, practiced by their ancestors but temporarily diminished due to residential schooling and its assimilatory results. Over the past twenty years, ceremonial uses of tobacco have gradually reemerged throughout the region.

Regardless of the practice's "authenticity" in the area, offering tobacco now serves as a marker of neotraditional Anishinaabe culture, identity, and pride. Nesper (2002: 142) explains the cosmological significance of tobacco in Western Great Lakes Anishinaabe culture:

> Historically and theologically, offerings of tobacco always alter the balance that the spirits redress with their beneficence. In the Ojibwe cosmos, humans are not sinners who sacrifice to produce harmony; instead, the gods are ambivalent but responsive to gifts made by needy, "pitiful" human beings. The practice turns on the relations of reciprocity assumed to exist between classes of living beings.

Tobacco offerings for spirits, other-than-human persons in the form of plants and animals (see Hallowell 1975), and human beings are all intended to demonstrate and maintain respectful, reciprocal social relationships.[3] During my time at Grassy, I saw tobacco offered in various ways, many of them corresponding to ethnographically documented conventions among Anishinaabe groups to the immediate south and described by Eddie Benton-Banai in *The Mishomis Book* (1988).

In the past, tobacco was offered before wild rice was harvested and before medicinal plants were gathered (Densmore 1979 [1929]; Danziger 1979). Some Grassy Narrows residents make similar offerings today. Several trappers told me of times they'd given tobacco upon finding a pine marten or beaver in their trap as a reciprocal show of gratitude and respect for the animal that had given its life. Historically, presentations of tobacco were also believed to calm storms and ensure safe passage over bodies of water (Densmore 1979 [1929]). One woman from Grassy described how she paused to offer tobacco during an unusually intense thunderstorm that struck northwestern Ontario that spring. She was on her way home from

Winnipeg when the sky turned a greenish color. She pulled her truck off the road to leave tobacco, she recalled, and made it home safely just before the worst of the storm hit. Perhaps for a similar reason, pinches of tobacco line the granite crevices beneath rock paintings accessible only from the waters of the Old Reserve.

Offering tobacco to individuals as a gift of appreciation or a sign of respect has also become relatively commonplace in northwestern Ontario. Commercially packaged pouches of loose tobacco are a favored gift for visiting speakers and small bags of tobacco were distributed at a powwow giveaway following the 2004 Environmental Youth Gathering at Slant Lake. Tobacco is also offered when requesting a favor of an admired elder. The placement of tobacco upon the scared fire mirrors this type of interpersonal exchange as well as the cosmological significance described previously; when people like Judy offer tobacco, they do so in hopes of humbly communicating their needs to a responsive spiritual realm.

After only ten minutes in the tipi, Judy's three older children emerge and resume their play. She lingers for several minutes before returning to her chair near the campfire with her two-year-old son at her side. Roberta holds a granddaughter of the same age on her lap. Relaxing around the fire sipping Red Rose tea with canned milk, people savor the unhurried pace and camaraderie. We barely notice as daylight fades slowly and the time ticks close to eleven o'clock. A red fox shows up looking for scraps. Looking scrawny in her summer fur, she visits the blockade almost every evening, walking the line between wariness and docile curiosity. In the cool of evening, the campfire flames brightly while overlapping conversations ebb and flow.

As on most nights at Slant Lake, close to half of the dialogue is in Anishinaabemowin. Like I do, children and youth from Grassy gather around the fire to listen intently as adults from the First Nation converse—even though we can only make out a few of the words. Sometimes we get the gist of things, but more often the sounds of the Ojibwe language are enough to hold our interest. Meanwhile, other non-Native visitors converse among themselves or with people from Grassy in English. Although it is still common to hear conversational Anishinaabemowin at Grassy Narrows, English is gradually replacing the Native language in daily use. This situation has raised the concern of educators, the elected band leadership, GNEG members, and scores of other First Nation residents.

The rapidity of language loss at Grassy Narrows becomes most strikingly apparent when comparing people of different age groups' language-use patterns and proficiencies. Elders most often speak fluent Anishinaabemowin and prefer to communicate in their first language. While everyone in the First Nation today speaks at least minimal English, elders report that they often have a difficult time understanding and making themselves understood when they must resort to it. Recognizing this fact, community meetings tend to be bilingual when elders are present, with formal introductions and prayers conducted in Anishinaabemowin and other proceedings translated into both languages.

Most people in their forties and fifties also learned Ojibwe as a first language, as children on the Old Reserve. They often speak Anishinaabemowin among themselves—both in person and on the telephone—with varying degrees of fluency and frequent code-switching to incorporate useful English terms. A majority of Grassy Narrows residents over the age of forty prefer to use Ojibwe whenever practicable. This holds true among those gathered at Slant Lake. As Roberta told me, she often feels caught between the two languages; although completely fluent in English, she can better express her thoughts and feelings in her first language. Reflecting on her attempts to communicate with people from Abitibi or the OMNR, Roberta added that this leads to frustration when she has no choice but to use English. Making a similar point, when Judy met with a small group of activists from another northwestern Ontario First Nation in 2005 she commented that, although their dialect had differed from her own, speaking with them in Anishinaabemowin had allowed them to understand one another in a way that would have been impossible in English.

Still, some people at the young end of this age spectrum consider themselves markedly less proficient in the Ojibwe language than older folks and at times feel better able to express themselves in English. Lillian—a forty-year-old woman fluent in conversational Anishinaabemowin and an Ojibwe-language instructor herself—told me there are things she has trouble saying in Anishinaabemowin. In most of these cases, she said, she ends up resorting to English to get her point across. Remembering how rich her grandmother's speech had been, Lillian evaluates her own abilities by way of contrast. She recalled how her grandmother would occasionally get upset with her when she was a girl, telling her she was starting to "be just like a white person" when she had to ask for clarification.

People in their twenties and thirties typically understand much of the Anishinaabemowin they hear, but tend to feel uncomfortable speaking more than a few phrases. For them, English is a dominant first language. Following this pattern of declining degree of fluency, the most severe language loss is seen among those younger than twenty. Most frequently, young people understand an assortment of Ojibwe words and phrases and make periodic use of them in an otherwise English linguistic context, but possess little conversational ability. While some Anishinaabemowin words—like *gookum* (grandmother), *miigwech* (thank you), *makwa* (bear), and various slang terms—seem unlikely to fall out of use in the near future, children and teenagers sometimes express embarrassment at not being able to speak their own language. One young woman of sixteen replied sheepishly when a man addressed her in Ojibwe, saying, "What did you say? I don't speak my language." Another girl, only six years old, clearly associated speaking Ojibwe with advancing age. She figured that, although she only knew a few Anishinaabemowin words now, she'd probably be able to speak Ojibwe when she got older.

Both a cause and an effect of the gradually declining use of Ojibwe at Grassy Narrows, when a conversational group contains people of mixed ages or outsiders who do not speak Anishinaabemowin, English is almost always employed. As in many Native North American communities, people at Grassy Narrows believe concerted efforts are now needed to ensure the survival of their language. Due to a combination of parents' residential school experiences and the prevalence of English media, exceedingly few young people in the community now learn Anishinaabemowin at home. For the past several years the Sakatcheway Anishinabe School has incorporated a language immersion program into the elementary grades in hopes of keeping the language alive.

Many people at Grassy Narrows see the Ojibwe language as an important part of their culture. It is a significant badge of Native— and specifically Anishinaabe—identity and a source and sign of cultural distinctiveness to be carried with pride. Mirroring the young woman's comment about not speaking *her* language, I've heard others demonstrate their Anishinaabemowin skill with almost personal pride, responding to my linguistic inquires with "it means _____ in *my* language." In this context, activists at Grassy Narrows frequently make use of Ojibwe place names in favor of English ones, increasingly choosing to refer to their community as Asubpeeschoseewagong rather than Grassy Narrows.

When the Slant Lake campfire conversation turns to Anishinaabe place-names, I ask what the site is called in Ojibwe. One man in his early fifties replies: Kakipitatapitmok, because it was "the end of the trail." Welcoming the dark of night, the loons and frogs resume their chorus. The resident boreal owl repeats its ghostly call. Life feels quietly enclosed by the flickering flames. As we contemplate the fire, Judy compares her life to that of her elder siblings. She shares her grief at how much her generation missed. Even some of her own brothers and sisters had the opportunity to live on the Old Reserve; they were able to experience life in the bush. She says that spending time at Slant Lake—perhaps a close approximation of what this life might have been like—makes up for some of what she missed.

When the conversation lulls, a few of us look up. The night sky is dark and unpolluted by city lights, although I'm surprised to find that even the small reserve community several miles away glows on the horizon. A man in his late forties mourns the loss of connection to the night sky he'd felt as a young boy living without electricity on the Old Reserve. Thousands of stars, crossed by the hazy stripe of the Milky Way galaxy, sparkle overhead. Perhaps the northern lights will make an appearance. As the night wears on, the crowd at Slant Lake diminishes one by one. Judy heads home to put her kids to bed. The CPT members disappear downhill to their A-frame. Part entertainment and part instruction, someone demonstrates how to make a moose call out of a coffee can and a flat shoelace. Laughter pierces the night at the flatulent sound. Well after midnight, Barbara and her husband make their way down the hill to their cabin. Others head off to sleep in cabins or tents.

In the flickering light of the two fires, a lone figure places one more log among the sacred flames.

Discussion: Lighting the Fire

Slant Lake's campfire may be the blockade's main social gathering place, but the sacred fire is its spiritual and symbolic heart. Located only forty feet apart, movement between the two fires is fluid and frequent. With intertwining significance, the fires symbolically encapsulate the wider cultural and political meanings of the Grassy Narrows blockade. Burning continuously from December of 2002 until the following fall and relit periodically thereafter, the sacred fire is a potent emblem of the blockaders' long-term political struggle to gain control of the GNTLUA. As a metaphor for Anishinaabe strength and a cultural symbol of spiritual connection, the sacred fire speaks to contemporary Anishinaabe aspirations to traditional ways of life. Though less consciously symbolic, the campfire makes similar statements. By spending time at Slant Lake, the blockaders are able—however momentarily—to symbolically remove themselves from the imposed political system and the cultural deterioration they equate with life on the reserve. Within Grassy's TLUA but outside of formal reserve boundaries, their constant presence at the blockade site lays claim to lands they perceive as rightly theirs and sends the message that Anishinaabe people can live without the strictures of Canada's Indian Act and Department of Indian Affairs.

By the time I arrived in northwestern Ontario, direct action against clearcutting in the GNTLUA had influenced how many of the First Nation's activists perceived their community, how they believed others perceived it, and how they understood their own roles within it. To activists at Grassy Narrows, theirs was undoubtedly a community on the rise. The following summer, Kitty evaluated the blockade's significance for Grassy's children and teenagers. In her view, the blockade had been a lesson in the value of direct action. Only in her mid-twenties, Kitty was proud to serve as a role model for her community's youth. Evoking a rich and fitting metaphor, she declared that the blockade had "lit the fire" in many of Grassy's young people. Their "fire," she added passionately—their desire and determination to challenge the sociopolitical status quo—would be central to the long-term survival of an Anishinaabe way of life.

Kitty's appraisal of the blockade's constructive consequences for the Grassy Narrows community reminded me of something Barbara had shared with me several months earlier. Sitting in the back of a warm van on a cold February day, I waited with Barbara while her elderly mother completed a transaction in a Kenora bank. Turning suddenly around in her seat, Barbara asked me if I'd ever seen the movie *Rocky*. I said yes; I'd seen it a long time ago and didn't remember it very well. Mostly, I was just surprised that, of all the movies in the world, she would bring up this one. This, she told me, was how she thought about her people and their culture. When I rented *Rocky* on

DVD in the months that followed, I saw how, in the beginning of the movie, the "Italian Stallion" is a demoralized boxer, down on his luck in his sport and his personal life. But Rocky trains hard, gains strength, and ultimately goes on to win forty-four fights. As Barbara had said, this is what is going on for Anishinaabe people today; this is the story of the Grassy Narrows blockade.

Continuity through Change:
The Anthropological Cultural Revitalization Framework

This chapter started with questions: Why was it that even when logging trucks ceased using the Jones Road route many residents of Grassy Narrows persisted in spending time at the blockade? Why, given that no actual "blockading" was taking place, did so many people continue to bring their families to the Slant Lake site? What Kitty and Barbara were able to convey through metaphor, anthropologists attempt to explain through theory.

Today, we recognize culture as dynamic and constantly changing. As Kehoe (1989: 124) writes, "Without change, adaptation, reformulation, revitalization, transformation (call it what you will), a society—Indian, European, *any* society—cannot continue." Cultural beliefs, practices, and traditions are now seen as continuously invented rather than static and fixed (Hobsbawm and Ranger 1983), and we now accept that "culture functions as a *synthesis* of stability and change, past and present, diachrony and synchrony" (Sahlins 1985: 144). Anthropologists, however, did not always embrace the dynamic nature of all cultures. In the not so distant past, many viewed the disappearance of American Indian culture as inevitable (Tarasoff 1980: 16, see also Bruner 1986). In the 1930s, Diamond Jenness (1977 [1932]: 260) wrote of the Ojibwa north of the Great Lakes:

> So, civilization, as it flows past their doors, seems to be entrapping them in a backwash that leaves only one issue, the absorption of a few families into the aggressive white race and the decline and extinction of the remainder.

More recently, Bernard James infamously declared in 1970 that "Ojibwa culture in the American reservations is . . . for all practical purposes, dead" (quoted in Danziger 1979: 202). Acculturation, use of modern technologies, and incorporation into the wage labor system, it was assumed, predestined Anishinaabeg in the United States and Canada for imminent "cultural death."

Even beyond compelling theoretical arguments about the processual, dynamic nature of culture, the alleged "death" of American Indian culture and cultural identity obviously never became a reality. Marshall Sahlins (1999) reminds anyone who may have forgotten that indigenous cultures have *not* disappeared, nor have Native peoples become just like members of their surrounding, colonizing societies. On the contrary, in recent decades an "indigenization of modernity" has swept across North America along with a reassertion of indigenous identity and pride. In many cases, Indian communities across the continent have reacted to the same circumstances anthropological observers once interpreted as foretelling their doom by working to renew and revitalize their culturally distinct ways of life (Nagel 1996).

The conjoined processes of cultural continuity and change have intrigued anthropologists for more than half a century. In the 1950s, Anthony Wallace put forward a theory he called cultural revitalization, characterizing a revitalization movement "as a deliberate, organized, conscious effort by members of a society to construct a more satisfying culture" (1956: 265). For Wallace, writing near the disciplinary end of a spatially bounded and ahistorical culture concept, cultural revitalization offered a way to begin thinking about culture change. The cultural revitalization framework can guide reflection on recent events at Grassy Narrows First Nation. Like the paradigmatic cases of cultural revitalization among the Seneca (see Wallace 1969) and the Ghost Dance that spread across much of the American West in the late nineteenth century (see Kehoe 1989), the Slant Lake blockade is a cultural and spiritual reaction to conditions of economic marginalization, political repression, and loss of traditional lands (Johnson et al. 1999b: 284). The lasting appeal of the Slant Lake blockade, then, can perhaps be explained in these terms: Slant Lake is not merely a blockade; it is a site of cultural revitalization and renewal.

Wallace outlined five distinctive stages of the revitalization process (Wallace 1956: 268–75). From the first stage—a "steady state" in which the cultural system operates efficiently and satisfactorily within the given environmental and social context—the process proceeds into a period of "increased individual stress," in which growing numbers of people experience discontent due to a decrease in the efficiency of culturally available "stress-reduction" practices. Wallace pointed out that a culture's techniques for dealing with the mental and physical stresses of life could be rendered less potent by multiple factors, including climate or environmental change, epidemic disease, conflict, and political subordination. Among the Anishinaabe people of Grassy Narrows, the acculturating, assimilatory forces of Euro-Canadian policy (as described in chapter 2), the more recent history of environmental devastation (seen in chapter 3), and the resulting endangerment of land-based subsistence (as chapter 1 depicts) further intensified these pressures.

The third stage of Wallace's revitalization process results from the prolonged experience of stress and the extended inability of familiar cultural patterns to ease it. Wallace called this stage the "period of cultural distortion." Cultural distortion may involve what Wallace, in his psychology-influenced terminology, called "regressive innovations." These could include alcohol abuse, extreme passivity, depression, and similar signs of long-term mental illness. He pointed out that some "regressive action systems become, in effect, new cultural patterns" (Wallace 1956: 269). Shkilnyk (1985) documented the period following the 1970 announcement of mercury poisoning in the English-Wabigoon River system as such a nadir of demoralization, hardship, and despair for the Grassy Narrows community. Wallace's fourth stage represents the "period of revitalization"—an era of creative response to ongoing social crisis. In Wallace's outline, revitalization is followed by a fifth stage—a new but altered cultural "steady state."

The original cultural revitalization model is not without limitations (see Harkin 2004a). While Wallace was heavily influenced by systems theoretical organismic analogies popular in the 1950s and 1960s (Wallace 2004: viii), anthropological paradigms have shifted over the past fifty years to encompass a more dynamic outlook. No longer, for example, can we accept the ideal of equilibrium; in recent decades, questions have arisen regarding the possibility of "revitalizing" something as inherently dynamic as culture and, as Michael Harkin rightly points out, the original cultural revitalization framework problematically "assumes a teleology in which a culture is in a state of decline and is destined to rise again" (2004b: 143). As well, the world is a very different place than it was fifty years ago. Indigenous peoples' attempts to forge better lives for themselves are mediated by a constantly shifting world order; the technological revolution and the rise of instant information exchange have shaped how we think about our world. In this sense, "members of a society" now means something very different than it did in the 1950s.

Still, Wallace's holistic conception of revitalization as intentional action for the purpose of altering social reality retains value as a compelling heuristic device. The cultural revitalization model suggests that change takes place when adaptation of cultural forms provides the best assurance that a society's distinctive traits and identity will endure. Whether enacted within indigenous communities or described by anthropological observers, revitalization in this broad sense hinges on cultural preservation *through* cultural change. While Wallace's original model struggled to overcome assumptions of cultural fixity, anthropologists have since transformed cultural revitalization into a dynamic and flexible theoretical lens (see Harkin 2004a). Recent analyses have revealed that revitalization movements build on indigenous cultural frameworks in innovative ways; they merge tradition and invention to meet the needs of the present moment and can be constructively explored as ingenious political resistance strategies intended to increase the power of indigenous communities relative to colonizing settler societies (McMullen 2004: 261; see also Kehoe 1989 and Lepowsky 2004: 48).

For activists at Grassy Narrows, cultural revitalization occurs where past, present, and future meet; it is lived in the here and now but designed to incorporate the best characteristics of the remembered past within a blueprint for a better future. I once asked a young Anishinaabe activist how she managed to maintain her positive attitude despite the dizzying array of challenges contemporary Native people confront. Where did she find her hope? Her clarity and perspective? She paused for a second and shrugged. "We were supposed to be *gone*," she replied. For anthropologists, cultural revitalization represents a theory of culture change and a conceptual tool. For indigenous activists striving to shape a better life for themselves and their children, it means hope.

Tragedies and Talks

In late July of 2003, people at Grassy Narrows learned that the trappers' lawsuit against Abitibi-Consolidated had been denied judicial review. Despite this setback, the blockaders showed no signs of backing down. In August, members of Grassy Narrows First Nation harvested the blueberries that grew throughout the GNTLUA. A handful of people also set out to gather the wild rice that thrived on lakes not connected to the river system and the crop-destroying water level fluctuations caused by its dams. Following a successful rice harvest, Shoon and Steve talked about selling some of their traditionally harvested rice commercially.

Following the comparative calm of midsummer, two incidents shook the Grassy Narrows First Nation community. On the evening of August 18th a young woman on her way home from Kenora's Lake of the Woods Hospital with her newborn son was seriously injured in a traffic accident on Jones Road (Gibson 2003a). An Ontario Provincial Police (OPP) cruiser attempting to pass a third vehicle at high speed despite the road's notoriously dangerous curves had collided head-on with the vehicle she and three others occupied. The Special Investigations Unit (SIU) that looked into the crash later determined that, although the officer's driving was at fault, the case did not warrant criminal charges (Alland 2003).

Only nine days later tragedy struck again. On the afternoon of August 27th a seventeen-year-old Grassy Narrows youth was shot and killed by an OPP officer. The shooting followed an early morning incident involving the young man and two other First Nation residents in which a shotgun had reportedly been fired. The OPP were called to the scene. It was not until afternoon that police finally cornered the young man, shotgun still in hand, in a wooded area within the reserve community. As they attempted negotiations, the young man allegedly moved the gun in the officers' direction multiple times. When nonlethal rubber bullets failed to subdue him, two of the officers fired their guns. One shot pierced his leg. The other fatally struck his head. First aid was attempted and an air ambulance was quick to respond, but the teenager was pronounced dead upon arrival at Kenora's hospital (Gibson 2003b).

Not surprisingly, tensions between Grassy Narrows residents and the OPP soared to new heights following these incidents. Stunned First Nation residents struggled to make sense of what had taken place in their community. Steve Fobister's email update stated that Grassy was "in a state of confusion" following the shooting. The young man's relatives were deeply angered that they had not been permitted to assist in the negotiations. They felt their involvement could have

prevented the loss of life (Gibson 2003d). In addition, some Grassy
Narrows residents interpreted the incident as a case of racially motivated police brutality. More explicitly than ever before, activists in
the community began to contemplate the connections between the
social and environmental injustices their people faced. The SIU
assigned to the case found that the officer had been legally justified in
the shooting given the young man's possession of a loaded weapon
and his refusal to drop the gun at police request (Gibson 2003c). An
inquest—required procedure when an individual dies in police custody—was planned for the following June (Gibson and Aiken 2003).

Meanwhile, the First Nation's elected leaders were making tenta-
tive plans to enter into talks with the Ontario Ministry of Natural
Resources and Abitibi-Consolidated. Deputy Chief Steve Fobister
made it clear to a *Miner and News* reporter that productive talks
would have to involve a higher level of provincial government than
local OMNR offices could provide (Barrera 2003g, 2003h). Some
members of Grassy's elected leadership were beginning to feel pressure
from the government to resolve the ongoing dispute surrounding the
blockade, but many of the most active blockaders seemed pessimistic
about the impending talks.

Despite the talks looming on the horizon, activists from Grassy
Narrows protested publicly once more. Accompanied by three members of CPT, a dozen First Nation residents staged a roadside "traffic
slowdown" alongside the Trans-Canada Highway just outside of
Kenora on August 29th. As opposed to an actual blockade, this event
was merely intended to draw public attention to Grassy Narrows'
plight. Protestors held up a large banner that read "The Treaty is Forever—Let's Protect It" as well as smaller anti-clearcutting signs (James
2003). Roberta Keesick reported a positive response to the demonstration; throughout the afternoon passing drivers had honked and
waved in support.

On September 11th of 2003, the meeting that had been in the
works for the past month-and-a-half finally took place at Abitibi's
Montreal headquarters. Grassy Narrows chief Simon Fobister, along
with Steve Fobister and one of the First Nation's elected councilors,
met with John Weaver, the CEO of Abitibi-Consolidated. A forest
manager from Abitibi's Kenora division and two other upper-level
Abitibi employees also attended the introductory session. No govern-

ment personnel took part. Following the meeting, Steve reported that Abitibi's representatives had hinted at their desire to generate economic growth for the First Nation, but that scant progress toward any resolution had been made. Steve also reported that Grassy's firm position had been made clear in the meeting. The blockade would remain.

Seven

Negotiations and Networks

The third phase of the blockade—roughly spanning the fall of 2003 through the fall of the following year—was a period of increasing tension. As the blockade's novelty wore off, Grassy Narrows residents' internal differences of opinion became increasingly hard to ignore. GNEG members continued to envision the blockade as a demonstration of Grassy Narrows First Nation's power relative to Canada, Ontario, and corporate interests. But some individuals were beginning to believe that the blockade was simultaneously a way for some First Nation members to gain power and prestige over others. For the blockaders, the emergence of these internal divisions was complicated by the need to strike a balance between attending to their own community, on the one hand, and concentrating on their expanding network of external supporters, on the other. Tensions also surrounded Grassy Narrows leaders' desire to present a cohesive image of their community; throughout the blockade's third phase, the First Nation's activists and elected leaders struggled to manage a complex dynamic that pitted their recognition of the differences within their community against externally directed images of a united front.[1]

The Grassy Narrows blockade's gradual transition from an active to a symbolic stand continued into the fall of 2003. The Christian Peacemakers Team left Slant Lake when the cold became too much for their thin-walled A-frame to withstand. While many of GNEG's core members continued to visit the Slant Lake site on an almost

149

daily basis—coming together for a shared potluck-style meal, to spend the night in the now-completed log cabin, or just to check on the sacred fire—the days of constant activity at the blockade came to an end as the chill of autumn filled the air.

Formal talks between Grassy Narrows First Nation and Abitibi-Consolidated commenced in November of 2003, but they seldom proceeded smoothly. Grassy's elected Chief and Council appeared willing to come to the table, but the fact that GNEG had acted independently from the very beginning raised questions about who possessed the authority to contemplate potential resolutions to the blockade conflict. With the commencement of the talks, internal divisions within the Grassy Narrows community that had lain dormant through the exhilarating early months of the blockade rose to the surface, leaving Steve Fobister—both an anti-clearcutting activist and the band's deputy chief—feeling caught in the middle. As he struggled with the daunting task of explaining the First Nation's position to corporate representatives, the band cancelled a string of meetings and frustration on all sides ensued.

As the seasons passed, Grassy Narrows activists continued their established pattern of direct action, engaging in public protests in Kenora and responding to the destruction of one First Nation member's trapline with a roving blockade. Increasingly, though, they directed their attention to the wider picture and to the burgeoning network of supporters that surrounded their cause.

Alliances

Although the blockaders had succeeded in halting the clearcutting closest to their community, industrial logging continued unabated in the more northerly parts of the Grassy Narrows Traditional Land Use Area. On October 2nd of 2003, J. B. Fobister posted a message on the website maintained by Friends of Grassy Narrows reporting the movement of logging equipment in the vicinity of Oak Lake Road, about sixteen miles north of Grassy. He declared, "A major protest (everywhere) I believe is in order." J. B. got his wish. Winnipeg-based Friends of Grassy Narrows organized a public rally in Kenora on October 16th. They called the event "Justice for Grassy Narrows." The group sent a call to action over the electronic media inviting people from Winnipeg to take part in the rally and offering to organize car-pools. Supporters in more distant locales were encouraged to hold sol-idarity events on the same date. In addition, FGN mailed an open letter to the Ministry of Indian Affairs, Ontario's Ministry of Natural Resources, and Abitibi-Consolidated. The letter opened by stating:

> The clear cutting being done by Abitibi-Consolidated at Grassy Narrows First Nation violates the community's aborig-inal and treaty rights to hunt and to fish in the area. Commu-nity members have erected a blockade which is entering its eleventh month in opposition to destruction of the Whiskey Jack forest. The federal government, the province, and Abitibi have each tried to shirk their responsibility by "pass-ing the buck" and claiming that this falls under the jurisdic-tion of the other two. This letter is addressed to all three entities to make the point clear: All three of you are responsi-ble for what is being done to the people of Grassy Narrows.

In the weeks leading up to the protest event, this letter was posted on the Friends of Grassy Narrows website for online viewing and endorsement.[2]

On the 16th, a mixed group of about sixty Grassy Narrows resi-dents and Winnipeggers marched through the streets of downtown Kenora, chanting and passing out informational leaflets. The protest-ers gathered at local MP and minister of Indian Affairs Robert Nault's offices, but found them closed. Some of the demonstrators speculated that his staff had been warned of the event and were afraid to face them. From there, they walked several blocks to the local Abitibi mill. In front of the mill, several Grassy Narrows activists spoke out against the clearcutting as a clear violation of their Aboriginal and treaty rights. Treaty Three grand chief Leon Jourdain was among those who participated in the rally. Like the FGN organizers of the event, Jourdain focused on the political dimensions of Grassy's strug-gle and the social challenges faced by Anishinaabe people in north-western Ontario; he told the crowd, "The history of our people, in relation to our country, is a history of denial and broken promises" (Aiken 2003a).

Responding to FGN's call, solidarity events were also held in cities across Canada. In British Columbia, a group of over fifty people gathered at the University of Victoria's student union to hear a young woman from Kenora speak in support of Grassy's blockade. Several Native musicians from the Victoria area performed at the event and nearly $300 was raised for the blockaders. In Thunder Bay, a smaller group—also calling itself Friends of Grassy Narrows and loosely affiliated with the Winnipeg-based group—assembled at the local Ontario Ministry of Natural Resources offices. And, in Montreal, a delegation of Grassy Narrows supporters associated with the Indigenous Peoples Solidarity Movement (IPSM) visited Abitibi's headquarters. There, they demanded to speak with John Weaver, the corporation's CEO. Although they did not succeed in contacting Weaver, Abitibi's media relations officer cordially listened to their complaints.

Causes, Compromises, Consequences

In his study of the Indian-French fur trading alliance in the Great Lakes region, historian Richard White uses the term "middle ground" to denote a "process of mutual invention" (1991: 50) wherein participants become "cocreators of a world in the making" (1991: 1). Different parties, White adds, enter the middle ground with different goals and different means for attaining them. Regarding the more recent context of indigenous-environmentalist alliances in Amazonia, Beth Conklin and Laura Graham (1995: 695–96) observe:

> Today a new kind of middle ground is developing between some fourth-world and first-world citizens. This contemporary middle ground is neither a geographic territory nor a social space where neighbors meet face-to-face. It is instead a political space, an area of intercultural communication, exchange, and joint political action.

Anishinaabe anti-clearcutting activists see establishing this kind of middle ground with supportive non-Natives as essential to their success. But what foundations underlie these alliances? And what compromises and consequences do they entail?

Many of the blockade's external supporters—especially those in distant urban locales—are non-Native environmentalists. Hundreds of environmentalists attended solidarity protests and fundraisers in

Toronto, Montreal, British Columbia, and Winnipeg and thousands more read about the blockade online or in newspaper reports. Although they have welcomed the generous material, moral, and tactical support of environmentalists and environmental organizations, activists at Grassy are well aware that doing so means emphasizing one aspect of their multifaceted agenda at the expense of others. While most environmentalists see ecological protection as an end in itself, stopping clearcutting within their Traditional Land Use Area is but one component of GNEG's much broader set of ambitions.

Non-Native environmentalists and indigenous activists arrive at their middle grounds by very different paths, carrying very different assumptions and aspirations. For this and other reasons, the middle ground of indigenous-environmentalist alliances is frequently unstable. Environmental groups choose to back indigenous campaigns for a variety of reasons; it helps them demonstrate their social responsibility and attract attention by inserting categorically popular indigenous peoples (see chapter 2) into their campaigns. Even more often, environmental groups have been eager to join forces with Natives who share their goal of ecological conservation. But, as Conklin and Graham (1995: 706) point out, "there is an inherent asymmetry at the core of the eco-Indian alliance. Indians' eco-political value is bestowed from the outside—the product of a historical moment that has seized on Indians in general and certain Indians in particular, as natural symbols of ecologically harmonious lifeways." Given Western society's collective imagining of indigenous peoples as profoundly and innately ecological, when Natives express interest—for whatever reason—in protecting their lands from industrial expansion, environmental groups have often been eager to climb on the bandwagon. Unfortunately, few of these enthusiastic allies stop to wonder *why* indigenous groups choose to take action; they see little need to question what they have already assumed.

Problematically, environmentalists often take for granted that Natives think and act in ways that fit stereotypical images of Ecological Nobility (see Krech 1999; Nadasdy 2005; Willow 2009). This requires envisioning the impossible existence of a monolithic "indigenous" viewpoint. It also implies a damaging denial of diversity, individual agency, and collective choice and, furthermore, presumes indigenous peoples' understandings of nature and uses of resources to be unrealistically consonant with Western conservation models.

Some environmentalists also seem to disregard the fact that indigenous peoples are part of a globally interconnected world, even when the same reality renders long-distance alliances possible in the first place. They envision Native communities as timeless and bounded entities and so trust that indigenous resource-use decisions into the infinite future can be counted on to mirror those of the allegedly sustainable past.

Stereotypical conceptions of indigenous people as inherently Ecological Indians persist not due to any mysterious intrinsic quality but because of the value of these ideas to those who perpetuate them. Indigenous activists and leaders have sometimes been able to benefit from representing themselves in ecological terms. Though they have been required to do so according to terms dictated by the dominant society (see Conklin and Graham 1995; Conklin 1997; Ramos 1998; Niezen 2003), some indigenous groups have capitalized on the Ecological Indian image as a springboard for getting their concerns heard by an international audience, often for the first time. In many cases, they have succeeded in drawing global attention and resources to local struggles and have managed to claim long-denied seats at the environmental bargaining table (see Ranco 2007).

But non-Natives have even more to gain from the Ecological Indian image. Although images of "noble savagery" have been infused with diverse specific connotations in different eras, one of their most long-standing functions surrounds the critique of Western industrial society (Berkhofer 1978). If Western society is viewed as hopelessly corrupted by consumerist greed and competitive individuality, for instance, Native society becomes symbolic of contrasting tendencies, including ecological enlightenment and communal harmony. It is not that surprising, then, that the environmental movement has played a key role in recasting the noble Indian in an ecological guise. Environmentalists, Kay Milton (1996: 109) suggests, *want* to believe in the existence of viable alternatives and paths to sustainability. "The myth of primitive ecological wisdom," she remarks, "is not just an incidental part of the romantic package carried by some environmentalists. It is fundamental to the radical environmental critique of industrialism, for without the assumption that non-industrial societies live sustainably in their environments, there would be no grounds for arguing that industrialism is the cause of environmental destruction" (see also Harkin 2007: 213).

In addition to providing serviceable tools for social critique and a wealth of imagined societal alternatives, images of Ecological Indians allow members of Western industrial societies to distance themselves from the legacies of colonialism. When contemporary indigenous activism is comprehended as a manifestation of Indian peoples' inherent ecological connection to the land, the political realities of Native resistance get pushed conveniently aside. While less transparently destructive than visions of Natives as bloodthirsty savages, the danger of "flattering" stereotypes like ecological nobility may lie in their very subtlety. Romantic portraits of indigenous people living in unspoiled landscapes shift attention away from serious political and social concerns (Buege 1996); aesthetically pleasing images mask agonizing tales of injustice and excuse the neglect and denial of legitimate Native claims to self-government and other fundamental rights.

Rooted as they are in profound underlying inequities, more pragmatic issues often surface to confound indigenous-environmentalist alliances. Assumptions about Ecological Indians—regardless of whether or not they contain any shred of veracity—have frequently set the stage for problematic disputes and accusations of indigenous "inauthenticity." Given that "images and ideas, not common identity or mutual economic interests, mobilize political cooperation among people separated by wide distances and differences of language, culture, and historical experience" (Conklin 1997: 713), what happens when environmentalists discover that real indigenous people are *not* inherent and eternal environmentalists? Or when they realize that most Native communities are at least as interested in land rights, cultural preservation, and political empowerment as in conservation? What happens when they are forced to comprehend indigenous people not as inhabitants of a static and distant past, but as coeval participants in a shared global system? Conklin and Graham (1995) suggest that these misunderstandings set the scene for such alliances' ultimate failure.

This has often been the case, but it doesn't have to be. For the most part, relationships between Grassy Narrows activists and environmental groups have been impersonal and relatively short-lived. It appears, however, that indigenous-environmentalist alliances are also being constructively reconfigured in the context of anti-clearcutting activism in northwestern Ontario. Several dozen non-Native environmentalists attended the 2003 and 2004 Environmental Youth

Gatherings at Slant Lake, including representatives of an assertive environmental group called Rainforest Action Network (RAN). Likely an outgrowth of the friendships and understanding established at these events, the partnership between the blockaders and RAN has been lasting and successful. Routinely spotlighting the inseparability of Native rights, cultural survival, and boreal forest preservation, RAN organized petitions, assisted with media communications, and pressured corporations to stop using wood from Grassy Narrows' Traditional Land Use Area in the years that followed.

While not the most numerous, the external supporters who have had the biggest impact on activism at Grassy Narrows have been associated with Friends of Grassy Narrows (FGN) and Christian Peacemaker Teams (CPT). As the open letter sent by FGN in conjunction with the October 16th protest exemplifies, rather than focusing on the environmental issues surrounding clearcutting in the boreal forest, FGN members have chosen to highlight the political side of the equation, presenting themselves primarily as defenders of Native rights. But why? On the surface, FGN appears to share many of GNEG's goals; while most FGN members are non-Native, the group advocates solidarity with First Nations activists and champions the blockaders' intertwined environmental, cultural, and political goals.

Many FGN members care deeply about Grassy Narrows' future. Some have made multiple trips to Slant Lake and developed constructive personal relationships with Grassy Narrows activists. But solidarity is not an end in itself. As Conklin and Graham (1995: 702) further suggest,

> Identification with Native cultures can be a political statement: it encapsulates a critique of Western cultural dominance and colonial regimes and locates those who identify with the Native in an oppositional position, morally distanced from their own societies' racism or colonial histories.

Indeed, many FGN members make no secret of their politically radical leanings. Through their alliance with Grassy Narrows activists, FGN members assemble an effective critique of Western industrial society's inherent injustice, consumerist greed, and systemic political corruption. By drawing attention to the striking case of the Grassy

Narrows blockade, they are able to share this political ideology with a broad public audience.

With their organizational mandate of witnessing and violence reduction, the Christian Peacemaker Team members stationed at Grassy Narrows from the beginning of the Slant Lake blockade until the fall of 2004 were also influential allies. In common with FGN, CPT acknowledged and supported the blockaders' complex set of objectives. Also like FGN, members of CPT built positive personal relationships with some First Nation residents. From CPT's constant presence, the blockaders gained a sense of security and a continuous stream of moral support. In turn, CPT was able to draw upon its association with Grassy Narrows to reinforce its stand against Western society's violence and inequity.[3]

Alliances with outsiders have had several important consequences for Grassy Narrows' activists. Beyond the material support these alliances generate, they enable a pooling of less tangible resources like social capital and media access. FGN's and CPT's logistical assistance, for example, made many of GNEG's protests in Kenora and Winnipeg a realistic possibility and FGN's—and later RAN's—internet presence drew considerable attention to Grassy's cause. But not all of the alliances' outcomes have been in Grassy Narrows activists' favor. Even as the rapid growth of their network of support confirmed for the blockaders the far-reaching significance of their work, GNEG's eagerness to partner with non-Native activists raised questions among skeptics within the Grassy Narrows community. Given the influence of so many outsiders, some First Nation members began to wonder, whose interests did blockade really represent?

Divisions

As the mid-October day of solidarity confirmed, although the Slant Lake site was growing quieter, the Grassy Narrows blockaders' network of support continued to expand. Dedicated Native and non-Native backers could now be found throughout Canada. To many of these distant supporters, the Grassy Narrows community appeared united in its efforts against Abitibi. On the ground, though, the blockade's future looked a bit less certain and considerably more complicated.

On the evening of November 11th, representatives of Grassy Narrows First Nation and Abitibi-Consolidated met at the Kenricia Hotel in downtown Kenora. The meeting was formally arranged between Grassy Narrows' Chief and Council and Abitibi's general manger, regional manager, and media spokesperson. Still, several key GNEG members—J. B., Judy, and Roberta among them—were also in attendance. Two members of the Christian Peacemaker Team stood by to document the affair. The session began with a brief presentation from Abitibi's general manager, who outlined the corporation's proposal for resolving the blockade dispute: Abitibi would establish a no-cut zone within a ten-kilometer radius of the reserve community. In addition, clearcutting would cease within twenty kilometers of the community, although other forms of logging could still take place in this zone subject to agreement among the community, the company, and the provincial government. In return, of course, the blockade would have to come down. Those who attended the meeting described the conversation that followed as tense. At one point, J. B. reportedly told the three Abitibi employees, "it's too bad it takes a blockade to get a meeting with you."

At the close of the meeting, the parties seemed no closer to reaching an agreement. Chief Simon Fobister concluded by stating that no deals could be made until the proposal had been taken back to the people of Grassy Narrows. Given that they hadn't agreed to anything, everyone at Grassy was surprised when Abitibi made the proposed resolution public the following day. The publicly released proposal echoed the ten-kilometer no-cutting zone and twenty-kilometer buffer presented the previous evening. The plan also included offers of financial support for a range of community and cultural activities (Knudson 2003) and training and economic development opportunities for First Nation members (Aiken 2003b). Abitibi personnel seemed optimistic about their proposal. Media spokesperson Marc Osborne told the media, "We're very committed to reaching an agreement" (Aiken 2003b) and "developing a dialogue with this community" (Knudson 2003). Abitibi general manager Don Hopkins also touted the plan, adding that it would give Grassy Narrows a strong voice on a land base covering more than 1,250 square kilometers (Aiken 2003b).

While some members of Grassy's elected leadership felt the proposal represented a positive first step, those most active in the blockade movement felt differently (Harries 2003). In their eyes, any agreement with Abitibi would miss the political point of the blockade; the only deal the blockaders would accept would have to be made at a government-to-government, nation-to-nation level. Abitibi's offer addressed—albeit on a minimal level—the blockaders' environmental concerns, but it failed to take their political objectives into account. GNEG's unwillingness to relax its position highlighted the multidimensionality of the blockaders' motives. It also underscored the fact that the company was missing—or ignoring—their point.

In the months that followed, heterogeneity within the Grassy Narrows community complicated the Chief and Council's efforts to reach an agreement with Abitibi. Not only were tensions mounting between the band's elected leadership and the leaders of the blockade, but the fact that not everyone at Grassy Narrows supported the blockade's direction was also becoming an increasingly pressing issue. Anthropological studies have shown that internal disputes and conflicts are "a normal part of social relationships and their ongoing maintenance, negotiation and renegotiation" (Edmunds 2007). In North America, divisions within Native communities have most frequently been described as pitting "traditionalists" against "progressives" (see Geertz 1994). While my experience has led me to view this distinction as overly simplistic—significant overlap, for example, exists between these groups and people may change their affiliation over time—keeping these broad categories in mind can help make sense of Grassy Narrows First Nation members' diverse viewpoints regarding the blockade.

Over the past decade, GNEG has positioned itself as a "traditionalist" group in contrast to the "progressive" Chief and Council. As in other Anishinaabe communities, internal conflict has also been predicated upon long-term competition between families, which has the ultimate effect of ensuring that no single kin group stays on top for too long (see Nesper 2002: 185–86). This pattern is further complicated by disparities of education, employment, and economic status. In this context, rival groups within Grassy Narrows First Nation strive constantly to establish and maintain legitimacy and to increase their standing relative to that of others. By emphasizing connections to traditional Anishinaabe culture—through, for example, adherence to customary patterns of authority and efforts to sustain and revitalize distinctive cultural practices—GNEG members validate their position as the community's traditional leadership.[4] In contrast, the Chief and Council's recognition by the federal Department of Indian Affairs, Ontario, and the Canadian public as the First Nation's official leadership functions to legitimize its continued influence. At the same time—as GNEG members are quick to point out—the Chief and Council's externally imposed Indian Act foundations render the elected leaders' claims to legitimate representation contestable.

In light of these political dynamics, Grassy Narrows residents' various views of the blockade can be approached as an arena in which complex internal power struggles play out. I once observed a man express his rage over the current state of affairs in his community. After more than a year of the blockade, he felt unmistakably and utterly resentful toward it. While this was the only instance of unconcealed rage directed at the blockade I ever witnessed, I can only suspect that at least a few other First Nation members must quietly hold similar views. As he told it, when powerful members of the community decided to take action they were met with praise, but when he attempted to do the same no one even noticed. For him, the blockade had become a daily reminder of the class differentials between individuals and families at Grassy Narrows. Personal frustrations aside, he had a valid point. While unlikely that any of GNEG's leaders would ever describe themselves as "powerful," they are among the most educated people at Grassy. The fact that some of the blockaders enjoy above-average economic situations compared to other First Nation residents likely also added insult to the frustrated man's injury.

While few Grassy Narrows residents felt so strongly or so negatively, dozens of people who participated in the blockade's early months became progressively less involved as time wore on. Many of these individuals initially saw the blockade as a positive step for their community, but didn't feel the sense of ownership or personal stake necessary to sustain their involvement. As one man indicated, the blockade was "not his project" anymore. Some former blockade supporters lost interest when they felt their presence could no longer make a difference. Impatient with the slow pace of the blockade, they continued to support it in principle, but believed that their physical presence at the site would have little effect. Despite this waning participation, core GNEG members were quick to assure me that these former blockaders would return if they felt their presence was truly needed. Other active participants in the blockade's early phases actually grew disenchanted with the blockade and its leadership and reacted by intentionally distancing themselves. As one woman explained, she felt increasingly excluded and "out of the loop." If no one told her when blockade-related events were taking place, she asked, how was she supposed to participate? By the fall of 2003, many people at Grassy seemed to share her outlook; although they continued to support the blockade in principle, they felt like they needed a membership card to penetrate its tight-knit social group.

Even more critically, some First Nation residents were beginning to perceive the blockade as an elitist project. Struggling on welfare and living day to day, many individuals and families simply did not have the luxury of spending time and resources on the blockade cause. Some of this lack of support was based on logistics; the Slant Lake site was located five miles from the reserve community, and many of the periodic "roving" blockades were even farther afield. Travel to the site thus required some form of vehicle and the financial resources to maintain it. Similarly, more than a few Grassy Narrows residents I met would be hard pressed to turn down offers of financial compensation or employment made by Abitibi in hopes of a quick resolution to the dispute. The fact that most GNEG members held down decent jobs meant they had little personal stake in the employment opportunities that cooperation with the logging industry could provide. Given GNEG's attempts to operate according to traditionally egalitarian patterns of leadership, these charges of elitism posed an ironic contradiction and, in the eyes of some, called the blockaders' authority into question. It was here, where the major lines of division within Grassy Narrows First Nation intersected, that GNEG and the blockade was most vulnerable to critique.

Talks and Tensions

With another round of talks scheduled for December 18th, Grassy Narrows activists came together to celebrate the blockade's first full year. Friends of Grassy Narrows members from Winnipeg joined them for a feast and powwow in the Slant Lake roundhouse on December

3rd. The atmosphere was celebratory. In early December of 2003, the elected band leadership was optimistic that a resolution to the blockade dispute would soon be achieved. Focusing on the big picture and eager to continue their stand, however, GNEG members did not share their optimism. While a brief *Miner and News* article marking the anniversary of the blockade focused on the former—suggesting that a solution might be found along the lines of revenue-sharing agreements already in place in other parts of Canada (Aiken 2003c)—many of the First Nation's activists weren't convinced. The blockaders prepared the Slant Lake site for the cold winter ahead.

The talks planned for mid-December never took place. Citing the band's lack of a united position, the First Nation called off the meeting at the last minute. Speaking on behalf of Grassy Narrows' Chief and Council, Steve Fobister explained that they had not yet received a clear mandate from the people and had therefore decided against proceeding with the talks (Aiken 2003d). He added that future meetings should include government representatives, not just corporate officials. Although the OMNR, Indian Affairs, and other offices had been contacted to request meetings, the First Nation had yet to receive any response. Steve, for one, was frustrated by the lack of progress. Abitibi representatives were also frustrated; they were already on their way from Montreal when they got news of the cancellation. In the wake of the canceled meeting, another was scheduled for mid-February, this time to be held at Grassy Narrows.

Before the meeting could take place, the Grassy Narrows blockaders took direct action once again, this time in response to an incident they took to signify the forest industry's continued blatant disrespect for their land and way of life. In the first days of February, a Grassy Narrows trapper reported the destruction of parts of his trapline by an Abitibi contractor. Located north of the English River, some of his access trails had been cut over and many of his marten box traps had vanished. According to J. B.'s informal GPS survey, the site appeared to be legally within Abitibi's cut block, but GNEG members and trappers reacted to the destruction with anger. On the evening of February 4th, 2004, over a dozen protestors gathered at the junction of Deer Lake and Segise roads to stage the first roving blockade since the previous June. The one-night protest was a direct response to the destruction of the trapline in question, but many Grassy Narrows activists were also upset that clearcutting in the

GNTLUA was continuing despite the band's recent negotiation attempts. As J. B. told me in the wake of the incident, the contractors just cut, with no regard for what's there.

Corporate personnel were troubled by the surge in blockade activity. On February 11th, Abitibi representatives from Montreal once again arrived in northwestern Ontario to meet with members of Grassy Narrows First Nation. Unlike the previous November's meeting, this day-long affair was held at Grassy Narrows and took the form of an open forum rather than a formal meeting with band leadership. More than anything else, the meeting provided an opportunity to discuss the recent roving blockade and the anger that provoked it. A short article in the *Miner and News* accurately described the event by stating that Abitibi got "an earful" from Grassy Narrows' trappers and others in the First Nation (Aiken 2004a). Discussion at the forum targeted clearcutting's adverse impacts on trapping. Many of the GNEG members who participated were trappers themselves and clearly identified themselves along these lines. Roberta Keesick, for instance, pointed out that fewer and fewer animals remained to trap; as a trapper, she declared, she simply could not tolerate clearcutting. Like other Grassy Narrows activists, Roberta also felt Abitibi was not really listening to people from Grassy. She cited as a case in point the fact that the company had already made up its mind about the next twenty-year Forest Management Plan, scheduled for imminent release in anticipation of a February 17th open house (Aiken 2004a).

Open House: Protesting the 2004–2024 Forest Management Plan (Again)

As the date approached, Kenora-based Abitibi staff and Grassy Narrows activists and supporters both geared up for the upcoming open house, where the now complete 2004–2024 Whiskey Jack Forest Management Plan would be presented for public commentary. Just as they had the previous spring during earlier phases of forest management planning, a large delegation of protestors anticipated attending the event.

On the 17th, several dozen First Nation residents—including a busload of middle and high school students and four chaperoning teachers from the Sakatcheway Anishinabe School—navigated the winding snow-covered road to Kenora, where they convened with close to thirty Friends of Grassy Narrows members. Together, the demonstrators peacefully marched from Kenora's scenic Harbourfront to the Lakeside Inn. The day was cold and bright. Still clutching their signs and banners, the protestors arrived in the lobby of the Lakeside Inn where they gradually shed the layers that had bundled them against the midday cold.

Barbara headed to town as soon as she finished working the lunch shift at her job in Grassy's school cafeteria. Her white van pulled up just as the march came to a close. Several activists gathered around to help unload boxes of snacks, homemade posters, and one white weasel costume. Inside the hotel's first-floor conference center, one large room housed the Whiskey Jack Forest Management Plan open house, sponsored jointly by the Ontario Ministry of Natural Resources (OMNR) and Abitibi-Consolidated. Like previous public open houses, the event provided an opportunity for the OMNR and industry to inform the public of their harvest plans for the coming years, gather feedback, and fulfill public consultation requirements.

This time around, non-Native blockade supporters had taken the lead in organizing the afternoon's events. Directly across the lobby from the official open house, members of Friends of Grassy Narrows and the Christian Peacemaker Team had booked an almost identical room where they intended to host an "open house" of their own. They hoped to present an otherwise unheard side of the story, focusing on the ecological and cultural devastation caused by clearcutting and spotlighting the logging industry's infringement on Native rights.

But the first thing on the protestors' agenda was a visit to the FMP open house. Activists and youth from Grassy gradually filtered into the room. Still holding the large white banner they'd prepared for the march, FGN members did the same. The banner read: "Clearcuts: Hurts First Nations, Hurts Workers, Hurts Kenora." Strategically intended to appeal to Kenora residents who would read it during the march, at the open house, or reproduced in media accounts, the banner made the point that Grassy Narrows residents were not the only ones harmed by industrial-scale clearcut logging. As Dave Brophy, writing for Friends of Grassy Narrows, put it in a long letter to the editor published by the *Kenora Daily Miner and News*, in addition to protesting clearcutting, the demonstrators also aimed to communicate something more: that clear-cut logging managed by a multi-national corporation not only perpetuates the cultural genocide to which First Nations in Canada have been subjected for generations, but also undermines workers' security and the economy of Kenora as a whole because it means dependence on private investors who have no real commitment to the local community. (Brophy 2004)

The group of protestors was a large one. Activists quickly overshadowed the dozen or so open house hosts and the small handful of Kenora citizens who had turned out to learn about and comment on the Forest Management Plan. Barbara, for one, was shocked by the meager public turnout. "So that's their consultation and nobody [from town] shows up," she commented, "no wonder they can do whatever they want."

As the pro-Grassy contingent flowed into the open house, some of the protestors suspiciously eyed the maps that lined a number of portable display walls and covered a wide table in the center of the room. The large space quickly became packed with close to eighty demonstrators. The prompt arrival of the press and several police officers—obvious despite their plainclothes dress—only added to the crowd. As the scene grew increasingly chaotic, a few students helped themselves to doughnuts provided by Abitibi and the OMNR. The weasel costume, worn well by a young woman from Grassy, made an appearance. Accompanying the diminutive weasel, a large non-Native man working as a heating plant engineer for the First Nation dressed as an outsized yellow muskrat for the occasion. Grassy Narrows activists capitalized expertly on the media presence at the event. As lights flashed for photo opportunities of the charismatic characters, the two costumed individuals stayed in character, responding to reporters' questions as "homeless residents of the Whiskey Jack Forest" upset by all the clearcutting.

Together, a group of students and adults from Grassy Narrows formed a circle on the floor, alternatively chanting and chatting while several Friends of Grassy Narrows continued to hold their signs—and the white banner—aloft. Despite the disorder, the protest remained peaceful. After nearly an hour at the open house, activists from Grassy Narrows and their supporters calmly dispersed to the room across the lobby. Grand Council Treaty Three and the Winnipeg division of Food Not Bombs had provided large boxes of sandwiches and drinks. Some people ate and socialized; others investigated an exhibit table depicting the trapping way of life and the detrimental impacts of clearcutting upon it or took in large photos of the clearcuts in Grassy's Traditional Land Use Area that were taped to the walls.

The main event was a screening of *As Long as the Rivers Flow*, an independent media film about the Grassy Narrows blockade's early months by Thunder Bay–based filmmaker Dave Clement (2003). For the most part, Abitibi and OMNR personnel declined the invitation to attend the screening, but one new OMNR hire watched intently. Following the film, the crowd dispersed quickly. Most GNEG members who attended the event considered it a success; although experience had taught them not to expect immediate results, the protest had effectively drawn attention to many of their concerns. Still, not everyone was content with how things had turned out. One woman from Grassy I spoke to after the event expressed disappointment; she contrasted the soaring support from groups like Friends of Grassy Narrows with the conspicuous absence of many of her own community's leaders. For better or worse, the protest would have amounted to little without the dedicated work of non-Native supporters.

Carrying Winter into Spring

In conjunction with the mid-February release of the 2004–2024 Whiskey Jack Forest Management Plan, Abitibi-Consolidated announced that the corporation was in the process of negotiating a deal with a contractor from Wabauskang First Nation. The deal would potentially supply Abitibi with some fifty thousand cubic meters of wood, mostly from the same area where the roving blockades had halted logging operations the previous summer (Kenora Daily Miner and News 2004). For First Nation leaders searching for compromises and solutions, the deal represented a positive step. For the most determined activists at Grassy, on the other hand, the Wabauskang deal looked like an intentional divide-and-conquer strategy; the blockaders worried that Abitibi's agreement with the neighboring First Nation might intensify divisions within their own community by further polarizing those who supported the blockade and those who advocated economic development.

Throughout the winter months, Grassy Narrows activists continued to spend time at Slant Lake. On almost any given evening, people could be found sitting around the sacred fire or warming themselves inside the log cabin. Children begged to be taken to the blockade; in their presence, the sloped path down to the frozen lake became a perfect sledding hill. A few times a month, GNEG members gathered at Slant Lake for potluck-style meals. While some seemed impromptu, others were planned several days in advance around a designated theme: a wild foods feast, a cowboy dinner. Under the orange tarps of the roundhouse roof, GNEG's core members and their families came together to share food and pass long winter evenings in good company. With the log cabin now meticulously winterized—insulated with pink commercial fiberglass and chinked with thin wooden slats—cold weather sleepovers at Slant Lake also became an attractive possibility. A small woodstove with a glass-paned door made the cabin a warm shelter against the chill of the boreal night. For those who experienced life on the Old Reserve, a night in the cabin was a nostalgic undertaking. Catalyzed by the log cabin's traditional setting—its lack of electricity, plumbing, and noisy neighbors—visitors remembered aloud the days before Grassy's relocation and reimagined the traditional life of generations past.

As the days lengthened and the snow began to melt, the slow but steady pace of anti-clearcutting activism continued. On April 22nd, activists from Grassy Narrows participated in an Earth Day Walk. Accompanied by support vehicles, sixteen walkers made the long journey from Grassy Narrows to Winnipeg relay style. When they arrived in the city, they were greeted by a rally organized by Friends of Grassy Narrows. Despite a few complaints about the difficult trip, GNEG members said they had been especially happy with the large turnout. About two hundred people—including residents of several regional First Nations and scores of non-Native environmentalist supporters—attended the event. All through the spring, core members of the GNEG worked to prepare for the second Annual Environmental Youth Gathering, planned for the last week in June. At the same time, many of the young people involved in the blockade worked to complete their academic year.

In mid-June of 2004, a high school student from Grassy Narrows First Nation became, as one witness was quick to point out, the first of his generation to sustain a birchbark canoe–making injury. The injury was not serious. Although the gash on his hand was deep, the nurse on duty at the reserve's clinic stitched it up and sent him on his way. Within a couple of hours, the young man returned to Slant Lake to participate in the canoe-making workshop he'd left and, it seemed, to show off his fresh wound. Back at the blockade, he rejoined a group of seven high school students and two dedicated teachers who were spending the week at Slant Lake building a traditional-style birchbark canoe out of locally available natural materials.

For the students, this workshop took the place of their final exam. A man from Sioux Lookout, a town several hours to the northeast, had been enlisted by the Native studies teachers at Grassy's Sakatcheway Anishinabe School to lead the workshop and was spending the week camping out in Slant Lake's log cabin. As canoe-building got underway, students and teachers sat in an outdoor circle, side-by-side on stackable school chairs. With knives, they painstakingly peeled the bark off bundles of *watap* (spruce root) they had gathered and soaked in water. The *watap* was then split to produce a flat edge. Peeling and splitting *watap* was a hazardous undertaking; it was the activity that led to the aforementioned injury, and everyone who

Figure 7.1. Building a birchbark canoe: peeling *watap*

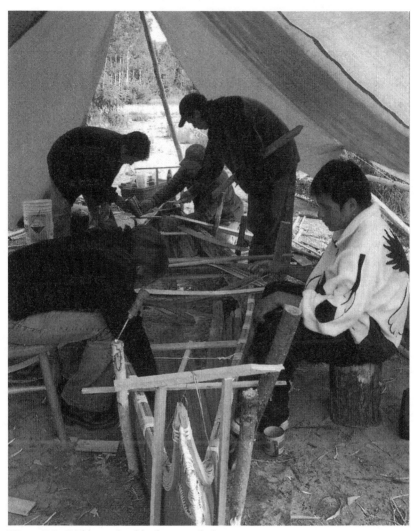

Figure 7.2. Building a birchbark canoe: lashings

participated left with sore fingers. But *watap* was a necessary part of the students' canoe. In the days that followed, the canoe's frame took shape. Using rocks, hot water, and clamps, the students learned how to mold long birchbark sheets into place. They took turns lashing the canoe's countless seams with *watap*, installing the vessel's ribs and sheathing and, finally, applying pitch and scraping high-contrast decorative images into the bark's thin membrane lining.

The workshop was open not only to students, but also to other interested people. Throughout the week, visitors from the Grassy Narrows community—blockaders and non-blockaders alike—stopped by to observe the canoe's progress. Some were just curious; others were interested in attempting a canoe of their own. Shoon dropped in several times, enthused by the opportunity to learn a new skill. He shared the stories he'd heard about the last birchbark canoe in Grassy. Back in the 1930s on the Old Reserve, Shoon said, an old man had owned a canoe just like the one the students were now building. When the man arrived at the clearing that served as the Old Reserve's communal meeting area, he always pulled his canoe up on shore. One day when he went back to retrieve it, it was gone. He looked all around but didn't see it. And then he looked up. A group of kids had picked up the canoe and strung it up the flagpole by one end. That's how light it had been.

As the chosen location for the canoe-building workshop, Slant Lake—and not the reserve—was again confirmed as a site of cultural revitalization. The workshop allowed the students and their Anishinaabe teachers to take part in revitalizing what they saw as an important but virtually vanished part of their cultural heritage. One teacher's eyes welled with tears of joy when she talked about watching the group work together like an extended family; this kind of communal work was how Anishinaabe people in her grandparents' generation had passed nearly every day. On the final day of the workshop, under an ominous sky, the canoe was ceremoniously launched from Slant Lake's shore. Two of the students brought their own small children to take part in the casual celebration. The wind was strong and the sky threatened to rain, but spirits were bright as the teachers took turns testing the canoe. All week, the students had been wondering if the product of their labor would float. Cutting through challenging waves with steadfast resilience, it did.

The 2004 Environmental Youth Gathering

June was a busy month at the blockade. From the 22nd through the 27th, the Slant Lake site buzzed with the activity of the second annual Environmental Youth Gathering. The 2004 Youth Gathering and the powwow that followed highlighted Grassy Narrows activists' dual focus on youth and networking as the two most prominent and promising dimensions of the blockade movement. On the first morning of the gathering, Kitty officially kicked things off with a small ceremony in the roundhouse. A documentary filmmaker visiting from Winnipeg was intent on recording the entire event.[5] Kitty waited cooperatively as he adjusted his camera for the orange roundhouse lighting before she smudged with sage. Her three-year-old daughter assisted by circulating an abalone shell containing the smoldering sage among the handful of people gathered for the affair. Then, in a voice as strong as its owner, Kitty sang to the beat of her hand drum.

Only four hours later, the crowd had quadrupled in size. Around twenty children and young adults had found rides from the reserve to the blockade. Judy and Roberta were present, along with Kitty and a few other blockade regulars. Testament to non-Native allies' significance to the Grassy Narrows blockade, the twenty-odd supporters who made the trip to Grassy for the Youth Gathering almost equaled attendance from the community itself. Friends of Grassy Narrows was well represented, and independent non-Native supporters were arriving from across Canada. As the day progressed, close to fifty people—the Grassy Men's Singers who'd been practicing at the Slant Lake powwow grounds, teachers from Sakatcheway Anishinabe School, members of Grassy's environmental group and the Christian Peacemaker Team, and other Youth Gathering attendees—filled the roundhouse to capacity. People conversed casually, relishing the opportunity to make new connections and reaffirm old ones.

With dinner behind schedule due to the latest power outage on the reserve, talk turned to Grassy's new sawmill project. The open-air mill was located adjacent to the community's garbage dump. With one small truck and milling equipment imported from Scandinavia, the logging operation utilized selectively cut trees harvested within the Grassy Narrows Traditional Land Use Area by hired band members. A solid log cabin could be constructed from seventy logs processed at the tiny mill. Members of GNEG said they saw the mill as a part of their long-term anti-clearcutting campaign; the mill simultaneously demonstrated a sustainable way to harvest wood from the boreal forest and encouraged community members to assert their right to use resources from the GNTLUA. In addition, the project's organizers hoped the mill could eventually solve the First Nation's housing shortage by providing better-quality homes at a lower price than those available through government programs. Before a hungry and restless roundhouse crowd, a couple of daring performers sang favorite blockade songs, including "Blockade Blues" and "Where Are You Warriors." After dinner, people from the reserve headed home. Visitors camping at Slant Lake also turned in early, tired from the day of travel and activity. The following day promised to be just as full.

A clearcut tour was first on the agenda for the Youth Gathering's second day. In the cool dampness of the rainy morning, twenty-eight people piled into a borrowed school bus to inspect the clearcuts to the north. Like the day before, the group included a mix of children and youth from Grassy and visiting non-Native supporters. The first stop was an old-growth spruce forest with prominent granite outcroppings and steep slopes that had made logging unfeasible. The forest was humid and thick with moss. Moose tracks were clearly visible in the spongy wet gravel of the road. Lady slippers and other wildflowers sprang from a green-carpeted forest floor. The crowded bus pressed on and came to a stop in the dry heat of one of the largest cuts. The contrast between forest and clearcut was palpable to everyone on board. Some of the kids from Grassy had never traveled this far up the road and were saddened by their first views of the clearcuts' barren enormity.

As the bus made its way back to Slant Lake, Kitty led the kids on board in a sing-along. Over and over so that everyone could commit it to memory, she repeated a song she and her sister had written. To the tune of "O Canada," she sang of the *ogitchidaa* who fight to protect their homelands, the *songade'e* that gives them the strength to stand up for their rights, and the hope that someday Turtle Island would be free. As noted in chapter 5, *ogitchidaa* means "warrior"—literally, "one who is big hearted"—in Anishinaabemowin. *Songade'e*, the term that inspired this book's title, similarly means "strong hearted." The phrase "Turtle Island" is also significant; with origins in widespread oral tradition that envisions the North American continent resting on the back of a giant turtle, the term references a neotraditional pan-Indian view of the land.[6] All told, the song celebrated the Grassy Narrows blockaders' determination to stop the destruction of their homeland and to stand united with others doing the same. Even further, it linked their community's struggle to a fight they perceived as extending across Native North America. By inverting the meaning of a familiar tune, Kitty and her sister paid their respects to the *ogitchidaa* who fight—often *against* the Canadian national project glorified by the original "O Canada"—for Native rights.

After the bus returned to Slant Lake, visitors were left to relax on their own until evening. A dinner of stew and bannock was served in the reserve's multipurpose complex. In the gymnasium, tables had been arranged in rows, with seats facing the small stage at one end. An Aboriginal rock band from Winnipeg called Eagle and Hawk had volunteered to do a free show. The band was popular with Grassy's children and teenagers, who made up two-thirds of the concert's sixty-person audience. Eagle and Hawk played original songs for their first set. Keeping with the mood of the Environmental Youth Gathering, many of the songs had First Nations and environmental themes; a tuned titled "Turtle Island" was particularly well received. For their second set, the band played an assortment of cover songs. At the end of the evening two teenage musicians from Grassy joined the band on stage.

After the high points of the clearcut tour and concert, the Youth Gathering continued for one more day. Casual workshops—semi-organized games and conversation sessions—took place at Slant Lake. Hoping to generate constructive dialogue between First Nations activists and non-Native supporters, Friends of Grassy Narrows facilitated an open discussion in the roundhouse. For supporters interested in helping the blockaders' cause, the session provided direction. With the Winnipeg-based filmmaker's camera rolling and the group seated in a large circle, some of the visitors asked what they could do to help. Kitty was quick to reply. Very soon, she said, they would need solid commitments from people willing to be "bodies at a blockade." So often, Kitty told the group, outsiders ask what they can do to support the blockade, but very few are willing to give up the comforts of city life in order to stay at Grassy long-term and stand with the blockaders. This kind of commitment, she said, would show Grassy's activists how much outsiders care about their cause. It would help keep them strong. Her words also hinted at the tensions within the Grassy Narrows community; too many people at Grassy had not committed to the blockade because of their attachments to school, work, or other personal demands. Kitty speculated that the dedication of outsiders might help these people see that they too should be standing up for their land and rights.

As it had been the previous year, the Youth Gathering was followed by two days of powwow. At its peak, close to one hundred people gathered to dance and one hundred more to watch from folding chairs and blankets arranged beneath the shade of a poplar-decked arbor. Most attendees were Anishinaabe; people from Grassy and other area First Nations turned out for the event. A comedian from Thunder Bay who went by the name of Moccasin Joe emceed the powwow. Right away, he grasped the youth-related theme of the event and began using it as a way to motivate spectators to get up and dance: "Look at all the young people out there," he announced, "Let's honor them; that's what it's all about." Given the comparative scarcity of Grassy Narrows adults throughout the Youth Gathering, the focus on young people seemed appropriate. On Sunday evening, the powwow wound down with a giveaway. Students from Grassy who had helped plan the Youth Gathering passed out locally made jams, tee-shirts, tobacco bags, children's activity books, socks, and dish towels. Judy and Roberta, in turn, presented each of the young organizers with an eagle feather in recognition of their hard work.

Searching for Consensus

The same week as the Environmental Youth Gathering, meetings between Grassy Narrows First Nation and Abitibi-Consolidated were scheduled to resume after a several-month hiatus. Responding to the First Nation's earlier invitation, local Ontario Ministry of Natural Resources personnel were also planning to attend the session. Like they did the previous December, however, the band cancelled the talks, once again citing their lack of a unified internal position. Further talks were postponed until fall. Instead of a normal part of social interaction, some of Grassy's leaders seemed to see their community's internal divisions as a problem to overcome. As one elected councilor told me, the postponement was a positive development, since the extra time would give them a chance to move toward consensus. Some of the blockaders were also happy to hear that the talks had been called off, but for a different reason; they remained adamant that any talks should take place at a nation-to-nation level and must involve the federal government instead of Abitibi.

Deputy Chief Steve Fobister continued to spearhead the search for consensus. He was careful to remind GNEG members that the meetings that had taken place up to this point were "exploratory discussions" rather than negotiations. With the hope of moving closer to an official position, Grassy Narrows' Chief and Council called a special assembly on July 7th and 8th of 2004. A pamphlet advertising "The Asubpeeschoseewagong Netum Anishinabek Assembly on Forestry" was distributed to households throughout the First Nation. The trifold leaflet stated the assembly's goal in bold type: "The expectation from this assembly is to put actions and plans together as a formal position from Grassy Narrows First Nation."

The two-day discussion took place in the same room that had housed the Eagle and Hawk concert two weeks before. A panel of band leaders was seated at a table along the front of the large room and an audience of about thirty other community members—two-thirds of them middle-aged men—sat in four rows of folding chairs. Core members of Grassy's environmental group were markedly absent. When I asked some of the blockaders why they hadn't attended, they told me they'd never heard anything about the event. Flyers had been distributed just the day before, so it's possible that they simply hadn't gotten the news. But some of Grassy's activists suspected they were being intentionally left out.

At the assembly, the walls near the multipurpose building's main door were graced with eighteen full-page color photos of clearcuts, a map of the Whiskey Jack Forest Management area produced by Abitibi, and a large-print reminder of the assembly's goal. A flipchart listed topics for discussion:

–Traditional Land Use and Forestry
–Land and Resources
–Chief and Council Report
–Strategy Sessions
–Community Planning.

As panel members spoke in turn over the course of the two-day meeting, most community members opted to listen quietly rather than share their own opinions. At length, Steve summarized the blockaders' view that the First Nation should refrain completely from bargaining with Abitibi. In their view, he said, including Abitibi in the mediation process gave the corporation a level of importance that no industrial entity should possess. At the same time, Steve pointed out, Treaty Three was made with the queen—and where was *she* in all of this? Chief Simon Fobister took less time to make his point. In his view, Abitibi was an instrument used to harm First Nation people. After all, it was Abitibi who trespassed on Native traplines to harvest wood. Neither the government (the party that let all of this happen) nor the corporation (the party that did the actual damage) should be let off the hook. As he saw it, Abitibi should be included in the ongoing attempt to resolve the blockade dispute.

As the assembly wore on, it became clear that the most profound disagreement had little to do with the blockade's existence; everyone who spoke at the assembly agreed that something needed to be done to slow the pace of clearcutting in the GNTLUA. Like the blockaders, they saw the need to protect their land, their rights, and their cultural heritage. Where people diverged, it now seemed, was over the inclusion of Abitibi at the bargaining table. On the assembly's first day, a casual lunch was served. Over soup and sandwiches, I asked Steve what he thought of the assembly so far. His response was gloomy. The attendance was so poor, he told me, and there seemed to be so many disagreements within the community. Indeed, even as the assembly reached full swing, a carload of GNEG members headed out on an "exploratory mission" along the logging roads, strategizing and searching for potential roving blockade sites.

Reconsidering Mercury's Legacy

For the people of Grassy Narrows, mercury poisoning has been a persistent source of anxiety since the 1970 discovery of contamination in the English-Wabigoon River system (see chapter 3). Concerns about the effects of methyl mercury on human and animal health remained below the surface—constant but more often than not overshadowed by other pressing affairs—for most of the summer of 2004. In the last month of the short northern summer two events inspired First Nation residents' renewed interest in the mercury poisoning that had impacted their waterways for decades. Blockaders and other band members alike focused on the ongoing health impacts of contamination and reflected on the enduring legacies they shared.

First, the findings of the ongoing Wild Meat Contaminant study were reported at a July 29th meeting. With Judy and Roberta as the project's coordinators, the links between the contaminant study and the blockade were unambiguous; both the study and the blockade focused on the viability of the GNTLUA's environment and on the consequences of industrial development for the community's cultural and physical health. Other interested people at the meeting included close to a dozen Grassy Narrows trappers, a nurse, and two members of Friends of Grassy Narrows who had driven in from Winnipeg for the event. Two outside researchers hired as technical consultants had also come to share their findings.

Bill Fobister—an accomplished trapper, former chief, and respected community elder—served as moderator and interpreter for the event. With Bill's skillful translation, preferences for both Anishinaabemowin and English were accommodated. Shoon spoke first. In Anishinaabemowin, he described how important food from the bush remains to many people in Grassy Narrows. This study, he said, is important to them because they want to know how much contamination is in the animals they eat. Another trapper followed with a similar declaration. The trappers and researchers seemed to be on the same page; both were worried about the health of the animals in the GNTLUA and about the potential consequences for human health.

Next, the researchers described their results. From 147 samples collected by the First Nation's hunters and trappers, the study had analyzed the levels of mercury and other heavy metals in the flesh of otter, beaver, muskrat, moose, rabbit, deer, mink, marten, fisher, lynx, fox, partridge (grouse), several species of ducks, jackfish (northern pike), whitefish, and pickerel (walleye). The study's conclusions confirmed many trappers' suspicion that something was amiss. Following Health Canada's guidelines for frequent consumers of fish, pickerel and jackfish in the region were both deemed to contain an unhealthy amount of mercury. Even more troubling, all eighteen otters tested had extremely high mercury levels.[7] On the other hand, the flesh of herbivorous species in the area had turned up no measurable mercury. The researchers warned trappers against eating the liver and kidney of any predatory species, but were told that there was no need to be concerned about their consumption of herbivores such as moose, deer, beaver, and rabbit. While the contaminant study's findings did not appear to alarm anyone at the meeting, they did serve as a reminder of the continuing risk mercury represented for the Grassy Narrows community.

The second event to stimulate interest in mercury poisoning occurred in late August of 2004. A team of Japanese doctors—headed by Dr. Masazumi Harada, one of the world's foremost experts on the impacts of mercury in the human body—arrived in northwestern Ontario to test mercury levels and symptoms in Grassy Narrows and Whitedog First Nation residents. Not coincidently, Harada was based near Minamata, Japan. His trip was a return visit; Harada and other Japanese experts had visited the First Nations on two occasions in the mid-1970s (Hutchison and Wallace 1977), and, in 2002, Harada had returned to northwestern Ontario to conduct a study on the long-term effects of mercury in the affected First Nations.[8]

A large crowd gathered at Grassy's health clinic on August 29th. The small clinic was overwhelmed with people waiting to be tested, translators, and Harada's numerous assistants. Testing took place not only in examination rooms, but spilled into the clinic's waiting area and break room as well. While Dr. Harada conducted basic nervous system examinations—examinees were asked, for example, to touch their nose with their eyes closed and to balance on one leg—other members of his team ran test stations where First Nation residents sorted marbles of various colors or felt sandpaper in order to assess fingertip sensitivity.

Over the course of Harada's two-day visit to Grassy Narrows, over sixty-five people from every segment of Grassy's population turned out to participate in the voluntary tests. Bill and Steve Fobister had arranged the doctors' visit, and both seemed pleased by their community's eager participation. As Steve pointed out, so many people at Grassy were desperate for solutions to their health problems. Citing one troubling example, he told me that ten children on the reserve—a number far exceeding the statistical norm—had recently been diagnosed with Multiple Sclerosis. Mercury, he speculated, might be to blame. In fact, at a press conference following his visit to the two First Nations, Dr. Harada estimated that 80 percent of the First Nation residents he examined showed symptoms of mercury poisoning. Further, it appeared that even though mercury levels in the river's fish were declining over time, for unknown reasons many people's symptoms were getting more instead of less severe (Aiken 2004b, 2004c).

After their visit to Grassy, members of the Japanese team made their way to Whitedog First Nation to conduct the same series of tests. On their last afternoon in the region, a small exhibition powwow was held in their honor. Despite the ongoing renovation of Whitedog's school, close to sixty people filled the gymnasium for the event. On the wall, someone had taped up a map of "Mercury River"—a map of the English-Wabigoon River system flowing west from Dryden and outlined in a toxic shade of pink. Following demonstrations of men's and women's traditional, men's grass, and women's jingle and shawl dances, representatives of both First Nations presented the Japanese guests with neatly wrapped gifts. Dr. Harada and three other doctors received eagle feathers in recognition of their work in the two communities. A feast of soup, manoomin, and bannock closed the event.

Neither the Wild Meat Contaminant study nor the Japanese medical team's visit were formally linked to the Grassy Narrows blockade. In fact, these events attracted dozens of people who had chosen *not* to get involved in anti-clearcutting activism. While most GNEG members associated the lasting effects of mercury with their current anti-clearcutting campaign—both, after all, depended upon a historically constituted awareness of the industrially altered environment as a potential health risk and a possible source of harm to Anishinaabe cultural life—the renewed interest in environmental health did not inspire more support for the blockaders' cause. Nor, it seemed, did anyone expect it to; the differences that divided Grassy Narrows residents ran too deep. Still, blockaders and non-blockaders alike coped with the physical and cultural impacts of mercury poisoning. In a way few other recent events had, reconsidering mercury's shared legacy brought the people of Grassy Narrows First Nation together for a common purpose.

With summer winding down, members of GNEG and the Christian Peacemaker Team gathered in the Slant Lake roundhouse for an evening potluck. As the small group feasted on chili and bannock, people fretted over Abitibi's plans to spray herbicides in the coming weeks. Perhaps due to the recent focus on environmental health, the spraying that always seemed perfectly timed to correspond to the annual blueberry harvest was on many minds. After dinner, everyone settled in for a round of blockade songs. For activists at Grassy Narrows, the third phase of the blockade had been filled with tension: tension between blockaders and elected leaders and between blockaders and non-blockaders, tension between projections of unity and realities of division, tension between the blockaders' internal and external agendas. With more talks with Abitibi on the Chief and Council's agenda and opinions within the First Nation more divided than ever, people at Slant Lake that evening felt a warm nostalgia for the late nights around the campfire of the blockade's first year.

Eight

Beyond the Blockade

As the chill of fall settled over Slant Lake once again, it seemed that the Grassy Narrows blockade was not simply slow moving—it was entering a new phase altogether. Periodic meetings between the band's Chief and Council, Abitibi-Consolidated, and the Ontario Ministry of Natural Resource (who had recently come to the table) were underway, despite the fact that consensus among First Nation members remained elusive. Responding to the disheartening situation at home, Grassy Narrows activists turned their attention outward.

As noted in chapter 2, Ronald Niezen defines *indigenism* as an emerging form of indigenous activism fueled by the development of global communication networks and the resulting consciousness of shared situations and goals (2003: 16). More than any other period, the fourth phase of the blockade exemplified indigenism in action. By the fall of 2004, blockaders were traveling far and wide to share their story and learn from the experiences and expertise of others. Block-ade-related events in this period were as likely to occur in the city of Winnipeg as at the blockade itself. Even more significantly, it now seemed that Grassy Narrows activists were prepared to pass the torch of resistance to other Native communities. In mid-January of 2005, Anishinaabe activists from Mishkeegogamang First Nation arrived at Grassy Narrows to meet the blockaders. In the months that followed, they staged their own blockades and posted the following statement—directed at the GNEG blockaders—on the Friends of Grassy Narrows website:

We welcome you to come and join us in our fight, as we share a history, and *it is your stand that has inspired us to take a stand.* Now that we are in the same situation as the people of Grassy Narrows and other First Nations, we are starting to recognize the trails [*sic*] and tribulations that the people of Grassy Narrows experienced, and the big obstacles and challenges that face you still today. We ask that you support us in any way you can, especially by using your *powerful network of allies and global supporters* to spread the word about our struggle to survive. In unity we stand strong, proud, and free. (April 6, 2005, emphasis added)

Grassy's activists had long been a part of a network; a technologically enabled "imagined community" (Anderson 1991) composed of indigenous activists and supporters that extended across North America and beyond. This imagined community was now becoming increasingly real. Since its inception, the Grassy Narrows blockade had inspired First Nations activists in all directions. As the blockade entered its fourth and final phase, motivating and encouraging others emerged as the blockaders' primary focus.

As the summer of 2004 drew to a close, Grassy Narrows activists were busy developing and sustaining their large network of colleagues and supporters. In the last days of August, the Grassy Narrows Environmental Group sent a representative to Montreal to attend an activist training conference sponsored by Rainforest Action Network (RAN).[1] A month later, a young man from Grassy visited Vladivostok, on Russia's northeastern coast, to attend a Taiga Rescue Network (TRN) symposium. Meanwhile, talks between the First Nation's elected leaders, Abitibi-Consolidated, and the OMNR began taking place on a bimonthly basis in Kenora, Winnipeg, Thunder Bay, or Montreal. After the rocky start in November of 2003 and cancellations in December of 2003 and June of 2004, meetings occurred in September and November of 2004 and again in January of 2005. Some GNEG members purposely chose not to participate in the negotiation process; others suspected that Grassy's Chief and Councilors were intentionally keeping them uninformed about upcoming sessions. While Abitibi officials remained optimistic that the talks would lead to a solution (Gauthier 2004a), all the First Nation members I spoke to—blockaders and elected leaders alike—felt that progress to this point had been slow indeed. The parties seemed as far as ever from seeing eye to eye.

By the fall of 2004, loggers still lacked access to the area they'd vacated during the previous year's roving blockades. For activists at Grassy, the cessation of logging in some parts of their Traditional Land Use Area was a reminder of past victories. They had succeeded—at least temporarily—in saving some of their land from clearcutting. To the contractors that had been evicted, however, the stacks of logs left at the site following their hasty withdrawal looked quite different. As one contractor put it, "There's a lot of money there just rotting . . . it's a terrible sight" (Gauthier 2004b).

"It looks like infighting, but it's not"

With logging still ongoing in the northern parts of the GNTLUA, GNEG's core members were determined to explore all potential avenues for slowing its pace. Speaking to non-Native environmentalist audiences—to people who might somehow be able to get the ear of corporate and government interests that had eluded First Nation members for so long—was part of this strategy. Among the many blockade-related events that took place in Winnipeg was a film screening and discussion held at the University of Manitoba on October 2, 2004.

At a Sustainable Campuses Conference that gathered over ninety university students from across Canada, anti-clearcutting activism at Grassy Narrows was allotted a late-afternoon breakout session. In a small but densely packed classroom, about thirty conference attendees waited patiently for the activists to arrive. As Judy, Barbara, and Roberta entered the room, one of several Friends of Grassy Narrows members at the conference popped *As Long as the Rivers Flow* (the Indymedia film about the blockade's first year) into the VCR. Everyone watched intently as GNEG's earlier actions at Slant Lake and in Kenora unfolded before their eyes. The film followed J. B. to a clearcut, where he expressed his sorrow and rage. It ended to the beat of the Grassy women's song: "We will sing and dance and fight and die as long as the rivers flow ya-hey-ya."

People were eager to learn more. In the discussion following the film, the Anishinaabe women fielded a half-hour of questions. Students at the conference wanted to hear about what was happening at the blockade now. Judy and Roberta provided an update. Although the cutting right around the reserve had stopped, Roberta told the group, portions of Grassy's Traditional Land Use Area was still being cut, including parts of her own trapline. Judy added that Kitty, the young mother so central to the Grassy Narrows blockade, had recently posted a public statement on Friends of Grassy Narrows' website implicating her as one of the instigators of the Slant Lake blockade. It had been Kitty's act, Judy explained, that set everything else in motion. Judy also mentioned the ongoing talks between the Chief and Council and Abitibi-Consolidated. With five meetings planned over the next few months, Judy worried aloud that their elected leaders were being "bulldozed" into an agreement. As an Indian Act government, she pointed out, the Chief and Council only has jurisdiction within the boundaries of the reserve. But, problematically, they were the ones doing all the negotiating. Sensing a swell of tension, one audience member posed a particularly thorny question. Did the blockaders feel Chief and Council had the authority to speak for them? For a few seconds, the room went silent. The three sisters from Grassy conferred quietly in Anishinaabemowin. Roberta filled in with a powerful clarifying statement: The blockaders didn't blame the people in those positions [Chief and Council] because this type of blame is exactly what government and industry want—divide and conquer.

When I talked to Judy about the same issue a few weeks later, she explained the tensions between Grassy's elected leadership and its blockaders in clear terms. "It looks like infighting, but it's not," she told me, "It's fighting the Canadian government." From the blockaders' point of view, the Indian Act system and those who participate in it are an extension of the Canadian government. In this context, an understanding of factionalism as "a disagreement over the means . . . [and] not the goal" (Siegel and Beals 1960: 109, quoted in Geertz 1994: 208) is germane to the Grassy Narrows case. Both GNEG and the elected band leadership want the best for their community. Both groups, too, share an ultimate goal of self-determination. But they disagree deeply regarding how to achieve these goals; while the Chief and Council chooses to work within the Indian Act system, the blockaders advocate moving beyond it.

A Visit from APTN: First Nations Media Communities

The following week was the height of fall, and the poplar leaves along Jones Road had turned a dazzling shade of bright yellow. A film crew was on its way from APTN (Aboriginal Peoples' Television Network) headquarters in Winnipeg to the Slant Lake blockade. APTN produces and airs programs intended primarily for indigenous Canadian audiences, although quite a few non-Natives with an interest in First Nations culture and issues also tune in. They could not have asked for a more perfect October day. Activists at Grassy Narrows had been informed by telephone of the planned visit and the crew had invited J. B. Fobister to come out to Slant Lake to star in a segment about the blockade, the community's youth, and cultural revitalization at Grassy Narrows intended for a weekly show called *Sharing Circle*.

Just after noon on October 9th, I pulled into Slant Lake to find J. B. sitting close to the sacred fire with a younger man who had been an active participant throughout the blockade. Although the Slant Lake site was rarely populated in the fall of 2004—especially in the middle of the day—their presence had an air of permanence. The sacred fire had been lit and the two men talked casually as they awaited the television crew's arrival. It wasn't long before four men pulled up in a black Jeep Cherokee with Manitoba plates. Looking polished and urban next to the men from Grassy, they joined them around the fire.

J. B. and the crew's director found plenty to discuss and their informal conversation continued for close to an hour. When the director candidly asked what he thought the loggers working in the area really wanted, J. B.'s reply was instant. As he saw it, the forest industry wanted every available log in Grassy's traditional territory. For me—familiar with J. B.'s outlook after months of dialogue—it was enlightening to sit back and listen as he set well-rehearsed themes to new words. J. B. appeared eager to portray the blockade as a grassroots challenge to the status quo. The blockade, he told the crew, had been separate from Grassy Narrows' Chief and Council all along—separate from Canada's Indian Act and its imposed band-governance system. The blockade at Slant Lake, J. B. said, was a way of stepping outside of this box.

The next vehicle to appear at Slant Lake was Judy DaSilva's gray minivan. Judy had rounded up a group of teenagers from around the reserve to take part in the filming session. As the visitors rose from their chairs and prepared to film a string of interviews in front of Slant Lake's traditional-style log cabin, the crew's director pulled J. B. aside. APTN's visit, he said, was important not only because of the attention it could bring to their cause, but because of the "media training" it offered activists at Grassy Narrows. He spoke with practiced authority: Everything that exists in the media is propaganda, he told him, and the footage produced today would be no exception. They could, however, slant the propaganda in a direction favorable for the Grassy Narrows blockade and First Nations people more generally. For a final shot, the director arranged a group of young people around the sacred fire, usually a site of quiet contemplation rather than a gathering place for youth. They appeared to be listening intently to what one young man had to say. The shot made for a compelling and symbolic (if artificially constructed) image—the youth of Grassy Narrows gathered around the sacred fire at Slant Lake to listen, learn, and renew their cultural heritage.

The APTN film crew's visit spoke loudly to the significance of the media for the Grassy Narrows blockaders. Like GNEG's non-Native supporters, the Aboriginal and alternative media recognized and promoted Grassy Narrows activists' influence—at least as far as blockade matters were concerned—as equaling that of the Chief and Council. Further, since the early days of their fight against clearcutting, GNEG members had worked to enter into and expand an existing network of First Nations activists. The media was an important catalyst for this network's development. The APTN crew, the thousands of Canadians who would potentially view the program being produced, and the activists at Grassy Narrows who spoke or posed for the camera on that October day were all part of a continuously evolving First Nations media community.

The indigenous movement depends upon and draws together a technologically enabled "imagined community" (Anderson 1991), a "mediascape" (Appadurai 1996) composed of indigenous people and their supporters. As a result of this dynamic, activists at Grassy Narrows are knowledgeable about ongoing struggles in places they have never been to that involve people with whom they have no direct contact. And, as Kitty's remarks at the Keys Lake beach in July of 2004 (see chapter 2) indicate, they feel a genuine sense of solidarity with distant Native groups based on mutual membership in this abstract community. Beyond the face-to-face interaction that occurs

when people travel to a conference, beyond the technologically facilitated communication that allows spoken or written words to flow
across many miles, the network of indigenous activists exists as a community of the mind.

In his discussion of the indigenous movement, Niezen (2003:
225n12) compares the rise of nationalism facilitated by the development of print media and the key role played by the proliferation of
electronic media in the growth of indigenism. In the latter case, those
considered "marginal" to the nation-state have been able to access
new channels of communication and create their own community of
resistance. This democratization of knowledge means that First
Nations activists now have access to a vast network of information
available through the Internet, television, and other media circuits.
Critically, it also means that they are able to shape how their communities are represented to the wider public; in this context, the media
has become a vehicle for the promotion of cultural revitalization,
renewal, and pride.

Renewing, Reinventing: Constructing a Wigwam at Slant Lake

Two carloads of longtime Friends of Grassy Narrows members also took
advantage of the beautiful weekend to make the trip from Winnipeg to
Grassy Narrows. The journey made for an attractive escape from the
city; it allowed FGN members to spend a peaceful weekend catching
up with friends and helping erect a wigwam to shelter the sacred fire.[2]
Careful not to disrupt the afternoon filming session, the visitors pulled
in at Slant Lake almost immediately after the APTN crew departed.
The blockade had experienced a changing of the guard. In a matter of
minutes, the focus at Slant Lake shifted from media-inspired perform-
ance to the physical work of wigwam construction.

The project was something the women of GNEG had been con-
templating for a long time. Recurring fires had plagued the canvas tipi
that stood over the sacred fire through the blockade's first two winters. After the original tipi burned to the ground it was replaced with
a similar model. This replacement burned as well but had remained at
the site, patched together with tarps, for many months. The tipis all
fared poorly in high winds and required frequent repairs. By October
of 2004, Judy and Roberta had decided that a large wigwam-style

structure would prove a more durable option. In addition, this new structure would be more specifically Anishinaabe; it would provide a concrete link to Grassy Narrows residents' cultural heritage.

For weeks, Judy and Roberta deliberated over the building plans: how many poles to include, what materials to use, how wide and how high the wigwam should be. The previous year, Roberta had built a similar structure on her trapline and had an orderly plan sketched out on paper. The women drew on her experience and consulted elders before reaching consensus. Preparations had taken place over the previous week: Judy's husband had been enlisted to cut twenty-four young poplar trees that would serve as the wigwam's frame. Judy and Roberta were soon present to direct the process, and a number of people from the reserve appeared to lend a hand or survey the action. As the work of construction got underway, the able-bodied visitors took turns digging holes for the wigwam's support poles by pounding a three-foot-long hollow metal rod into the ground with the back of an axe. As soil oozed from the top of the rod, the holes grew gradually deeper. It was a time-consuming, backbreaking, and (in my estimation) dangerous process. All of the wigwam's poles were in place by nightfall, sticking straight up into the air in an open circle.

As it grew darker and colder, most of the twenty-odd people now on hand worked together to bend and tie four of the poles together at the top in order to form the wigwam's symmetrical support system. No one seemed to have considered the difficulty of reaching the poles' tips—nearly fifteen feet overhead—and a lasso mechanism was devised. Work continued by firelight. Wigwams like this used to be put up in one day, Roberta mentioned casually, by small groups of women. Granted this wigwam was an extra-large one, but her point was well taken: Traditional Anishinaabe women had been dedicated and highly skilled workers.[3] With the central frame complete and the chill of night descending quickly, remaining work on the wigwam was saved for another day.

As Kimberly Christen (2006: 425) observes, "Tradition is mobile and fixed, part of a dialogue between community members and outsiders, linked to material needs and cultural responsibilities. Tradition is always in the making." For the activists of Grassy Narrows First Nation, the wigwam erected in the fall of 2004 represented a unique merger of innovative and traditional ideas, materials, processes, and meanings. Like the tipis that enclosed the fire previously, the wigwam's door faced east. Around the fire at each cardinal direction a different colored tobacco tie placed atop a thin wooden pole corresponded to the emblematic shades of the medicine wheel. Reflecting Anishinaabe as well as pan-Indian traditionality, the wigwam led people to ponder their heritage and the ways of life experienced by their great-grandparents in a way few other structures could.

Over the next month, the wigwam gradually moved toward completion. Judy and Roberta could often be found at Slant Lake, bending and shaping the poplar frame and, finally, securing a tan canvas as the wigwam's domed roof. A few days after the group construction effort of October 9th, the two sisters worked on the wigwam late into a night of bitter cold and wind. The following day, Judy reflected on the experience. Pushing your limits like this makes your spirit stronger, she said. She told me how whenever she worries about her children spending time out in the cold, she remembers how her ancestors survived life in the bush. Living in dwellings much like the new wigwam at Slant Lake, *they* had been able to withstand such cold.

Intended to host gatherings and meetings, the Slant Lake wigwam was much larger than those of days past. Emblematic of the blockade and its ongoing political resistance as well as the cultural revitalization so many blockaders valued, the wigwam's symbolic presence matched its large physical size. Fittingly, the wigwam represented the blockaders' links to a larger-than-life "traditional" past. For indigenous peoples long denied control of their own histories, reclaiming the meanings of the past and expressing them in the present often become important projects of cultural renewal. The past, Jonathan Friedman (1994: 141) theorizes, "is always practiced in the present, not because the past imposes itself, but because subjects in the present fashion the past in the practice of their social identity." Just as a historical text may refract rather than perfectly reflect the place and time it describes (Whitehead 1997), for twenty-first-century Anishinaabeg, the traditional past becomes a mirror not only of what was, but also of what people today desire it to be.

For the blockaders, the world of the traditional is socially and orally—if not personally—remembered. Perceptions of traditionality shape a distinct cultural identity that motivates activists at Grassy Narrows to persist in their struggle to sustain their environment, their culture, and their political rights. Like the building of the birchbark canoe the previous spring, the wigwam erected in the fall of 2004 was one way the people of Grassy Narrows attempted to assert not just a Native identity, but a specifically Anishinaabe one as well. A synthesis of tradition and modernity shaped the wigwam's physical construction from start to finish. Critically, this complex fusion also shaped how the blockaders at Grassy experienced the construction process and how they viewed the final product of their labor. As First Nation members and outsiders worked together, they solidified their personal and political ties while simultaneously responding to a perceived pragmatic necessity.

Walking Together

Throughout the fall, meetings between Grassy Narrows' Chief and Council, Abitibi-Consolidated, and the OMNR continued. Although Steve Fobister persisted in his search for consensus, it was becoming increasingly obvious that a united Grassy Narrows First Nation position would never exist. The blockade also remained a busy place. Yet, as GNEG's leaders pointed out, the energy at Slant Lake seemed to have changed. With the sacred fire no longer burning continuously and only a part-time presence at the site, the blockade was no longer a constant vigil. Even within the tight-knit group of activists, some blockaders lamented that communications seemed to be breaking down. With the second anniversary of the blockade less than a month away, whether or not the date would be marked by celebration was still undecided.

On November 11th, it was the blockaders' turn to drive the highway between Grassy Narrows and Winnipeg once again. Judy DaSilva had been invited to speak at a Multi-Faith Forum on the Environment. Held in the multipurpose room of a local church, a long table for the six panelists faced eight round tables for guests. Several Friends of Grassy Narrows members and three Christian Peacemakers sat amid roughly fifty other attendees. Each of the speakers—a Baha'i man, a Muslim woman, two Quakers, one interdenominational Christian, and Judy—were given ten minutes apiece. Judy's talk was last on the evening's program. Casually dressed in her usual ribbon skirt and tee-shirt and speaking from the heart, the strength of Judy's personality and emotions reverberated through the room.

Judy began by sharing some of the thoughts that had entered her mind as she traveled into the city that day. Sometimes, Judy said, she feels like a second-class citizen on her own land. She wanted to be sure everyone understood that the Indian reserves dotting northwestern Ontario and Manitoba are far from the only Anishinaabe land, that Winnipeg itself overlies her people's land as well. This awareness needs to extend across the entire continent; wherever we go in North America, Judy told the audience, we are always on Native land. She continued in a stream-of-consciousness fashion, gathering her strength as she spoke. She contrasted the square buildings of the city—the church hosting the forum was no exception—with the rounded forms of Anishinaabe culture. In her world, she pointed out, everything is circular.[4] Everything is open. Next, Judy lingered for several minutes on the topic of Native rights. Anishinaabe people's rights come from the land, Judy told the group. They are forever. She said she could picture her feet touching the ground and the rights flowing up through them. Finally and directly, Judy's main message was clear—it is about "putting aside grudges and understanding that we're all in this together, whether we like it or not." Natives and non-Natives must walk together and work together if the earth is to survive. At the end of her talk she invited everyone to walk with her and her people. At an environmental forum, Judy had spoken seamlessly of Native rights, Anishinaabe ways, and her hopes for the future of the earth. She received an enthusiastic round of applause.

Networking with non-Native environmentalists was clearly important to Judy and the other members of GNEG. They were, after all, willing to travel for hours to participate in events like this one, usually with little compensation. So, did the blockaders at Grassy Narrows consider themselves "environmentalists"? I once asked Judy—viewed by many outsiders as the quintessential indigenous environmental crusader—if she thought of herself as an environmentalist. After all, she'd been nominated for numerous environmental awards and had been portrayed in dozens of media reports as one of the region's most prominent environmental spokespersons. But for her, she told me, all of this was just a label.

Grassy Narrows activists acknowledge environmentalism as an external category. They are well aware of the differences that divide their outlooks and objectives from those of non-Native environmentalists; as we have seen, non-Native environmentalists and First

Nations activists tend to have very dissimilar goals and agendas; while environmentalists typically view ecological protection as paramount, the Grassy Narrows blockaders see the environment as inseparable from their cultural and political goals. Still, as Tsing (2005) points out, common movements can and do arise in the face of social and political difference. The Grassy Narrows blockaders have regarded environmentalism as a place where their interests and the interests of outsiders can productively intersect. Like their adoption of Earth Day and their use of "environmental" terminology, Judy's participation in the Multi-Faith Forum on the Environment signaled the blockaders' perception of the environmental movement as a prospective middle ground and a productive maneuvering point for their networking efforts.

Beyond the Blockade

On the 3rd of December, the blockade's second anniversary passed with little fanfare. It seemed that most of Grassy's activists had gone to Kenora for the day or were doing their holiday shopping in Winnipeg. Still, Kenora's *Miner and News* recognized the anniversary with a front-page article. With a war metaphor for a headline—"All Quiet on Northern Front Two Years after Grassy Narrows Blockade Began"—the piece alluded to the tensions that continued to surround the blockade (Aiken 2004d). The article sympathetically observed that the blockade had "become an important symbol for defenders of treaty rights and environmentalists." Dave Canfield, the mayor of Kenora as well as a local Abitibi employee, felt differently about Grassy Narrows' ongoing stand. Canfield emphasized the hardship the blockade heralded for a town with a struggling timber-based economy. "The world's changing and you don't need any added volatility," he told the *Miner and News* reporter (Aiken 2004d). With no media presence, around twenty-five blockaders and blockade supporters quietly celebrated the anniversary with a December 9th gathering in the Slant Lake roundhouse. As winter deepened, Grassy Narrows activists spent the holiday season at home with family and friends.

In mid-January of 2005, on a day so cold the air formed a cloud of vapor around any living body, a group of activists from Mishkeegogamang First Nation paid a visit to Grassy Narrows and the Slant Lake blockade. Only five days before, close to one hundred people from Mishkeegogamang and other Native communities in the Sioux Lookout, Ontario area had marched in protest of forestry practices in their region. With plans to protest again the following month, the visitors came to Grassy Narrows hoping to learn from the experience of the GNEG blockaders. With the windchill in the negative forties, few people were out and about. Even the reserve's dogs dozed like draftstops, curled in front of doors to absorb warmth seeping out from woodstove-heated interiors (a few others lay tail-to-face in the road, soaking in the solar heating that made the ice-covered blacktop slightly warmer than the surrounding air). Still, word of the visitors' arrival spread quickly by telephone as they drove around the reserve in their white van.

J. B. was ready to lead the group out to Slant Lake, and the three women and two men from Mishkeegogamang quickly piled on extra layers of clothing. The blockade turn-around had been plowed several days earlier and was still passable. As everyone filed into the wigwam and took seats on icy chairs, the sacred fire glowed faintly. J. B. added wood, but the bright flames did little to warm the frozen air. J. B. smirked as he told the visitors that the one thing everyone had learned at the blockade was how to build a fire. His tone became serious, then, as he summed up the lessons of the Grassy Narrows blockade.

Over the next hour and a half, J. B. supplied a well-thought-out inventory of what had worked well at Grassy Narrows and what he thought they could have done better. He passed these hard-won lessons to the people of Mishkeegogamang First Nation:

- Act now, before it's too late. If you look around near the city of Thunder Bay, there are no large trees left, only young ones. Take action before this happens to your land too.
- You can't always count on your Chief and Council to take care of things like this. In a lot of cases they are better at talk than they are at action.
- Have confidence in what you can accomplish. Three years earlier, people at Grassy started thinking about blockading

when they realized that other kinds of protest weren't working. At that point, only a few people had supported the
idea. Two years ago, when they finally decided to go ahead
with the blockade, they ended up having sixty people come
out on the first day.

- Keep things as peaceful as possible. Do not include any
  weapons or violence in your actions.
- Recognize the important role of the media and send out as
  many press releases as you can. This is how you widen your
  base of support.
- Involve sympathetic outsiders, including non-Natives and
  environmental groups. Educate yourself about your rights.
  Learn about the Supreme Court decisions that set positive
  precedents for Native rights and lands and apply what you
  learn from as many angles as possible.

Most importantly, J. B. told the visitors, they need to truly believe in
their rights and themselves. They must believe the land is theirs. The
treaties their forbearers signed over one hundred years ago, he said,
had been treaties of peace and friendship rather than land surrender
treaties (see chapter 2). "We've proven something here in Grassy," J.
B. proclaimed. Together, the blockaders had proven—to themselves if
not to the provincial government and general public—that their
people had never given up their land.

One of the women had started shivering perceptibly, but the conversation continued as activists from the two First Nations compared
notes. As at Grassy Narrows, logging—especially clearcutting—was
the Mishkeegogamang activists' primary concern. The visitors were
also worried about mining in their immediate vicinity; core and
sample drilling, they said, had already released toxins into their waterways. Activists from both communities, it turned out, had taken similar routes to direct action, participating in corporate/OMNR open
houses before escalating to conventional protests and finally to blockades. As the conversation started to wane, J. B. told the visitors that
they seemed to be off to a better start than the blockaders at Grassy
had been in the beginning; the people of Mishkeegogamang had managed to mobilize a lot of support in a short time. On the way out of
the wigwam, J. B. spoke optimistically of the value of working
together and supporting each other.

Leaving Slant Lake at dusk, I contemplated the significance of the Mishkeegogamang First Nation members' visit. People from other Native communities were now approaching the blockaders in order to learn from their years of experience. It seemed that activists at Grassy Narrows First Nation were ready to pass the torch. As the sun slid beneath the horizon, things slipped into perspective. The blockaders had not yet been able to stop clearcutting within the GNTLUA entirely, nor had they gained control over their traditional lands, but they had succeeded in other important ways. The Grassy Narrows blockade had earned its place as a key chapter in the history of First Nations activism and contributed to the ongoing struggle for Anishinaabe cultural revitalization and self-determination. For GNEG members and dozens of young people at Grassy, participation in the blockade had ushered in a new sense of community and cultural pride. For First Nations activists elsewhere, the blockade had become a model and an inspiration.

At an icy morning march on February 10th, about thirty Anishinaabe activists walked the short distance from the Sioux Lookout Indian Friendship Centre to the local Ontario Ministry of Natural Resources office to convey their opposition to the St. Raphael Signature Site, a proposed multi-use management area. Following the march, the protestors slowed traffic so they could distribute informational leaflets to passersby and sent a letter to area First Nations asking for unity and support. On that day, the Mishkeegogamang activists proudly carried the torch of the Grassy Narrows blockade through the streets of Sioux Lookout.

Conclusion

The Blockade Is Still There

This isn't just a hobby. It is something you do *forever*. It is your life.
—Judy DaSilva, November 2004

I set out to discover what motivated members of Grassy Narrows First Nation to take direct action to protect their homeland from industrial clearcutting. As the story of the Grassy Narrows blockade makes clear, one-dimensional portraits that romanticize and naturalize relationships between indigenous peoples and the environments they live in fail to do justice to the complexity of their motives. History, politics, and culture mediate Grassy Narrows activists' views of the environment and contour their visions of its best possible future.

I have argued that we must attend to all of these things—to historical, political, and cultural elements as well as environmental ones—in order to effectively answer some of environmental anthropology's most fundamental questions: How can we make sense of the multifaceted relationships that hold peoples and places together? How do people give cultural meaning to the environments in which they live? And why do they treat them as they do? Overly simplistic imaginings of indigenous peoples' relationships to the environment continue to contour anthropologies of environment and landscape and shape popular perceptions of First Nations activism. This narrative analysis of Anishinaabe anti-clearcutting activism advocates a way to move beyond this dilemma: We must look to the rich cultural and political contexts that inform and underlie indigenous activists' connections to the lands they work so tirelessly to protect.

Like the blockade itself, the historical foundations of Anishinaabe anti-clearcutting activism must be examined through a multifocal lens. A wide range of factors inspired anti-clearcutting activism at Grassy Narrows First Nation. As described in chapter 1, in the space of only a few generations land-based subsistence shifted from a relatively unquestioned way of life to an explicit marker of Anishinaabe cultural identity. Now at least as symbolically meaningful as economically important, the practice of traditional subsistence, the wild foods it yields, and the land base it requires have become essential— although increasingly threatened—ingredients in Grassy Narrows activists' struggle for cultural preservation and political self-determination. As chapter 2 explains, long-term changes in the political climate and the wider indigenous empowerment movement also contributed to the rise of activism at Grassy Narrows. And, as chapter 3 shows, from the relocation of the 1960s and mercury poisoning of the 1970s to the industrial-scale logging so conspicuous today, changes in the immediate environment surrounding Grassy Narrows and resulting transformations in First Nation members' conceptions of the natural world have guided the development of the community's anti-clearcutting movement.

I returned home in the spring of 2005 to begin the challenging task of telling the story of the Grassy Narrows First Nation blockade. Yet, even now, the blockade and its story are far from over. As we prepared to say our goodbyes, one woman at Grassy resolutely assured me that the blockade was still there, that her people still believed in it. The environmental, political, and cultural concerns that moved First Nation members to action remain as valid—and as urgent—as ever. For the next year, the situation at Grassy remained essentially unchanged. Talks between the First Nation's Chief and Council, Abitibi-Consolidated, and the OMNR had not produced a solution and shifted back into hiatus. Blockaders continued to travel to Winnipeg and other cities for speaking engagements and conferences. The blockade's network of non-Native supporters continued to grow and members of Grassy's environmental group continued to serve as influential role models for other First Nations activists in other communities. As before, the sacred fire at Slant Lake was rekindled on a regular basis and the site remained a frequent gathering place for Grassy Narrows activists and their families.

The summer of 2006 saw a resurgence of blockade activity. On June 16th, Grassy Narrows youth and elders convened at Slant Lake for a three-day conference on healing and leadership. A logo I hadn't seen before appeared prominently on the poster produced to advertise the event. The new emblem depicted a solitary blockader standing, arms outstretched, in front of the intense headlights of a logging truck. The figure was outlined in bright red. Superimposed in the foreground and completing the colors of the medicine wheel stood three smaller figures. Inspired by a photograph taken in the early days of the blockade, the image was a vivid reminder of the blockaders' lengthy struggle and unwavering determination. Around the same time, a new sign was erected at the Slant Lake blockade. The large billboard was visible to anyone traveling north on the gravel road. In plain view of non-Native hunters and anglers, the sign was a concrete extension of the blockaders' public education project. White with red lettering, it proclaimed:

> Let it be known that this sign marks the centre of the Asub-peeschoseewagong Anishinaabe territory. From time immemorial this land has been occupied by and cherished by Asubpeeschoseewagong Anishinaabek. The land is integral to our identity and existence as a people. From this point as far as the Asubpeeschoseewagong Anishinaabek have traveled is by divine right declared Anishinaabe territory. What the creator gave to the Anishinaabe only the creator can take away.

For more than three years, the Slant Lake blockade had been the spatial and symbolic center of activism at Grassy Narrows First Nation. As the new sign boldly proclaimed, the blockaders now claimed it as the heart of Asubpeeschoseewagong land, identity, and life.

In mid-July, Rainforest Action Network collaborated with the Grassy Narrows Environmental Group to host an "Earth Justice Gathering" at the Slant Lake site. Approximately one hundred First Nations activists and non-Native environmentalists from across North America attended a week of workshops. The gathering made national news when protestors blockaded a stretch of the Trans-Canada

Highway near Kenora on July 13th. There, they erected a large metal tripod over the highway. A non-Native activist dangled from the formation and a large banner attached to the structure read "Save Grassy Narrows Boreal Forest" (CBC 2006; Bujold and Aiken 2006). Although the protestors left the scene peacefully the same evening, a second blockade at a nearby provincial highway bridge led to ten arrests—the first ever associated with the Grassy Narrows blockade. Three Grassy Narrows First Nation members were among those taken into custody.

The partnership between Grassy Narrows and RAN grew stronger as the seasons passed. In mid-January of 2007, Grassy Narrows declared a moratorium on clearcutting and other industrial activity within its Traditional Land Use Area. Supported and publicized by RAN, Grassy's open letter was directed at government leaders and industry:

> We now declare a moratorium on further industrial activity in our Traditional Territory until such a time as the Governments of Canada and Ontario restore their honour and obtain the consent of our community in these decisions that will forever alter the future of our people . . . . If you choose to ignore our rights we will have no choice but take more action with our supporters in the forest, in the markets, in the legislature, and in the courts to assert our rights as the Indigenous people of this land. We will determine the course of our own future and we will care for our Traditional Territory.[1]

Meanwhile, RAN launched a public campaign pressuring corporations to stop using wood from the area. The group's strategy was based on supply chain logic: Many of the trees cut in the Whiskey Jack Forest traveled to Abitibi's pulp mill in Fort Francis, Ontario and later across the Rainy River to the Boise Cascade paper plant in International Falls, Minnesota for processing. Boise Cascade owned two retail office supply chains—Grand & Toy and OfficeMax—where paper products containing this wood were sold. RAN's efforts culminated in an International Day of Action that brought organized protests to Grand & Toy and OfficeMax stores in over thirty North American cities on January 30, 2008 (Tiner 2008). Less than a month later, Boise Cascade responded to RAN's actions. Citing a recent Amnesty

International (2007) report calling on corporations to find alternative sources of wood fiber, the company stated on February 27th that it would cease purchasing wood from Grassy Narrows' traditional territory without the community's support (Earley 2008).

On May 11, 2008 the Ontario Ministry of Natural Resources and Grassy Narrows First Nation entered into a memorandum of understanding to initiate formal negotiations—expected to take up to four years to complete—under the guidance of former Canadian Supreme Court justice Frank Iacobucci. And then it happened. Exactly five-and-a-half years after the blockade began, AbitibiBowater (the result of a 2007 merger between Abitibi-Consolidated Incorporated and Bowater Incorporated) announced its intention to stop using wood from the Whiskey Jack Forest in its paper products and relinquish its license to log in the area. As AbitibiBowater CEO David Paterson acknowledged in a June 3rd letter to Ontario minister of natural resources Donna Cansfield, "We have made the decision to discontinue using wood from the Whiskey Jack Forest while the Government of Ontario and the Grassy Narrows First Nation conduct their negotiations."[2] Corporate representatives explained the decision in economic terms; with new sources of wood becoming available elsewhere due to a downturn in demand, waiting four years to determine the future tenability of logging in the Whiskey Jack simply did not fit the company's business interests (Gorrie 2008).

With the door left open for other companies to step into the license voluntarily vacated by AbitibiBowater (slated to run through 2023) Grassy Narrows' activists had no plans to abandon the blockade anytime soon. As J. B. Fobister commented in the wake of the victory, "Grassy will not stop until we are in control of our lands and until our territories have been withdrawn from all clear-cut logging. Our moratorium on industry without our consent still stands, and we will enforce it."[3] Still, the Grassy Narrows blockade can in many ways be considered a remarkable success. The fact that citizens of Grassy Narrows have managed, at least for the time being, to save their trees and traditional territory from the largest newsprint company in the world is a remarkable achievement. As well, although challenging inequity within the wider North American socioeconomic system remains a multigenerational project, the blockade has inspired other First Nations communities to join the ongoing fight for Native rights. Canada's endorsement of the United Nations Declaration on the

Rights of Indigenous Peoples in November of 2010 indicates that public sentiment and policy are becoming increasingly responsive to an international "politics of embarrassment" (see Niezen 1998) and is regarded by many Native leaders as a long overdue step in the right direction (Cultural Survival 2010). Of equal importance, the blockade launched an era of cultural consciousness, revitalization, and pride among Grassy's activists and youth that is likely to have positive repercussions for years to come.

But the fight was never easy. As Steve Fobister told me in January of 2005, he felt he'd "aged ten years in the last three." So, why continue? Why keep doing activist work? Months of reflection on this question led me to a surprisingly straightforward conclusion. People everywhere do what they perceive as necessary to their mental, physical, and spiritual survival. Very few of us would abandon the things we cherish most—our children and families, our cultural identities and fundamental rights—for the sake of even the noblest of causes. Instead, we choose to act *because* these things are so dear to us. We act in order to sustain and secure their future. When the people of Grassy Narrows took action to protect their land, they did so with the recognition that the fate of the earth and the fate of so much more are tightly interwoven. Kitty explained her decision to initiate the blockade on that cold December day:

> We grew up hunting and fishing and just living off the land. We still have our culture and beliefs. That's what we wanted to save that day. Laying those logs on the road wasn't just against clearcutting, it was for *everything* that affects Anishinaabeg negatively today.[4]

Environmental anthropologists, activists, and organizers can learn from this perspective. In this spirit, I conclude with some of the Grassy Narrows blockade's most important lessons.

Environmental issues are social and political issues.

The story of the Grassy Narrows blockade clearly illustrates the intertwined complexity of environmental, cultural, and political dimensions of Anishinaabe activism. Yet, the same dynamic inseparability applies to all of our lives, regardless of where we live or how compartmentalized our societies appear. Environmental justice scholar Bunyan Bryant (1995: 217) put it well:

> The solutions to social and environmental problems require us to move beyond thinking about environmental and social problems in conventional terms. We must begin thinking about them not as separate from one another, but in terms of their intricate relations with one another. We can no longer afford to champion the rights of trees and nonhuman life without also championing the rights of all people, regardless of race, sex, income, or social standing.

Along the same lines, a provocative essay on "The Death of Environmentalism" (Shellenberger and Nordhaus 2004) suggests that in our "post-environmental" era—when environmentalism's doom and gloom approach has repelled so many of its constituents—the environmental movement's survival depends upon broadening how it conceptualizes environmental problems.[5] As Shellenberger and Nordhaus (2004: 9) point out, "Environmentalism is today more about protecting a supposed 'thing'—'the environment'—than advancing the worldview articulated by Sierra Club founder John Muir, who nearly a century ago observed, 'When we try to pick out anything by itself, we find it hitched to everything else in the Universe.'" From the Grassy Narrows case, we can take the essential lesson that social, cultural, political, and environmental issues can only be comprehended collectively.

We are part of the natural world.

It follows that conceiving of humanity—with its broad spectrum of interests—as external to the natural systems environmentalists work to protect is also an untenable point of view. Shellenberger and Nordhaus (2004: 12) state:

> The concepts of "nature" and "environment" have been thoroughly deconstructed. Yet they retain their mythic and debilitating power within the environmental movement and the

public at large. If one understands the notion of "environ-ment" to include humans, then the way the environmental community designates certain problems as environmental and others as not is completely arbitrary.

In contrast to Western society's dichotomous conceptual construc-tions of nature/culture and human/environment, most indigenous peoples have never seen themselves as separate or separable from the natural world. This is true among the Hagan highlanders of New Guinea for whom, Marilyn Strathern explains, "there is no culture, in the sense of the cumulative works of man, and no nature to be tamed and made productive" (1980: 219) and, although complicated by gen-erations of colonial intervention, it is also true for Anishinaabe people in northwestern Ontario where land-based subsistence and emplaced cultural identity combine to give such distinctions a hollow ring. We would do well to internalize this point, to realize that we are part of the ecological systems we simultaneously destroy and protect.

Our future is shared.

Grassy Narrows First Nation—in common with countless other indigenous communities—is currently facing the environmentally destructive consequences of a far-reaching, short-sighted, and profit-driven world system. While others among us have been able to buy a few more years of comfortable denial, it may be only a matter of time before the same catastrophe encompasses us all. Our path forward, to repeat what Judy DaSilva told her audience in November of 2004, will mean "putting aside grudges and understanding that we're all in this together, whether we like it or not." We would be wise to listen.

In his treatment of Lumbee Indian campaigns for cultural and politi-cal recognition, Gerald Sider raises an intriguing question: Why do indigenous Americans keep struggling, even in the face of so many repeated defeats? "Native American peoples," he theorizes, "have had to continue to struggle just to continue to survive" to the point that the struggle itself has become an important part of their cultural iden-tity (Sider 1993: 279). After more than a decade of anti-clearcutting protest, Grassy Narrows activists' struggle has become a fundamental and entrenched part of their collective cultural sensibility. Their long-term resistance has itself become part of their distinctiveness; it has become a source of cultural identification and a strategy for cultural survival.

Like indigenous peoples elsewhere, the people of Grassy Narrows aspire to be recognized both as equal within mainstream society and as distinctly themselves. They fight to preserve a cultural identity with foundations in modern interpretations of a traditional past and, even more importantly, to have a meaningful say in determining the shape of their future. Based on the long-term accomplishments of the blockade, members of Grassy Narrows First Nation are able to envision their community as on the rise; they see themselves as strong, as willing to take a stand, and as people who will not abandon their struggle any time soon. When I last visited northwestern Ontario, Steve Fobister wasted no time updating me on the blockade's status. His words had a familiar ring: "The blockade is still there."

Notes

Introduction

1. Because of the potential legal consequences of these actions, I do not include names here. In order to retain anonymity, I also avoid using names in socially sensitive contexts. For less sensitive material, when a person's full name has become a part of the public record, I use it in this work. When this is not the case, I use only first names or, when requested by individuals, pseudonyms. The meaning, development, and political implications of the term "Traditional Land Use Area" are discussed in chapter 4.
2. In his well-known critical analysis, Shepard Krech (1999: 21) defines the Ecological Indian as "the Indian in nature who understands the systemic consequences of his actions, feels deep sympathy with all living forms, and takes steps to conserve so the earth's harmonies are never imbalanced and resources never in doubt."
3. Although, in a few instances, I encountered difficulty finding industry representatives willing to speak openly with me, I seriously doubt that *anyone* in the Grassy Narrows blockade community would have taken the time to talk seriously with an outside researcher who wasn't also a supporter. They have justified reasons for their hesitancy.
4. This conflict-based model of research (Marcus 1998) is exemplified clearly in the work of Landsman (1988) and Satterfield

(2002: 161), who describes conflict as "a central site of culture in action."

5. This tipi was replaced in the fall of 2004 with a more durable—and more quintessentially Anishinaabe—wigwam-style structure.
6. Benton-Banai (1988), for example, breaks down the word's morphemes as follows: *Ani* (from whence) *Nishina* (lowered) *Abe* (the male of the species). At an Anishinaabe language conference I attended in February of 2005, ten different possible origins for the word were discussed.

Chapter 1.
Anishinaabe Cultural History and Land-Based Subsistence

1. Several individuals also run small stores out of their homes. These tend to operate on irregular schedules, sell only a few specialized items, and go in and out of business frequently.
2. While scholars concur that the clan system was patrilineal, considerable debate about this issue exists among contemporary Anishinaabe people. An informational page produced by Grand Council Treaty Three further suggests that females in many cases took their mother's clan while males assumed the clan of their father.
3. Nelson (1983), for comparison, provides an excellent description of the Koyukon seasonal round.
4. I was told by a band employee that around 80 percent of Grassy Narrows citizens bring in no earned income at any given time. Canadian government statistics give a fuller picture; the 2006 census lists the rate of labor force participation as 53.6 percent and the official unemployment (those actively seeking employment but unable to find it) rate as 33.3 percent, http://bit.ly/ge6XPe (accessed February 3, 2011).
5. In the late 1940s, the provincial government began a program of resource licensing that included the official designation of traplines and their holders.
6. Hunting, here, categorically includes fishing and trapping activities.
7. As in northern Wisconsin, the strict enforcement of fish and game regulations was associated with a perceived potential for

tourism and recreation; in order to attract tourists, a bountiful supply of harvestable animal resources was necessary.

Chapter 2. From Aboriginal Policy to Indigenous Empowerment

1. In *The Origins of Indigenism*, Ronald Niezen describes the "battle of the 'S'" that has been an ongoing source of disagreement between indigenous peoples and states in the international law arena. "On the surface," Niezen writes, "the controversy surrounding the 'S' appears to be a mere product of the pedantry of jurists; but hanging upon the 'S' is the question of whether indigenous peoples are the same 'peoples'—with an 'S'—so prominent in the Charter of the United Nations . . . and who therefore must be recognized as possessing all the rights that flow from that status, including the right to self-determination" (2003: 161).

2. The relationship between Aboriginal rights and Aboriginal title is complex, with title to land serving simultaneously as a subset of and as a basis for Aboriginal rights. Aboriginal rights are possessed by Canadian First Nations peoples by virtue of their Aboriginality and occupation of a particular area since time immemorial (Miller 1991b; Nadasdy 2003).

3. On the one hand, Native people in Canada perceive Aboriginal rights as encompassing a broad range of economic, social, cultural, and political rights, including the right to a land base with a separate political jurisdiction. Asch notes that "these rights flow, first of all, from the fact that the Aboriginal peoples were in sovereign occupation of Canada at the time of contact, and secondly from the assertion that their legitimacy and continued existence has not been extinguished by the subsequent occupation of Canada by immigrants" (1984: 30). On the other hand, while Canada's federal government acknowledges the fundamental right of First Nations to preserve their cultures and govern themselves and recognizes the impossibility of a "one-size-fits-all" approach (Canada 1995: part 2), it has tended to interpret Native communities' political sovereignty in a more limited manner that emphasizes First Nations' internal affairs (see Canada 1995).

4. Grand Council Treaty Three is a regional Provincial and Territorial Organization that operates throughout the area covered by

Treaty Three of 1873. It is a prominent organization in north-western Ontario that provides services, information, and resources for Treaty Three Anishinaabe communities.

5. Also known as Riel's Rebellion or the Métis Rebellion. In 1869–1870 the Métis people of the Red River Colony violently protested the Hudson Bay Company's sale of their territories to Canada.

6. Because of Treaty Three's accomplishments, in fact, the government was compelled to alter Treaties One and Two to make them fairer to the First Nations involved. In addition, Treaty Three served as a model for the numbered treaties that followed, with many First Nations negotiators requesting they receive identical terms.

7. Many scholars see it as highly unlikely that the concept of ceding lands was discussed at treaty negotiations due to the incompatibility of the concept with the indigenous worldview (Cardinal ND: 17). In addition, records note that the treaty was read aloud immediately before it was signed, but it is doubtful that the document could ever have been accurately translated into oral Anishinaabemowin (Grand Council Treaty Three 1992). Regarding treaties in the United States, John Nichols (2000) believes it highly unlikely that an accurate translation of the treaty from written English into oral Anishinaabemowin would have been possible. Not only was the quality of interpretation in the nineteenth century dubious, he points out, but the two languages also have radically different manners of constructing sentences and words and rely on very divergent underlying conceptual systems. Furthermore, the Anishinaabe language contains few words that could have been used to describe the legal concepts of property and ownership.

8. The Indian Act was not Canada's first or only act pertaining to Indians. Two 1850 precedents, the "Act for the better protection of the lands and property of the Indians in Lower Canada" and the "Act for the protection of Indians in Upper Canada from imposition, and the property occupied or enjoyed by them from trespass and injury" had some similarities to the later Indian Act (Miller 1991a: 109).

9. For an overview of programs and services sponsored by Aboriginal and Northern Affairs Canada, see http://www.ainc-inac.gc.ca/index-eng.asp.

10. In addition to the historical factors behind these views, we can also consider cultural explanations: Hallowell proposes the existence of a characteristic psychology of blame, stating that for Anishinaabeg, "a culturally constituted psychological set operates which inevitably directs the reasoning of individuals toward an explanation of events in personalistic terms. *Who* did it, *who* is responsible, is always the crucial question to be answered" (Hallowell 1975: 170).

11. The 1973 *Calder* case was the first widely recognized triumph for First Nations peoples in the Canadian judicial system. As noted early in this chapter, this case established the precedent for governmental recognition of Aboriginal title. At the time, the Nisga'a of British Columbia's Nass River Valley had never signed a treaty (though they had been petitioning the Crown to negotiate for years), yet the British Columbia government failed to acknowledge Nisga'a claims to traditional lands. The Nisga'a took their case to the provincial court system, where it was initially defeated. Upon appeal to the Supreme Court, a technical issue prevented Nisga'a victory, but the concept of Aboriginal title was nevertheless recognized. It was, as Coates (2000) puts it, a legal defeat, but a political and moral victory. Even more significantly, the *Calder* case set the stage for future land claims negotiations; after *Calder*, the federal government resolved to commence comprehensive negotiations with all non-treaty Native groups in Canada.

12. The 1990 *Sparrow* case commenced when Ronald Sparrow, a British Columbia Native from Musqueam First Nation, was charged with fishing for salmon using a drift net that exceeded Department of Fisheries and Oceans size regulations. His victory, upon appeal, in Canada's Supreme Court affirmed First Nations peoples' right to traditional subsistence in the form of hunting, trapping, fishing, and gathering on the basis of Section 35 of the 1982 Constitution Act's recognition and affirmation of Aboriginal and treaty rights. In fact, only conservation and public health and safety were accorded greater importance than First Nations rights. *Sparrow* is also celebrated because of the precedent it set for treaty interpretation and constitutional entrenchment of Native rights. In *Sparrow*, "the court rule[d] that Aboriginal and treaty rights could evolve over time and should be interpreted in a 'generous and liberal manner'" (Coates 2000: 89). *Sparrow*

further affirmed constitutional protection of Aboriginal peoples against provincial legislative power (Miller 1991a).

13. The local newspaper was quick to point out that those involved in the occupation were a small minority of the local Indian population (Kenora Daily Miner and News 1974d).

14. These words are visible in a photo printed in the *Kenora Daily Miner and News* on August 16, 1974.

15. Dudley George did not die in vain; following the Ipperwash Inquiry's final report, Ontario announced plans to return the Provincial Park to its original owners in December of 2007 (Toronto Star 2007). The Report of the Ipperwash Inquiry is available at http://www.attorneygeneral.jus.gov.on.ca/inquiries/ipperwash/report/index.html.

16. The global indigenous movement presents some fascinating paradoxes. Indigenism is a relatively recent phenomenon, yet it draws upon notions of timelessness, tradition, and connection to ancient ways of life. And, while the term may be new, indigenism "invokes people's sense of permanence and their ability to survive and stay close to their cultures and homelands despite almost insurmountable odds" (Niezen 2003: xi–xii). As a global movement founded upon specifically local types of identity, the indigenous movement generates another interesting irony. As Brysk (2000: 42) indicates, "the content of indigenous political movements contests globalization, but the process of Indian rights activism depends upon and deepens it." Even as indigenous activists strive to present a unified front, "the concerns of most indigenous people remain deeply local and rooted in particular colonial struggles" (Sissons 2005: 8, see also Warren and Jackson 2002). Indigenism, therefore, simultaneously conceals and glorifies its own diversity. It represents, on the one hand, a global community facilitated by an international network and, on the other, a conscious rebellion against globalization's alleged "homogenizing" forces. As part of a collective global moment, indigenous peoples occupy a unique position in an interconnected world system. In this light, indigenism can be seen as an innovative response to globalization that demonstrates the accuracy of the now widely accepted anthropological insight that "globalization is not the story of cultural homogenization" (Appadurai 1996: 11).

17. In 1971, the UN launched a study of the situation and rights of indigenous peoples around the world. Completed in 1986, the

resulting report is commonly known as the Cobo Report after its chief author, José Martinez Cobo of Ecuador (Cobo 1986). With Cobo's investigation still underway, the UN established a Working Group on Indigenous Populations in 1982 (UNOHCHR 1995), which began drafting a declaration on the rights of indigenous peoples shortly after its formation. The draft declaration was completed in 1995; after years of contention, it was formally adopted on September 13, 2007 in a vote of 143 to 4. Canada— along with the United States, New Zealand, and Australia—initially voted against the declaration (Keating 2007).

18. Actors within the contemporary indigenous movement play active roles in ongoing processes of cultural self-representation. Indigenous activists create such representations in part for their own use; they serve to shape goals and alliances, and they foster a constructive and culturally rooted indigenous—along with a more specifically Cree, Kayapo, or Anishinaabe—sense of self. Recognizing, conversely, that indigenism depends upon externally created conceptual categories and the backing of outsiders, indigenous peoples have also learned to capitalize on their own categorical popularity by adjusting how they present themselves in order to resonate strongly with a non-indigenous public (see Conklin and Graham 1995; Conklin 1997; Ramos 1998; Niezen 2003). Viewed from this angle, indigenous peoples' outwardly projected representations of their cultures become potent political devices. Indigenism functions simultaneously as a vehicle for the development of cultural identity and as a political tool; it is both internal and external; both image and implement.

Chapter 3. A World Transformed

1. I draw primarily on oral history shared by individuals at Grassy Narrows First Nation between 2003 and 2005. Regarding mercury poisoning and its impacts at Grassy Narrows, these stories are corroborated by Hutchison and Wallace (1977), Troyer (1977), McLeod (1977), and Shkilnyk (1985). Erikson and Vecsey (1980) and Shkilnyk (1985) also cover Grassy Narrows' relocation experience.

2. Native communities throughout Canada have been thrust into similar disarray based on identical assimilationist policies. The

Innu community of Davis Inlet, Labrador provides what is perhaps the most infamous example of the disastrous consequences of relocation (LaDuke 1999: 67–70; Penashue 2001; Samson 2003). Similarly, Ronald Niezen (1998: chapter 5) describes the James Bay Cree experience of relocation and its consequences.

3. Throughout the 1970 season, the government attempted to discourage people from eating the contaminated fish. Signs that read "Fish for Fun" in bold letters and featured an image of a fish in a frying pan with an "X" over it were posted at boat landings. It didn't take the media long to point out that the Fish for Fun campaign did Native commercial and subsistence fishermen no good (CBC 1970). Many of the signs were quickly marked by graffiti or ripped down and none were posted in subsequent years.

4. Following hydroelectric development and subsequent flooding, the mercury naturally present in the bedrock of the James Bay region began to leech from sediments underlying the newly formed reservoirs. Richard Scott (2001) traces the James Bay Cree experience of mercury poisoning as well as the history of mercury poisoning in Canadian First Nations more generally.

5. Responding to these concerns, a few dozen activists, hunters, and trappers at Grassy Narrows—working in conjunction with the nearby Wabauskang First Nation community and two scientific consultants—initiated an ongoing wild meats contaminant study in 2001. The study aimed to investigate the bioaccumulated levels of toxins, especially mercury and dioxins, in the flesh of wild animal species frequently eaten by community members. Based on the continuing economic and cultural value of food "from the bush," many people at Grassy see learning about the types and quantity of contamination in such foods as an indispensable project. The contaminant study and its findings are described in more detail in chapters 4 and 7.

Chapter 4. Beginnings

1. In later years, the Grassy Narrows Environmental Group also called itself the Grassy Narrows Environmental Committee. To avoid confusion, I use the original name.

2. LaDuke documented Grassy's fight against nuclear waste storage in her subsequent publications (LaDuke 1999, 2004).
3. This statement has been published online at http://www.envirowatch.org/chrissy.htm (accessed December 10, 2006).
4. Although Abitibi-Consolidated held the license to log and manage the Whiskey Jack, other area mills received some of the trees cut in the area. The 1999–2019 FMP indicated that 40 percent of the harvest would be black spruce (mixed with some slightly less desirable jack pine) destined for Abitibi's paper mill. Another 40 percent of the proposed cut would be poplar intended for Kenora's newly constructed Trus Joist. The remaining 20 percent of the harvest was allocated for the Kenora Forest Products sawmill (Stewart 1999).
5. Scarification implies a large-scale "tilling" of the land in order to prepare it for forest planting and tending. Its detractors argue that it compacts the soil and contributes to monocropping in the forest industry.
6. This letter was posted at http://freegrassy.org/wpcontent/uploads/2010/03/LettersJan99_ToWashingtonPost_ToMinNR_Enviro_WJF99-04.pdf (accessed March 20, 2005), but is no longer available.
7. In addition to speaking to Grassy Narrows activists about this visit, I was able to view footage of the visit shot by a University of Winnipeg filmmaker. In one scene, a Kayapo elder and J .B. Fobister are shown standing in a clearcut, deep in conversation. The Kayapo man is visibly upset about what he sees.
8. The letter requested that representatives from each of these offices meet with the people of Grassy Narrows First Nation to "discuss and to hopefully resolve these issues" and cited the Royal Proclamation of 1763, Treaty Three, Section 35 of 1982 Constitution Act, and the *Delgamuukw* decision as bases of their rights. When these letters failed to produce the desired meeting, Bill Fobister sent an additional letter to local Minister of Parliament Bob Nault asking that he raise these issues to the House of Commons.
9. Shortly before this book went to press, the trappers won this important case. In August of 2011, Ontario's Superior Court ruled that the province has no legal authority to authorize timber operations that infringe on federal treaty promises protecting

indigenous peoples' traditional hunting and trapping rights. (For more information, see http://freegrassy.org/2011/08/01/grassy-trappers-win-major-legal-victory/, accessed September 12, 2011).

Chapter 5. The Blockade

1. From a 2004 public statement entitled "No More!" Originally posted online at http://www.friendsofgrassynarrows.com (accessed October 6, 2004), but no longer available at this location.
2. In the next portion of the notice, the area of concern is described using logging roads as primary landmarks. In addition, Moozomoo Saigun and Shkin Dii Saigun are mentioned as hunt boundaries. Speakers of Anishinaabemowin will note the fictional and humorous—and therefore all the more symbolic—nature of these place-names.
3. Over a decade earlier, an OPP officer was shot and killed while responding to a call at Grassy Narrows. This tragic incident continues to color current officers' views; being stationed at Grassy, one OPP officer told me, was one of the worst possible placements in the province. On the other hand, many First Nation members—especially youth—perceive the OPP as unnecessarily violent and slow to respond to their calls for assistance. Although rumors of injunctions sometimes spread with the roving blockades, no arrests of Native activists or their non-Native supporters took place until the summer of 2006.
4. The Sustainable Forest Management Plan was produced as part of a CSA (Canadian Standards Association) certification process. It is independent of the Forest Management Plan (FMP) critiqued by members of Grassy Narrows First Nation.
5. Nishnawbe Aski Nation (NAN) represents the Treaty Nine area, which covers the large portion of northwestern Ontario not covered by Treaty Three. It includes forty-nine communities, many of them remote.
6. GNEG's 1999 letter to the *Washington Post* also affirmed the importance of working with non-Native outsiders. It stated, "As indigenous cultures around the world are destroyed one by one, so too will all other people see social, economic, spiritual, and moral degradation. . . . This is not just our issue, this is an earth issue."
7. As described in chapter 2, the 1997 *Delgamuukw* decision estab-

lished the obligation of the government to consult with First Nations on issues relating to their traditional lands or territories. Grassy Narrows activists were familiar with this precedent and frequently cited the *Delgamuukw* precedent along these lines.

8. The *ogitchidaa* see it as their responsibility to assist wherever they are needed in the manner of a regional peacekeeping force for Anishinaabe communities of Ontario and Manitoba. Most First Nations activists consider membership in the Ojibwe Warrior Society an important honor, conferred by invitation and ceremonial induction. Traditionally, according to Kohl's (1985 [1860]: 121) observations of Ojibwe life in the summer of 1855, "the title 'odgidjida' is to the Indians the highest on earth. In order to gain it, they will run to the end of the world." Today, both men and women fill the role of *ogitchidaa*; for women, the *–kwe* suffix is added to the term. Like the members of the Mohawk Warrior Society (see York and Pindera 1991), many *ogitchidaa* and *ogitchidaakwe* dress in camouflage and black clothing.

9. These tensions seemed to parallel the "dual political structure" (Nesper 2002) of traditional Anishinaabe society. Peace chiefs were often older leaders who advocated a thoughtful approach. War chiefs, on the other hand, tended to be younger and were more disposed to immediate action and risk (Kohl 1985 [1860]; Hickerson 1962).

10. TVO (TV Ontario) is equivalent to public television in the Unites States. A segment on the Grassy Narrows First Nation blockade was included in a program called *Studio 2*.

11. Although some people who attended the gathering felt Hill had little in common with the activists at Grassy Narrows, her presence helped to draw media attention to the event and to lend it credence among non-Native environmental activists. Julia Butterfly Hill is known for her 2001 book entitled *The Legacy of Luna: The Story of a Tree, a Woman and the Struggle to Save the Redwoods* (Hill 2001).

Chapter 6. Blockade Life

1. As I quickly learned, at Slant Lake women are encouraged to tend to the sacred fire so long as they are not on their menstrual "moontime." While some First Nations communities consider it

an exclusively male responsibility, the women at Grassy have played a central role in maintaining the sacred fire vigil.

2. The English and Wabigoon rivers merge at Ball Lake, to the north and upstream of the reserve but still within Grassy Narrows' Traditional Land Use Area. While the rivers are most frequently referred to as a single system, in this location the Wabigoon River is still independent of the English. Although the Dryden mill was ordered to cease all discharge of mercury in March of 1970, some Grassy residents suspect that it continues to pollute the river with dioxins and other toxins.

3. Frances Densmore also describes northern Minnesota Ojibwe beliefs and practices regarding tobacco in the early 1900s. "Tobacco was regarded as a gift from the manido," she writes, "and for this reason it was supposed to have "magic power," in that it increased the efficacy of a request and made an obligation or agreement more binding" (Densmore 1979 [1929]: 145). In this context, tobacco was employed by Native negotiators in many of their treaties with the United States (see also Danziger 1979).

Chapter 7. Negotiations and Networks

1. While anthropologists have critiqued movements based on the politics of identity as problematically essentializing, in many cases successful "organizing requires the projection of "sameness" to outsiders" (Stephen 2005:66). Spivak (1993) refers to this dynamic as "strategic essentialism."

2. Originally posted online at www.friendsofgrassynarrows.com (accessed October 8, 2004), but no longer available at this location.

3. Even as FGN and CPT members work tirelessly to build bridges between Natives and non-Natives, their socially critical projects require that Natives remain externally positioned as mirrors for Western society's ills (see Berkhofer 1978). While this accords well with these allies' concern for Grassy Narrows' ability to remain politically and culturally distinct from the wider Canadian society, the fact that FGN and CPT simultaneously attempt to overcome difference and make use of it hints that these alliances, too, may be fundamentally unstable.

4. With this in mind, the physical markers of cultural revitalization at the Slant Lake site can be comprehended as symbolic means to authenticate the traditional Anishinaabe identity of people who spend time at the blockade. The wigwam constructed to shelter the sacred fire in the late fall of 2004, discussed later, offers a striking example.

5. Tadashi Orui's documentary film, *The Scars of Mercury*, was released in 2009.

6. This theme is present in the Ojibwe re-creation story as told by Eddie Benton-Banai (1988: 29–34).

7. While people at Grassy do not intentionally consume them, the high level of mercury in otters—a species high on the food chain—indicates the presence of a bioaccumulating substance like mercury throughout the ecosystem.

8. *The Scars of Mercury* (Orui 2009) includes footage from Dr. Harada's visit and highlights Grassy Narrows residents' ongoing struggle to cope with mercury contamination.

Chapter 8. Beyond the Blockade

1. Among North American environmental groups, the San Francisco–based RAN is known for its comparatively direct and confrontational tactics.

2. The sacred fire no longer burned continuously, though, as Judy once informed me, this was okay; a visiting traditional healer, she explained, told her that the fire had burned for so long and so many people had put their energy and prayers into it that it had created an energy connection so strong it didn't need the fire to sustain it. At least for the blockaders, the fact that the fire had gone out did little to detract from its symbolic potency.

3. Frances Densmore's observations of wigwam construction in 1925 at Mille Lac, Minnesota support the Grassy women's claim; while men assisted in the construction process, Densmore (1979 [1929]: 24–26) notes that women were in charge of the work.

4. The concept of the circle is important in a neotraditional and pan-Indian view of the world. A frequently cited example comes from the words of Black Elk, the famed Lakota spiritual leader

(Neihardt 1932: 194–96): "Everything the Power of the World does is done in a circle. The sky is round, and I have heard the earth is round like a ball, and so are all the stars. The wind, in its greatest power, whirls. Birds make their nests in circles, for theirs is the same religion as ours. The sun comes forth and goes down again in a circle. The moon does the same and both are round. Even the seasons form a great circle in their changing, and always come back again to where they were. The life of a man is a circle from childhood to childhood, so it is in everything where power moves."

Conclusion. The Blockade Is Still There

1. This letter was signed by Grassy Narrows chief Simon Fobister as well as environmental group members, blockaders, trappers, elders, and youth and posted online at http://www.amnesty.ca/grassy_narrows/voice_of_the_people.php (accessed April 16, 2010).
2. Paterson's letter was posted at http://freegrassy.org/wp-content/uploads/Abitibi_to_MNR_re_GN.pdf (accessed August 8, 2009).
3. This message from J. B. Fobister was posted on Rainforest Action Network's blog at http://understory.ran.org/2008/06/05/message-from-jb-fobister-in-grassy-narrows (accessed March 10, 2009).
4. From Kitty's 2004 public statement entitled "No More!" Originally posted online at http://www.friendsofgrassynarrows.com (accessed October 6, 2004), but no longer available at this location.
5. Inspired by the reaction to their 2004 essay, Shellenberger and Nordhaus published a book-length manifesto in 2007 entitled *Break Through: From the Death of Environmentalism to the Politics of Possibility*.

Bibliography

Abercrombie, Thomas A. 1998. Pathways of Memory and Power: Ethnography and History Among an Andean People. Madison: University of Wisconsin Press.

Abitibi-Consolidated. 2004a. Draft Sustainable Forest Management Plan: Whiskey Jack Forest Defined Forest Area. October 14, 2004.

Abitibi-Consolidated. 2004b. Summary of the Draft Forest Management Plan: Whiskey Jack Forest 2004–2024.

Agyeman, Julian. 2005. Sustainable Communities and the Challenge of Environmental Justice. New York: New York University Press.

Aiken, Mike. 2003a. Clearcutting Protest Brought to Kenora. Kenora Daily Miner and News. September 17, 2003.

Aiken, Mike. 2003b. Abitibi Proposes Resolution for Grassy Narrows. Kenora Daily Miner and News. November 13, 2003.

Aiken, Mike. 2003c. Some Optimism One Year Later. Kenora Daily Miner and News. December 3, 2003.

Aiken, Mike. 2003d. Talks with Abitibi Cancelled at Last Minute by Band. Kenora Daily Miner and News. December 23, 2003.

Aiken, Mike. 2004a. Abitibi Gets an Earful at Grassy Narrows Forum. Kenora Daily Miner and News. February 12, 2004.

Aiken, Mike. 2004b. Mercury Expert to Revisit Grassy Narrows. Kenora Daily Miner and News. August 5, 2004.

Aiken, Mike. 2004c. Japanese Expert Gives Second Opinion of Mercury Poisoning. *Lake of the Woods Enterprise*. September 4, 2004.

Aiken, Mike. 2004d. All Quiet on Northern Front Two Years after Grassy Narrows Blockade Began. *Kenora Daily Miner and News*. December 2, 2004.

Alland, Sandra. 2003. SIU Concluded First Grassy Narrows Investigation. *Kenora Daily Miner and News*. October 5, 2003.

Amnesty International. 2007. The Law of the Land: Amnesty International Canada's Position on the Conflict over Logging at Grassy Narrows. Ottawa: Amnesty International Canada.

Anderson, Benedict. 1991. *Imagined Communities*. London: Verso.

Anderson, Kim. 2000. A Recognition of Being: Reconstructing Native Womanhood. Toronto: Sumac Press.

Appadurai, Arjun. 1988. Putting Hierarchy in Its Place. *Cultural Anthropology* 3(1): 36–49.

Appadurai, Arjun. 1996. *Modernity at Large: Cultural Dimensions of Globalization*. Minneapolis: University of Minnesota Press.

Asad, Talal, ed. 1973. *Anthropology and the Colonial Encounter*. Amherst, NY: Humanity Books.

Asch, Michael. 1984. Home and Native Land: Aboriginal Rights and the Canadian Constitution. Toronto: Methuen.

Asch, Michael. 1988. *Kinship and the Drum Dance in a Northern Dene Community*. Edmonton: University of Alberta Press.

Barrera, Jorge. 2003a. UN Human Rights Inspectors Make Visit to Local First Nation Today. *Kenora Daily Miner and News*. May 6, 2003.

Barrera, Jorge. 2003b. Grassy Band Throws Up Another Blockade. *Kenora Daily Miner and News*. June 6, 2003.

Barrera, Jorge. 2003c. Company to Mull Blockade This Week. *Kenora Daily Miner and News*. June 9, 2003.

Barrera, Jorge. 2003d. Truck Hit by Vandals. *Kenora Daily Miner and News*. June 10, 2003.

Barrera, Jorge. 2003e. No End in Sight for Running Blockade Battle. *Kenora Daily Miner and News*. June 13, 2003.

Barrera, Jorge. 2003f. MNR Stumped by Blockade Issue. *Kenora Daily Miner and News*. June 26, 2003.

Barrera, Jorge. 2003g. Grassy Narrows to Start Talks with Province. *Kenora Daily Miner and News*. July 22, 2003.

Barrera, Jorge. 2003h. Band Wants Real Talks with Province to End Blockade Stand-Off. *Kenora Daily Miner and News.* July 23, 2003.

Basso, Keith. 1996. *Wisdom Sits in Places: Landscape and Language among the Western Apache.* Albuquerque: University of New Mexico Press.

BC (British Columbia) Treaty Commission. 1999. *A Lay Person's Guide to* Delgamuukw. Vancouver: BC Treaty Commission.

Bender, Barbara. 1993. *Landscape: Politics and Perspective.* Providence, RI: Berg Publishers.

Benton-Banai, Edward. 1988. *The Mishomis Book: The Voice of the Ojibway.* Hayward, WI: Indian Country Communications.

Berger, Thomas R. 1991. A Long and Terrible Shadow: White Values, Native Rights in the Americas since 1492. Vancouver: Douglas and McIntyre.

Berkhofer, Robert F. 1978. The White Man's Indian: Images of the American Indian from Columbus to the Present. New York: Vintage.

Biolsi, Thomas. 2005. Imagined Geographies: Sovereignty, Indigenous Space, and American Indian Struggles. *American Ethnologist* 32(2): 239–59.

Blackburn, Carole. 2005. Searching for Guarantees in the Midst of Uncertainty: Negotiating Aboriginal Rights and Title in British Columbia. *American Anthropologist* 107(4): 586–96.

Bland, June. 1998. Grassy Narrows Residents Protest. *Kenora Daily Miner and News.* December 29, 1998.

Bland, June. 1999a. Protestors Placard Forest Capital Kick-Off. *Kenora Daily Miner and News.* January 18, 1999.

Bland, June. 1999b. Threats to Blockade at Grassy Narrows. *Kenora Daily Miner and News.* March 11, 1999.

Brightman, Robert. 1993. *Grateful Prey: Rock Cree Human-Animal Relationships.* Berkeley: University of California Press.

Brody, Hugh. 1981. *Maps and Dreams.* Prospect Heights, IL: Waveland Press.

Brophy, Dave. 2004. Letter to the Editor. *Kenora Daily Miner and News.* February 27, 2004.

Bruner, Edward M. 1986. Ethnography as Narrative. In *The Anthropology of Experience.* Victor W. Turner and Edward M. Bruner, eds. Pp. 139–55. Urbana: University of Illinois Press.

Bryant, Bunyan. 1995. Summary. In *Environmental Justice: Issues, Polices, and Solutions*. Bunyan Bryant, ed. Pp. 208–19. Washington, DC: Island Press.

Brysk, Alison. 2000. From Tribal Village to Global Village: Indian Rights and International Relations in Latin America. Stanford: Stanford University Press.

Buege, Douglas J. 1996. The Ecologically Noble Savage Revisited. *Environmental Ethics* 18(1): 71–88.

Bujold, Shelly, and Mike Aiken. 2006. Activists Blockade Trans-Canada Highway. *Kenora Daily Miner and News*. July 13, 3006.

CBC (Canadian Broadcasting Corporation). 1970. *Mercury Rising: The Poisoning of Grassy Narrows*. Http://archives.cbc.ca/IDD-1-701178/disasters_tragedies/ grassy_narrows_mercury_pollution, accessed August 12, 2010.

CBC (Canadian Broadcasting Corporation). 2004. InDepth: Ipperwash: Dudley George. CBC News Online. January 21, 2004.

CBC (Canadian Broadcasting Company). 2006. Environmentalists Block Highway Near Kenora to Protest Logging. CBC News Online. July 13, 2006.

Canada (Federal Government). 1966 [1871–1874]. Treaty No. 3 Between Her Majesty the Queen and the Saulteaux Tribe of Ojibbeway Indians at the Northwest Angle on the Lake of the Woods with Adhesions. Ottawa: Queens Printer.

Canada (Federal Government). 1986. Grassy Narrows and Islington Indian Bands Mercury Pollution Claim Settlement Act. Ottawa: Department of Justice Canada.

Canada (Federal Government). 1995. Aboriginal Self-Government: The Government of Canada's Approach to Implementation of the Inherent Right and the Negotiation of Aboriginal Self-Government. Ottawa: Minister of Public Works and Government Services Canada.

Canadian Parks and Wilderness Society (CPAWS). No Date. Fact Sheet #4: Good Boreal Forestry. Ottawa: CPAWS.

Canadian Royal Commission on Aboriginal Peoples. 1996. People to People, Nation to Nation: Highlights from the Report of the Royal Commission on Aboriginal Peoples. Ottawa: Minster of Supply and Services Canada.

Cardinal, Sheldon. No Date. *Delgamuukw*—The Implications for the Prairie Treaty First Nations.

Casey, Edward. 1996. How to Get from Space to Place in a Fairly Short Stretch of Time: A Phenomenological Prolegomena. In *Senses of Place*. Steven Feld and Keith Basso, eds. Pp. 13–52. Santa Fe, NM: School of American Research Press.

Chamberlin, J. Edward. 2003. If This Is Your Land, Where Are Your Stories? Finding Common Ground. Toronto: Vintage Canada.

Checker, Melissa. 2005. Polluted Promises: Environmental Racism and the Search for Justice in a Southern Town. New York: New York University Press.

Checker, Melissa, and Maggie Fishman. 2004. Introduction. In *Local Actions: Cultural Activism, Power, and Public Life in America*. Melissa Checker and Maggie Fishman, eds. Pp. 1–25. New York: Columbia University Press.

Christen, Kimberly. 2006. Tracking Properness: Repackaging Culture in a Remote Australian Town. *Cultural Anthropology* 21(3): 416–46.

Christian Peacemaker Teams (CPT). No Date. Christian Peacemaker Teams Asubpeeschoseewagong Brochure.

Churchill, Ward. 1996. From a Native Son: Selected Essays on Indigenism, 1985–1995. Boston: South End Press.

Churchill, Ward. 2002. Struggle for the Land: Native North American Resistance to Genocide, Ecocide, and Colonization. San Francisco: City Lights.

Clarren, Rebecca. 2007. Partners in Conservation. *Nature Conservancy* 57(4): 12.

Clayton, Reg. 2003a. Harvest Plan Emulates Fire Patterns. *Lake of the Woods Enterprise*. April 5, 2003.

Clayton, Reg. 2003b. Protestors Seek End to Whiskey Jack Clear Cuts. *Lake of the Woods Enterprise*. April 5, 2003.

Cleary, Linda M., and Thomas D. Peacock. 1998. *Collected Wisdom: American Indian Education*. Needham Heights, MA: Allyn and Bacon.

Clement, Dave. 2003. *As Long as the Rivers Flow: The Grassy Narrows Blockade Story*. Thunder Bay, ON: Thunder Bay Indymedia Film.

Clifford, James, and George E. Marcus, eds. 1986. *Writing Culture: The Poetics and Politics of Ethnography*. Berkeley: University of California Press.

Coates, Ken. 2000. *The Marshall Decision and Native Rights*. Montreal: McGill-Queen's University Press.

Cobb, Daniel M. 2007. Continuing Encounters: Historical Perspectives. In *Beyond Red Power: American Indians Politics and Activism since 1900*. Daniel M. Cobb and Loretta Fowler, eds. Pp. 57–69. Santa Fe, NM: School of American Research Press.

Cobb, Daniel M., and Loretta Fowler, eds. 2007. *Beyond Red Power: American Indian Politics and Activism since 1900*. Santa Fe, NM: School of American Research Press.

Cobo, José Martinez. 1986. *The Study of the Problem of Discrimination against Indigenous Populations*. Vol. 1-5. United Nations Document E/CN.4/Sub.2/1986/7. New York: United Nations.

Comaroff, John, and Jean Comaroff. 1992. *Ethnography and the Historical Imagination*. Boulder, CO: Westview Press.

Conklin, Beth A. 1997. Body Paint, Feathers, and VCRs: Aesthetics and Authenticity in Amazonian Activism. *American Ethnologist* 24(4): 711–37.

Conklin, Beth A., and Laura R. Graham. 1995. The Shifting Middle Ground: Amazonian Indians and Eco-Politics. *American Anthropologist* 97(4): 695–710.

Cronon, William. 1983. *Changes in the Land: Indians, Colonists, and the Ecology of New England*. New York: Hill and Wang.

Cruikshank, Julie. 1990. *Life Lived Like a Story: Life Stories of Three Yukon Native Elders*. Lincoln: University of Nebraska Press.

Cruikshank, Julie. 2005. *Do Glaciers Listen?* Vancouver: University of British Columbia Press.

Cultural Survival. 2010. Canada Endorses the UN Declaration on the Rights of Indigenous Peoples. http://www.culturalsurvival.org/news/canada/canada-endorses-un-declaration-rights-indigenous-peoples. Updated November 12, 2010, accessed January 29, 2011.

Danziger, Edmund Jefferson. 1979. *The Chippewas of Lake Superior*. Norman: University of Oklahoma Press.

Daugherty, Wayne E. 1986. *Treaty Three Research Report*. Ottawa: Treaties and Historical Research Centre, Indian and Northern Affairs Canada.

Dawson, Simon J. 1873. Notes Taken at Indian Treaty Northwest Angle, Lake of the Woods, from 30th Sept. 1873 to Close of Treaty. Typed copy, Indian and Northern Affairs Canada, MG 29, C67, 35.

Deerchild, Rosanna. 2003. Tribal Feminism Is a Drum Song. In *Strong Women Stories: Native Vision and Community Survival*. Kim Anderson and Bonita Lawrence, eds. Pp. 97–105. Toronto: Sumac Press.

Degnen, Catherine. 2001. Country Space as a Healing Place: Community Healing at Sheshatshiu. In *Aboriginal Autonomy and Development in Northern Quebec and Labrador*. Colin H. Scott, ed. Pp. 357–78. Vancouver: University of British Columbia Press.

Deloria, Phillip J. 1998. *Playing Indian*. New Haven: Yale University Press.

Densmore, Frances. 1979 [1929]. *Chippewa Customs*. Minneapolis: Minnesota Historical Society Press.

Descola, Philippe. 1986. *In the Society of Nature: A Native Ecology of Amazonia*. Cambridge, UK: Cambridge University Press.

Dombrowski, Kirk. 2001. Against Culture: Development, Politics, and Religion in Indian Alaska. Lincoln: University of Nebraska Press.

Doyle, Timothy, and Doug McEachern. 1998. *Environment and Politics*. London: Routledge.

Dusang, Clarence. 1974. Session Held Over Protest. *Kenora Daily Miner and News*. July 24, 1974.

Earley, Steven B. 2008. Letter from Steven B. Earley, Boise Woodlands Manager to Chris Gibbons, Smartwood Program Chain-of-Custody Associate dated February 27, 2008.

Edmunds, Mary. 2007. Managing Conflict Through Native Title Claims in Australia. *Anthropology News* 48(8): 11.

Englund, Henri. 2002. Ethnography After Globalism. *American Ethnologist* 29(2): 261–86.

Erasmus, Georges, and Joe Sanders. 1992. Canadian History: An Aboriginal Perspective. In *Nation to Nation: Aboriginal Sovereignty and the Future of Canada*. Diane Engelstad and John Bird, eds. Pp. 3–11. Concord, ON: Anansi Press.

Erikson, Kai, and Christopher Vecsey. 1980. A Report to the People of Grassy Narrows. In *American Indian Environments*. Christopher Vecsey and Robert W. Venables, eds. Pp. 152–161. Syracuse, NY: Syracuse University Press.

Fabian, Johannes. 1983. *Time and the Other: How Anthropology Makes Its Object*. New York: Columbia University Press.

Feit, Harvey, and Robert Beaulieu. 2001. Voices from a Disappearing Forest: Government, Corporate, and Cree Participatory Forest Management Practices. In *Aboriginal Autonomy and Development in Northern Quebec and Labrador*. Colin H. Scott, ed. Pp. 119–48. Vancouver: University of British Columbia Press.

Feld, Stephen, and Keith Basso, eds. 1996. *Senses of Place*. Santa Fe, NM: School of American Research Press.

First Nation International Court of Justice. 1996. The First Nation of Turtle Island and Her Majesty the Queen in Right of Canada (Transcripts of Proceeding). Vol. 1 Toronto, File no. F.N. 001/95. Unpublished document.

Fixico, Donald L. 2003. *The American Indian Mind in a Lineal World: American Indian Studies and Traditional Knowledge*. New York: Routledge.

Fixico, Donald L. 2007. Witness to Change: 50 Years of Indian Activism and Tribal Politics. In *Beyond Red Power: American Indians Politics and Activism since 1900*. Daniel M. Cobb and Loretta Fowler, eds. Pp. 2–15. Santa Fe: School of American Research Press.

ForestEthics. No Date. Overview of Ontario Forests and Forestry. Forestethics.org/article.php? id=1226, accessed February 1, 2006.

Friedman, Jonathan. 1994. *Cultural Identity and Global Process*. London: Sage Publications.

Friesen, Jean. 1981. Presentation on the Making of Treaty Three. Delivered at the Native Studies Conference, Brandon University. November 1981.

Gauthier, Dan. 2004a. Grassy Narrows to Resume Talks with Abitibi. *Kenora Daily Miner and News*. September 2, 2004.

Gauthier, Dan. 2004b. Wood Cutters Kept Away from Whiskey Jack Forest Until Deal Is Reached. *Kenora Daily Miner and News*. September 2, 2004.

Geertz, Armin W. 1994. The Invention of Prophecy: Community and Meaning in Hopi Indian Religion. Berkeley: University of California Press.

Gibson, Janet. 2003a. Woman Recovering After Police Cruiser Collision. *Kenora Daily Miner and News*. August 21, 2003.

Gibson, Janet. 2003b. Grassy Narrows Teen Killed in Standoff. *Kenora Daily Miner and News*. August 28, 2003.

Gibson, Janet. 2003c. Officer Legally Justified in Shooting: SIU. *Kenora Daily Miner and News*. October 28, 2003.

Gibson, Janet. 2003d. Community, SIU and Police Discuss Shooting Death. *Kenora Daily Miner and News*. November 6, 2003.

Gibson, Janet, and Mike Aiken. 2003. Inquest Set to Review Shooting Death of Grassy Teen. *Lake of the Woods Enterprise*. June 5, 2004.

Ginsburg, Faye. 2004. Foreword. In *Local Actions: Cultural Activism, Power, and Public Life in America.* Melissa Checker and Maggie Fishman, eds. Pp. ix–xvii. New York: Columbia University Press.

Godin, Wes. 2002a. Grassy Narrows Protesting Clear-Cut Practices. *Kenora Daily Miner and News.* December 4, 2002.

Godin, Wes. 2002b. Grand Chief Supports Protest's Efforts to Gain Respect for Lands. *Kenora Daily Miner and News.* December 10, 2002.

Godin, Wes. 2003a. Grassy Narrows Residents Maintaining Road Blockade. *Kenora Daily Miner and News.* January 3, 2003.

Godin, Wes. 2003b. MNR Proposes Meeting to Resolve Blockade. *Kenora Daily Miner and News.* January 15, 2003.

Godin, Wes. 2003c. Grassy Narrows Continuing Blockade with Support of Treaty Three. Kenora *Daily Miner and News.* January 21, 2003.

Godin, Wes. 2003d. Day-long Blockade Standoff Ended. *Kenora Daily Miner and News.* February 7, 2003.

Godin, Wes. 2003e. Protest Builds, Comes to Kenora. *Kenora Daily Miner and News.* February 13, 2003.

Godin, Wes. 2003f. Coon-Come to Show Support for Grassy Narrows Blockaders. *Kenora Daily Miner and News.* February 26, 2003.

Godin, Wes. 2003g. National Chief Visits Grassy Narrows. *Kenora Daily Miner and News.* February 28, 2003.

Godin, Wes. 2003h. Grassy Narrows Protest Taken on Road to Toronto. *Kenora Daily Miner and News.* March 18, 2003.

Godin, Wes. 2003i. Drums of Protest Beating. *Kenora Daily Miner and News.* March 27, 2003.

Godin, Wes. 2003j. Year's Work in Whiskey Jack Forest Is Outlined. *Kenora Daily Miner and News.* March 27, 2003.

Godin, Wes. 2003k. Grassy Narrows Voices Protest to Clear-Cutting. *Kenora Daily Miner and News.* April 1, 2003.

Gorrie, Peter. 2008. Protest Prompts Abitibi Pullout. *Toronto Star.* June 5, 2008.

Goulet, Jean-Guy. 1998. *Ways of Knowing.* Lincoln: University of Nebraska Press.

Grand Council Treaty Three. 1974. *While People Sleep.* Kenora, ON: Grand Council Treaty Three.

Grand Council Treaty Three. 1992. *We Ask for Fair Play: Wild Plant Usage.* Kenora, ON: Treaty and Aboriginal Rights Research Brochure.

Grand Council Treaty Three. No Date a. *Where Blue Sky Meets Sunset Country: Treaty Three Territory.* Kenora, ON: Undated Brochure.

Grand Council Treaty Three. No Date b. The Paypom Treaty. Grassy Narrows Band. 1979. Presentation of the Grassy Narrows Band to the Governments of Canada and Ontario at the Opening Session of the Mediation Process. Grassy Narrows Environmental Group. 1999. Position Paper.

Grinde, Donald A., and Bruce E. Johansen. 1995. *Ecocide of Native America: Environmental Destruction of Indian Lands and People.* Santa Fe, NM: Clear Light Publishers

Gupta, Akhil. 1998. Postcolonial Developments: Agriculture and the Making of Modern India. Durham, NC: Duke University Press.

Gupta, Akhil, and James Ferguson. 1997. Culture, Power, Place: Ethnography at the End of an Era. In *Culture, Power, Place: Explorations in Critical Anthropology.* Akhil Gupta and James Ferguson, eds. Pp. 1–32. Durham, NC: Duke University Press.

Gupta, Akhil, and James Ferguson, eds. 1997. *Culture, Power, Place: Explorations in Critical Anthropology.* Durham, NC: Duke University Press.

Habermas, Jürgen. 1968. *Knowledge and Human Interests.* Boston: Beacon Press.

Hallowell, A. Irving. 1975. Ojibwa Ontology, Behavior, and World View. In *Teachings from the American Earth: Indian Religion and Philosophy.* Dennis and Barbara Tedlock, eds. Pp. 141–178. New York: Liveright.

Hallowell, A. Irving. 1992. Edited by Jennifer Brown. *The Ojibwa of Berens River, Manitoba: Ethnography into History.* Fort Worth, TX: Harcourt Brace College Publishers.

Harada, Masazumi, Masanori Hanada, Takashi Miyakita, Tadashi Fujino, Kazuhiti Tsuruta, Akira Fukuhara, Tadashi Orui, Shigeharu Nakachi, Chihiti Araki, Masami Tajiri, and Itsuka Nagano. 2005. Long-Term Study on the Effects of Mercury Contamination on Two Indigenous Communities in Canada (1975–2004). Tadashi Orui, trans. Research on Environmental Disruption 34(4). http://freegrassy.org/wp-content/uploads/ Harada_report_2004_FINAL.pdf, accessed August 21, 2010.

Harkin, Michael E. 2004a. Introduction: Revitalization as History and Theory. In *Reassessing Revitalization Movements: Perspectives from*

North America and the Pacific Islands. Michael E. Harkin, ed. Pp. xv–xxxvi. Lincoln: University of Nebraska Press.

Harkin, Michael E. 2004b. Revitalization as Catharsis: The Warm House Cult of Western Oregon. In *Reassessing Revitalization Movements: Perspectives from North America and the Pacific Islands.* Michael E. Harkin, ed. Pp. 143–61. Lincoln: University of Nebraska Press.

Harkin, Michael E. 2007. Swallowing Wealth: Northwest Coast Beliefs and Ecological Practices. In *Native Americans and the Environment: Perspectives on the Ecological Indian.* Michael E. Harkin and David Rich Lewis, eds. Pp. 211–32. Lincoln: University of Nebraska Press.

Harries, Kate. 2003. Grassy Narrows: Still Fighting to Live. *Toronto Star Tribune.* November 30, 2003.

Harries, Kate. 2004. Mercury Still a Risk, Japanese MD Says. *Toronto Star Tribune.* August 30, 2004.

Harries-Jones, Peter. 1991. Introduction. In *Making Knowledge Count: Advocacy and Social Science.* Peter Harries-Jones, ed. Pp. 3–19. Montreal: McGill-Queens University Press.

Heidegger, Martin. 1977 [1927]. Introduction to *Being and Time.* In *Martin Heidegger: Basic Writings.* David Farrell Krell, ed. Pp. 343–63. San Francisco: Harper Collins Publishers. Originally published in German in 1927 as *Sein und Zeit.*

Henry, J. David. 2002. *Canada's Boreal Forest.* Washington, DC: Smithsonian Institution.

Hickerson, Harold. 1962. The Southwestern Chippewa: An Ethnohistorical Study. *Memoirs of the American Anthropological Association* 64(3): Part 2. Memoir 92.

Hickerson, Harold. 1970. *The Chippewa and Their Neighbors: A Study in Ethnohistory.* New York: Holt, Rinehart, and Winston, Inc.

Hill, Julia Butterfly. 2001. The Legacy of Luna: The Story of a Tree, a Woman and the Struggle to Save the Redwoods. San Francisco: Harper.

Hirsh, Eric. 1995. Introduction. In *The Anthropology of Landscape: Perspectives on Place and Space.* Eric Hirsh and Michael O'Hanlon, eds. Pp. 1–30. Oxford, UK: Oxford University Press.

Hirsh, Eric, and Michael O'Hanlon, eds. 1995. *The Anthropology of Landscape: Perspectives on Place and Space.* Oxford, UK: Oxford University Press.

Hobsbawm, Eric, and Terrence Ranger, eds. 1983. *The Invention of Tradition*. Cambridge, UK: Cambridge University Press.

Hodgson, Dorothy. 2002. Comparative Perspectives on the Indigenous Rights Movements in Africa and the Americas. *American Anthropologist* 104(4): 1037–49.

Holm, Tom, J., Diane Pearson, and Ben Chavis. 2003. Peoplehood: A Model for the Extension of Sovereignty in American Indian Studies. *Wicazo Sa Review* 18(1): 7–24.

Holland, April. 1974. Native People Urged to Work Together. *Kenora Daily Miner and News*. August 22, 1974.

Holland, April, and Joe Ralko. 1974. Mayor Views Positive Results. *Kenora Daily Miner and News*. July 31, 1974.

Hughes, Lotte. 2003. *The No-Nonsense Guide to Indigenous Peoples*. London: Verso.

Hutchinson, Sharon. 1996. *Nuer Dilemmas: Coping with Money, War, and the State*. Berkeley: University of California Press.

Hutchison, George, and Dick Wallace. 1977. *Grassy Narrows*. Toronto: Van Nostrand and Reinhold.

Jackson, Michael. 1996. Introduction. In *Things as They Are: New Directions in Phenomenological Anthropology*. Michael Jackson, ed. Pp. 1–50. Bloomington: University of Indiana Press.

James, Peter. 2003. Grassy Narrows Continues Protest. *Kenora Daily Miner and News*. September 2, 2003.

James, Wendy. 1973. The Anthropologist as Reluctant Imperialist. In *Anthropology and the Colonial Encounter*. Talal Asad, ed. Pp. 41–69. Amherst, NY: Humanity Books.

Jenness, Diamond. 1977 [1923]. *The Indians of Canada*. Toronto: University of Toronto Press.

Johnson, Troy R., Joane Nagel, and Duane Champagne, eds. 1999a. *American Indian Activism: Alcatraz to the Longest Walk*. Urbana: University of Illinois Press.

Johnson, Troy R., Duane Champagne, and Joane Nagel. 1999b. American Indian Activism and Transformation: Lessons from Alcatraz. In *Contemporary Native American Political Issues*. Troy R. Johnson, ed. Pp. 283–314. Walnut Creek, CA: AltaMira Press.

Jourdain, Leon. 2003. Natural Resource Revenue for Aboriginal Peoples: An Alternative to Genocide. Paper Presented at the Ninth National Forest Conference. May 1, Ottawa.

Keating, Neal B. 2007. UN General Assembly Adopts Declaration on the Rights of Indigenous Peoples 143-4. *Anthropology News* 48(8): 22–23.

Kelly, Fred, John Kelly, James MacMillan, and Shirley Lyon. 1977. *A Socio-Economic Impact Evaluation for Treaty Three Area Development Projects.* Winnipeg: University of Manitoba Natural Resources Institute.

Kehoe, Alice Beck. 1989. *The Ghost Dance: Ethnohistory and Revitalization.* Fort Worth, TX: Holt, Rinehart, and Winston.

Kenora Daily Miner and News. 1965. Indians Are Frustrated; Uprising Sure to Follow. *Kenora Daily Miner and News.* November 17, 1965.

Kenora Daily Miner and News. 1974a. Conference Orderly on Weekend. *Kenora Daily Miner and News.* July 22, 1974.

Kenora Daily Miner and News. 1974b. 150 Indians Occupy Anicinabe Park. *Kenora Daily Miner and News.* July 23, 1974.

Kenora Daily Miner and News. 1974c. Indian Issue Talks Underway. *Kenora Daily Miner and News.* July 25, 1974.

Kenora Daily Miner and News. 1974d. Natives Don't Approve of Occupation: Survey. *Kenora Daily Miner and News.* July 26, 1974.

Kenora Daily Miner and News. 1974e. Indian Sentry Fires Gun Shot at Group. *Kenora Daily Miner and News.* August 12, 1974.

Kenora Daily Miner and News. 1974f. Militants Lay Down Arms. *Kenora Daily Miner and News.* August 19, 1974.

Kenora Daily Miner and News. 1986. Parliament Passes Settlement Act Covering Grassy, Islington Bands. *Kenora Daily Miner and News.* June 5, 1986.

Kenora Daily Miner and News. 2003. Grassy Narrows Strikes Again. *Kenora Daily Miner and News.* June 11, 2003.

Kenora Daily Miner and News. 2004. Abitibi and Wabauskang Negotiating Forestry Deal. *Kenora Daily Miner and News.* February 17, 2004.

Kenora Miner and News Staff and the Canadian Press. 1984. $10 Million Package Approved. *Kenora Daily Miner and News.* September 19, 1984.

Kirsch, Stuart. 2006. *Reverse Anthropology: Indigenous Analysis of Social and Environmental Relations in New Guinea.* Stanford: Stanford University Press.

Kirsch, Stuart. 2007. Indigenous Movements and the Risks of Counterglobalization: Tracking the Campaign against Papua New Guinea's Ok Tedi Mine. *American Ethnologist* 34(2): 303–21.

Knudson, Tom. 2001. State of Denial. *Sacramento Bee*. April 27, 2003.

Knudson, Tom. 2003. Newsprint Maker Offers Deal to End Clearcutting Fight. *Sacramento Bee*. November 14, 2003.

Kohl, Johann Georg. 1985 [1860]. *Kitch-Gami: Life among the Lake Superior Ojibway*. Minneapolis: Minnesota Historical Society Press.

Krech, Shepard. 1999. *The Ecological Indian: Myth and History*. New York: W.W. Norton and Company.

Kuper, Adam. 2003. The Return of the Native. *Current Anthropology* 44 (3): 389–95.

LaDuke, Winona. 1999. *All Our Relations: Native Struggles for Land and Life*. Cambridge, MA: South End Press.

LaDuke, Winona. 2004. *Indigenous Peoples, Power and Politics: A Renewable Future for the Seventh Generation*. Minneapolis: Honor the Earth Publications.

Lake of the Woods Enterprise. 2004. Grassy Gets Help for Forest Plan for Canadian Boreal Initiative. *Lake of the Woods Enterprise*. December 25, 2004.

Lake of the Woods Museum. 1999. Our Logging Heritage. *Kenora Daily Miner and News*. February 15, 1999.

Landsman, Gail H. 1988. *Sovereignty and Symbol: Indian-White Conflict at Ganienkeh*. Albuquerque: University of New Mexico Press.

Lassiter, Luke Eric. 2005. *The Chicago Guide to Collaborative Ethnography*. Chicago: University of Chicago Press.

Lepowsky, Maria. 2004. Indian Revolts and Cargo Cults: Ritual Violence and Revitalization in California and New Guinea. In *Reassessing Revitalization Movements: Perspectives from North America and the Pacific Islands*. Michael E. Harkin, ed. Pp. 1–60. Lincoln: University of Nebraska Press.

Levi, Jerome M. 2002. A New Dawn or a Cycle Restored: Regional Dynamics and Cultural Politics in Indigenous Mexico, 1978–2001. In *The Politics of Ethnicity: Indigenous People in Latin American States*. David Maybury-Lewis, ed. Pp. 3–50. Cambridge, MA: Harvard University Press.

Lewis, David Rich. 2007. Skull Valley Gestures and Politics of Nuclear Waste. In *Native Americans and the Environment: Perspec-*

tives on the Ecological Indian. Michael E. Harkin and David Rich Lewis, eds. Pp. 304–42. Lincoln: University of Nebraska Press.

Lischke, Ute, and David T. McNab. 2003. Actions of Peace. In *Blockades and Resistance: Studies in Actions of Peace and the Temagami Blockades 1988–89*. Bruce W. Hodgins, Ute Lischke, and David T. McNab, eds. Pp. 1–9. Waterloo, ON: Wilfrid Laurier Press.

Low, Setha M., and Denise Lawrence-Zúñiga, eds. 2003. *The Anthropology of Space and Place: Locating Culture*. Malden, MA: Blackwell Publishing.

Lund, Duane R. 1995. *The Indian Wars*. Cambridge, MN: Adventure Publications.

MacDonald, Mary N., ed. 2003. *Experiences of Place*. Cambridge, MA: Harvard University Press/Center for the Study of World Religions.

MacKinnon, James. 1995. Shaking Hands with Wolverine. *Monday Magazine*. Victoria, BC. August 31, 1993.

Malinowski, Bronislaw. 1984 [1922]. *Argonauts of the Western Pacific*. Long Grove, IL: Waveland Press. Reprint Edition.

Malkki, Liisa H. 1997. National Geographic: The Rooting of Peoples and the Territorialization of National Identity among Scholars and Refugees. In *Culture, Power, Place: Explorations in Critical Anthropology*. Akhil Gupta and James Ferguson, eds. Pp. 52–74. Durham, NC: Duke University Press.

Marcus, George E. 1998. *Ethnography through Thick and Thin*. Princeton, NJ: Princeton University Press.

Maybury-Lewis, David. 1997. *Indigenous Peoples, Ethnic Groups, and the State*. Needham Heights, MA: Allyn and Bacon.

McDonald, Anne, and Hiroshi Isogai. 2001. *From Grassy Narrows*. Tokyo: Shimizukobundo Shobo.

McLeod, Joseph. 1977. *And the Rivers Our Blood*. Toronto: NC Press.

McMullen, Ann. 2004. "Canny About Conflict": Nativism, Revitalization, and the Invention of Tradition in Native Southeastern New England. In *Reassessing Revitalization Movements: Perspectives from North America and the Pacific Islands*. Michael E. Harkin, ed. Pp. 261–77. Lincoln: University of Nebraska Press.

McNab, David T. 1999. *Circles of Time: Aboriginal Land Rights and Resistance in Ontario*. Waterloo, ON: Wilfrid Laurier University Press.

Mercredi, Ovide, and Mary Ellen Turpel. 1993. *In the Rapids: Navigating the Future of First Nations.* Toronto: Viking/Penguin Canada.

Mihesuah, Devon A., ed. 1998. *Natives and Academics: Researching and Writing about American Indians.* Lincoln, Nebraska: Bison Books.

Miller, J. R. 1991a. *Skyscrapers Hide the Heavens: A History of Indian-White Relationships in Canada.* Toronto: University of Toronto Press.

Miller, J. R. 1991b. Aboriginal Rights, Land Claims, and the Struggle to Survive. In *Sweet Promises: A Reader on Indian White Relations in Canada.* J. R. Miller, ed. Pp. 405–20. Toronto: University of Toronto Press.

Milton, Kay. 1993. Introduction. In *Environmentalism: The View from Anthropology.* Kay Milton, ed. Pp. 1–17. London: Routledge.

Milton, Kay. 1996. *Environmentalism and Cultural Theory: Exploring the Role of Anthropology in Environmental Discourse.* London: Routledge.

Mittelstaedt, Martin. 2000. Abitibi Sued over N. Ontario Logging. *Toronto Globe and Mail.* April 6, 2000.

Morphey, Howard. 1995. Landscape and the Reproduction of the Ancestral Past. In *The Anthropology of Landscape: Perspectives on Place and Space.* Eric Hirsh and Michael O'Hanlon, eds. Pp. 184–209. Oxford, UK: Oxford University Press.

Nadasdy, Paul. 2003. *Hunters and Bureaucrats: Power, Knowledge, and Aboriginal-State Relations in the Southwest Yukon.* Vancouver: University of British Columbia Press.

Nadasdy, Paul. 2005. Transcending the Debate over the Ecologically Noble Indian: Indigenous Peoples and Environmentalism. *Ethnohistory* 52(2): 291–331.

Nagel, Joane. 1996. *American Indian Ethnic Renewal: Red Power and the Resurgence of Identity and Culture.* New York: Oxford University Press.

Neihardt, John. 1932. *Black Elk Speaks.* Lincoln: University of Nebraska Press.

Nelson, Richard. 1983. *Make Prayers to the Raven: A Koyukon View of the Northern Forest.* Chicago: University of Chicago Press.

Nesper, Larry. 2002. *The Walleye War: The Struggle for Ojibwe Spearfishing and Treaty Rights.* Lincoln: University of Nebraska Press.

Nesper, Larry, Anna J. Willow, and Thomas F King. 2002. The Mushgigagamongsebe District: A Traditional Cultural Property of the Sokaogon Ojibwe Community. Report submitted to the Army Corps of Engineers, St. Paul District, by the Mole Lake Sokaogon Community of the Great Lakes Chippewa Indians. Crandon, Wisconsin.

Neu, Dean, and Richard Therrien. 2003. *Accounting for Genocide: Canada's Bureaucratic Assault on Aboriginal Peoples*. Blackpoint, NS: Fernwood Publishing.

Newton, Jon. 1979. The Kenora Syndrome. *The Journal*. November 1, 1979: 7–14.

Nichols, John D., and Earl Nyholm. 1995. *A Concise Dictionary of Minnesota Ojibwe*. Minneapolis: University of Minnesota Press.

Nichols, John D. 2000. The Translation of Key Phrases in the Treaties of 1837 and 1855. In *Fish in the Lakes, Wild Rice, and Game in Abundance*. James McClurken, ed. East Lansing: Michigan State University Press.

Niezen, Ronald. 1998. *Defending the Land: Sovereignty and Forest Life in James Bay Cree Society*. Boston: Allyn and Bacon.

Niezen, Ronald. 2003. *The Origins of Indigenism: Human Rights and the Politics of Identity*. Berkeley: University of California Press.

Nute, Grace Lee. 1941. *The Voyageur's Highway: Minnesota's Border Lake Land*. St. Paul: Minnesota Historical Society.

Orui, Tadashi. 2009. *The Scars of Mercury*. Winnipeg: Sou International Ltd. Films.

Peers, Laura. 1994. *The Ojibwa of Western Canada: 1780–1870*. Winnipeg: University of Manitoba Press.

Pels, Peter, and Oscar Salemink, eds. 2000. *Colonial Subjects: Essays on the Practical History of Anthropology*. Ann Arbor: University of Michigan Press.

Penashue, Peter. 2001. Healing the Past, Meeting the Future. In *Aboriginal Autonomy and Development in Northern Quebec and Labrador*. Colin H. Scott, ed. Pp. 21–29. Vancouver, British Columbia: University of British Columbia Press.

Phelan, Bryan. 1999a. Clearcuts Disturb Grassy Narrows Residents. *Kenora Enterprise*. Sunday, January 3, 1999.

Phelan, Bryan. 1999b. Protestors May Call for Boycott of Abitibi Paper. *Kenora Enterprise*. Sunday, January 3, 1999.

Phelan, Bryan. 2001. Two Takes: The Meaning of Treaty Three, Part Two. *Lake of the Woods Area News* 31(1): 25–27. March 2001.

Pile, Steven, and Michael Keith. 1997. *Geographies of Resistance*. London: Routledge.

Power, Michael. 2003a. Clearcut Protestors Stage Kenora March. *Lake of the Woods Enterprise*. February 23, 2003.

Power, Michael. 2003b. National Chief Visits Protestors. *Lake of the Woods Enterprise*. March 2, 2003.

Price, Richard. Introduction. 1987. In *The Spirit of the Alberta Indian Treaties*. Richard Price, ed. Pp. ix–xiii. Edmonton: University of Alberta Press.

Ramos, Alcida Rita. 1998. *Indigenism: Ethnic Politics in Brazil*. Madison: University of Wisconsin Press.

Ranco, Darren J. 2007. The Ecological Indian and the Politics of Representation. In *Native Americans and the Environment: Perspectives on the Ecological Indian*. Michael E. Harkin and David Rich Lewis, eds. Pp. 32–51. Lincoln: University of Nebraska Press.

Raunet, Daniel. 1996. *Without Surrender, Without Consent: A History of the Nisga'a Land Claims*. Vancouver, BC: Douglas and McIntyre.

Rebuffoni, Dean. 1977. Mercury in the Northwoods. *Minneapolis Tribune Picture Magazine*. September 11, 1977.

Redford, Kent H. 1990. The Ecologically Noble Savage. *Orion Nature Quarterly* 9(3): 25–29.

Rodman, Margaret C. 2003. Empowering Place: Multilocality and Multivocality. In *The Anthropology of Space and Place: Locating Culture*. Setha M. Low and Denise Lawrence-Zúñiga, eds. Pp. 204–223. Malden, MA: Blackwell Publishing.

Rosaldo, Renato. 1989. *Culture and Truth: The Remaking of Social Analysis*. Boston: Beacon Press.

Said, Edward. 1979. *Orientalism*. New York: Vintage Books.

Sahlins, Marshall. 1985. *Islands of History*. Chicago: University of Chicago Press.

Sahlins, Marshall. 1999. What Is Anthropological Enlightenment? Some Lessons of the Twentieth Century. *Annual Review of Anthropology* 28: i–xxiii.

Samson, Colin. 2003. *A Way of Life That Does Not Exist: Canada and the Extinguishment of the Innu*. London: Verso.

Samuel, Stephen. 1996. Wolverine's War. http://www.begreen.com/wolverine.html, accessed July 19, 2006.

Santos-Granero, Fernando. 1998. Writing History into the Landscape: Space, Myth, and Ritual in Contemporary Amazonia. *American Ethnologist* 25(2): 128–48.

Satterfield, Terre. 2002. *Anatomy of a Conflict: Identity, Knowledge, and Emotion in Old-Growth Forests*. Vancouver: University of British Columbia Press.

Satz, Ronald N. 1991. Chippewa Treaty Rights: The Reserved Rights of Wisconsin's Chippewa Indians in Historical Perspective. *Transactions* 79 (1). Madison: Wisconsin Academy of Sciences, Arts, and Letters.

Schenck, Theresa M. 2007. *William W. Warren: The Life, Letters, and Times of an Ojibwe Leader*. Lincoln: University of Nebraska Press.

Scott, Colin H. 2001. On Autonomy and Development. In *Aboriginal Autonomy and Development in Northern Quebec and Labrador*. Colin H. Scott, ed. Pp. 3–20. Vancouver: University of British Columbia Press.

Scott, Richard T. 2001. Becoming a Mercury Dealer: Moral Implications and the Construction of Objective Knowledge for the James Bay Cree. In *Aboriginal Autonomy and Development in Northern Quebec and Labrador*. Colin H. Scott, ed. Pp. 175–205. Vancouver: University of British Columbia Press.

Shellenberger, Michael, and Ted Nordhaus. 2004. The Death of Environmentalism: Global Warming in a Post-Environmental World. Released at the October 2004 meeting of the Environmental Grantmakers Association. http://www.thebreakthrough.org/images/Death_of_Environmentalism.pdf, accessed January 19, 2007.

Shellenberger, Michael, and Ted Nordhaus. 2007. *Break Through: From the Death of Environmentalism to the Politics of Possibility*. New York: Houghton Mifflin.

Shkilnyk, Anastasia. 1985. *A Poison Stronger Than Love: The Destruction of an Ojibwa Community*. New Haven, CT: Yale University Press.

Sider, Gerald. 1993. *Lumbee Indian Histories: Race, Ethnicity, and Indian Identity in the Southern United States*. Cambridge, MA: Cambridge University Press.

Siegel, Bernard J., and Alan R. Beals. 1960. Conflict and Factionalist Disputes. *Journal of the Royal Anthropological Institute* 90(1): 107–17.

Sissons, Jeffrey. 2005. *First Peoples: Indigenous Cultures and Their Futures*. London: Reaktion Books.

240 BIBLIOGRAPHY

Spivak, Gayatri. 1993. *Inside the Teaching Machine*. New York: Routledge.
Stavenhagen, Rodolfo. 2004. Report of the Special Rapporteur on the Situation of Human Rights and Fundamental Freedoms of Indigenous People. Addendum: Mission to Canada. December 2004. (UN Document E/CN 4/2005/88/Add. 3).
Stephen, Lynn. 2005. Gender, Citizenship, and the Politics of Identity. In *Social Movements: An Anthropological Reader*. June Nash, ed. Pp. 66–77. Malden, MA: Blackwell Publishing.
Stewart, Bob. 1999. Whiskey Jack Forest Plan Out for Final Inspection. *Kenora Daily Miner and News*. March 8, 1999.
Strathern, Marilyn. 1980. No Nature, No Culture: The Hagen Case. In *Nature, Culture and Gender*. Carol MacCormack and Marilyn Strathern, eds. Pp. 174–222. Cambridge, UK: Cambridge University Press.
Taiga Rescue Network. 2005. Supporting Grassy Narrows. *Taiga News* Issue 50, Spring 2005. http://www.taigarescue.org, accessed March 24, 2005.
Tanner, Adrian. 1979. *Bringing Home Animals: Religious Ideology and Mode of Production of the Mistassini Cree Hunters*. St. Johns: Memorial University of Newfoundland Press.
Tanner, Adrian. 1999. Culture, Social Change, and Cree Opposition to the James Bay Hydroelectric Development. In *Social and Environmental Impacts of the James Bay Hydroelectric Project*. James F. Hornig, ed. Pp. 124–40. Montreal: McGill-Queen's University Press.
Tarasoff, Koozma. 1980. *Persistent Ceremonialism: The Plains Cree and Saulteaux*. Ottawa: National Museum of Canada.
Taylor, John Leonard. 1987. Two Views on the Meanings of Treaties Six and Seven. In *The Spirit of the Alberta Indian Treaties*. Richard Price, ed. Pp. 9–45. Edmonton: University of Alberta Press.
Tilley, Christopher. 1994. *A Phenomenology of Landscape: Places, Paths and Monuments*. Providence, RI: Berg.
Tiner, Tina. 2008. Narrows Escape. *Now Magazine* 27(42). http://www.nowtoronto.com/news/story.cfm?content=163639, accessed October 9, 2008.
Toronto Star. 2007. Ipperwash Land Returned to Indians. *Toronto Star*. December 21, 2007.

Troyer, Warner. 1977. *No Safe Place*. Toronto: Clarke, Irwin, and Company.

Tsing, Anna. 2005. *Friction: An Ethnography of Global Connection*. Princeton, NJ: Princeton University Press.

Tsing, Anna. 2007. Indigenous Voice. In *Indigenous Experience Today*. Marisol de la Cadena and Orin Starn, eds. Oxford, UK: Berg.

Turner, Terrence. 1991. Representing, Resisting, Rethinking: Historical Transformation of Kayapó Culture and Anthropological Consciousness. In *Colonial Situations: Essays on the Contextualization of Ethnographic Knowledge*. George W. Stocking, ed. Pp. 285–313. Madison: University of Wisconsin Press.

United Nations Office of the High Commissioner for Human Rights (UNOHCHR). 1995. Fact Sheet No. 9 (Rev. 1), The Rights of Indigenous Peoples. Geneva, Switzerland: UNOHCHR.

United Nations Permanent Forum on Indigenous Issues. 2005. About UNPFII/History. http://www.un.org/esa/socdev/unpfii/aboutPFII/hisotry_home1.htm, accessed March 13, 2006.

Vansina, Jan. 1985. *Oral Tradition as History*. Madison: University of Wisconsin Press.

Vecsey, Christopher. 1987. Grassy Narrows Reserve: Mercury Pollution, Social Disruption, and Natural Resources: A Question of Autonomy. *American Indian Quarterly* 11(4): 278–314.

Vizenor, Gerald. 1984. *The People Named the Chippewa: Narrative Histories*. Minneapolis: University of Minnesota Press.

Wallace, Anthony F. C. 1956. Revitalization Movements: Some Theoretical Considerations for Their Comparative Study. *American Anthropologist* 58: 264–81.

Wallace, Anthony F. C. 1969. *Death and Rebirth of the Seneca*. New York: Vintage Books.

Wallace, Anthony F. C. 2004. Foreword. In *Reassessing Revitalization Movements: Perspectives from North America and the Pacific Islands*. Michael E. Harkin, ed. Pp. vii–xi. Lincoln: University of Nebraska Press.

Warren, Kay B. 1998. *Indigenous Movements and Their Critics: Pan-Maya Activism in Guatemala*. Princeton, NJ: Princeton University Press.

Warren, Kay B., and Jean E. Jackson. 2002. Introduction: Studying Indigenous Movements in Latin America. In *Indigenous Move-

ments, Self-Reorientations and the State in Latin America. Kay B. Warren and Jean E. Jackson, eds. Pp. 1–46. Austin: University of Texas Press.

Warren, William. 1984 [1885]. *History of the Ojibway People.* St. Paul: Minnesota Historical Society.

Wenzel, George. 1991. *Animal Rights, Human Rights: Ecology, Economy, and Ideology in the Canadian Arctic.* Toronto: University of Toronto Press.

White, Richard. 1991. *The Middle Ground: Indians, Empires, and Republics in the Great Lakes Region, 1650–1815.* Cambridge, UK: Cambridge University Press.

Whitehead, Neil L. 1997. *The Discoverie of the Large, Rich and Bewtiful Empyre of Guiana by Sir Walter Ralegh: Transcribed, edited and introduced by Neil L. Whitehead.* Norman: University of Oklahoma Press.

Williams, Raymond. 1973. *The Country and the City.* Oxford, UK: Oxford University Press.

Willow, Anna J. 2009. Clear-Cutting and Colonialism: The Ethnopolitical Dynamics of Indigenous Environmental Activism in Northwestern Ontario. *Ethnohistory* 56(1): 35–67.

Willow, Anna J. 2010. Cultural Revitalization in Anishinaabe and Anthropological Discourse. *American Indian Quarterly* 34(1): 33–60.

Willow, Anna J. 2011. Conceiving Kakipitatapitmok: The Political Landscape of Anishinaabe Anti-Clearcutting Activism. *American Anthropologist* 113(2): 262–76.

Wolf, Eric. 1982. *Europe and the People without History.* Berkeley: University of California Press.

York, Geoffrey. 1990. *The Dispossessed: Life and Death in Native Canada.* London: Vintage.

York, Geoffrey, and Loreen Pindera. 1991. *People of the Pines: The Warriors and Legacy of Oka.* Boston: Little, Brown, and Company.

Index

Abitibi-Consolidated, 91; defense of clearcutting, 109–110; and First Nations economic development, 116, 147, 158, 161, 166; headquarters, 146, 152; lawsuit against, 48, 101, 144, 215–216n9; mill in Kenora, 84, 151; pull out, 201; response to blockade, 124–125. *See also* forest management planning; logging; negotiations

Aboriginal Peoples Television Network, 185–186

aboriginal rights, 40–42, 52, 95, 209n2–3

agency, of individuals, 5, 6

alcohol, 72, 76, 132

alliances. *See* environmentalists, alliances with; supporters

American Indian Movement, 54–55, 56

Amnesty International, 200–201

Anderson, Benedict. *See* imagined community

Anderson, Kim, 61

Anicinabe Park occupation, 55–59

Anishinaabe, 28; etymology, 17, 208n6; population, 28

Anishinaabemowin, 18, 28, 121, 210n7; and cultural identity, 138; language loss, 136–138

annual round. *See* land-based subsistence

anthropology: and advocacy, 8–9; and American Indians, 8–10, historical, 5

Appadurai, Arjun, 6, 7, 186, 212n16

As Long as the Rivers Flow: scenes from, 111–112, 113, 115; screenings of, 166, 183

Asch, Michael, 41, 209n3

Assembly of First Nations, 112

Asubpeeschoseewagong Netum Anishinabek, as designation for Grassy Narrows, 3, 17, 18, 175, 199

Ball Lake Lodge, 31, 75

Banks, Dennis, 56

243